BETWEEN CHINA AND EUROPE

LONDON SCHOOL OF ECONOMICS MONOGRAPHS ON SOCIAL ANTHROPOLOGY

Managing Editor: Charles Stafford

The Monographs on Social Anthropology were established in 1940 and aim to publish results of modern anthropological research of primary interest to specialists.

The continuation of the series was made possible by a grant in aid from the Wenner-Gren Foundation for Anthropological Research, and more recently by a further grant from the Governors of the London School of Economics and Political Science. Income from sales is returned to a revolving fund to assist further publications.

The Monographs are under the direction of an Editorial Board associated with the Department of Anthropology of the London School of Economics and Political Science.

BETWEEN CHINA AND EUROPE

PERSON, CULTURE AND EMOTION IN MACAO

JOÃO DE PINA-CABRAL

LONDON SCHOOL OF ECONOMICS MONOGRAPHS ON SOCIAL ANTHROPOLOGY
Volume 74

First published 2002 by
Continuum
The Tower Building, 11 York Road, London, SE1 7NX
370 Lexington Avenue, New York, NY 10017–6503

© João de Pina-Cabral, 2002

All rights reserved. No part of this publication may be reproduced, or transmitted in any form or by any means, electronic or mechanical, including photocopying, recording or any information storage or retrieval system, without permission in writing from the publishers.

British Library Cataloguing-in-Publication Data
A catalogue record for this book is available from the British Library.

ISBN
0–8264–5748–7 (hardback)
0–8264–5749–5 (paperback)

Library of Congress Cataloging-in-Publication Data
Pina-Cabral, João de
  Between China and Europe : person, culture and emotion in Macao / João de Pina-Cabral.
    p. cm.—(London School of Economics monographs on social anthropology ; v. 74)
  Includes bibliographical references and index.
  ISBN 0–8264–5748–7—ISBN 0–8264–5749–5 (pbk.)
  1. Macau (China : Special Administrative Region)—History. I. Title. II. Series.

DS796.M2 P55 2002
951.26—dc21   2001047480

Typeset by Waverley Typesetters, Galashiels
Printed and bound in Great Britain by Biddles Ltd, Guildford and Kings Lynn

CONTENTS

List of Figures	ix
List of Tables	ix
Permissions	x
Acknowledgements	xi

Chapter 1: MACAO BAMBOO	1
Periods in the city's history	4
The *incidentes* – instability and permanence	6
About this book	17
Chapter 2: THE CITY'S PROFILE	21
The historical origins of Macao's ethnic composition	21
People in motion	23
The population of Macao in the transition period	26
Main economic activities	28
Broad lines of cultural differentiation	32
Broad ethnic categories	36
Conclusion	48
Chapter 3: HOLLERING IN BRONZE: MEMORY AND CONFLICT	51
The *hoppo* and 'Macao's subjection'	54
The Governor's impossible task	60

CONTENTS

A new *modus vivendi*   64
The colonial period   66
A martyr and a hero   71
Mesquita during the Cultural Revolution   72
Some guy on a horse   75
Conclusion   77

Chapter 4: PARADOXES: GAMBLING AND THE IMPERIAL CIVIL SERVICE EXAMINATION   79

Gambling monopolies in Macao   80
Waan2 or *do2*?   82
Popular gambling games   87
The *vaeseng* lottery   90
The history of the gambling syndicates   93
The examination paradox   99
Conclusion: the three paradoxes   100

Chapter 5: EQUIVOCAL COMPATIBILITIES: PERSON, CULTURE AND EMOTION   105

A confrontation of hegemonies   106
A critique of the isomorphic model of social reproduction   108
The court case   109
Macao's legal system   110
Slavery in Macao   114
The trade in persons in Macao   116
The Chinese concept of person   120
Conclusion   125

Chapter 6: STONE SILENCES: ORGANIZED AMNESIA   127

An non-existent monument   127
Silences and identities   128
Ambiguous belongings   130
Zhou Enlai's response   132
A third silence   134
A Christian coda   137

CONTENTS

Chapter 7: NAMES: PERSONAL IDENTITY AND
ETHNIC AMBIGUITY ... 141
Ethnicity and the person ... 141
Naming systems ... 146
Interethnic naming ... 150
Conclusion ... 156

Chapter 8: CORRELATE ASYMMETRIES: GENDER,
CLASS AND ETHNICITY ... 159
The matrimonial context of production ... 160
The asymmetry in interethnic sexual relations ... 165
The matrimonial context of reproduction ... 168
The caesura of the 1970s: marriage patterns ... 171
The caesura of the 1970s: domestic environment ... 174
Conclusion: correlate asymmetries ... 176

Chapter 9: HABITS OF THE HEART: MODERN WOMEN
AND FILIAL PIETY ... 179
Marriage property transfers ... 181
Matrimonial insecurity ... 185
Working women ... 190
Filial daughters ... 192
Diverging devolution ... 195
Conclusion ... 200

Chapter 10: TRIAD WARS AND THE END OF
PORTUGUESE ADMINISTRATION ... 205
Outlaws of the marsh ... 208
A synopsis of the Triad Wars ... 213
The Triad Wars as an *incidente* ... 218
Conclusion ... 220

Appendix: GOVERNOR'S TELEGRAM CONCERNING
STATUES ... 222

Glossary of Cantonese Words ... 223

CONTENTS

Notes 226
Bibliography 240
Index 250

LIST OF FIGURES

Figure 1 Map of Macao – 1997 xiv

Figure 2 Year of entry of residents in Macao born in the PRC 28

Figure 3 Language of schooling – Macao 1985 33

Figure 4 Statue of Ferreira do Amaral in Lisbon 52

LIST OF TABLES

Table 1 Population for 1991 and 1996 27

Table 2 Thai and Filipino residents – 1991 and 1996 47

Table 3 Percentage of females among Thai and Filipino migrants – 1991 and 1996 48

PERMISSIONS

Parts of this text have previously appeared in print as articles, I am grateful to the editors of these journals and collected volumes for permission to include them here. Passages of Chapter 1 came out in *Os Fundamentos da Amizade* (C.C.C. Macau, Lisbon 1999); an earlier and longer version of Chapter 2 was published as a chapter of the *History of the Portuguese Expansion* (Círculo de Leitores, Lisbon 1998); the second half of Chapter 4 came out in *Oceanos* (Lisbon 1997); a shorter and earlier version of Chapter 5 came out in *Ethnologie Française* (Paris 1999); Chapter 7 came out under a different title in *Social Anthropologist* (Cambridge 1994).

ACKNOWLEDGEMENTS

In writing this book I had in mind Theodore de Bary's warning that 'the past of a people is never completely done for, never something wholly dispensable to them' (1996: 37) Thus, I dedicate the book to the local people (*boon dei yan*) of Macao of the twenty-first century, whichever way they come to define themselves. Macao is a place of indetermination, but it is also a city with a rich past and an auspicious future. The world has moved inexorably towards greater communicability between nations and cultures. Places of passage, such as Macao, today face a window of opportunity that they must deliberately take into their own hands.

I am grateful to Jorge Morbey and Nelson Lourenço, who convinced me to take up the challenge of studying Macao in 1990. The Government of Macao and, in particular, the Cultural Institute and its successive presidents – Carlos Marreiros and Gabriela Pombas Cabelo – were a constant source of collaboration and support. At the Institute, I am also especially indebted to Teresa Sena. Many were the people of Macao who helped me further my research. Being incapable of thanking them all, I will name only two – Henrique de Senna Fernandes and Gary Ngai.

Unfortunately, after several years of negotiation, the Orient Foundation never managed to reach a final decision as to whether or not they wished to support my research. Thus, after 1995, it became impossible to continue fieldwork and my visits to south China became shorter and sporadic.

Most of all, I am grateful to the Institute of Social Sciences of the University of Lisbon, which provides its members with conditions to pursue their own independent research that are nearly unique in the world today. In preparing the final draft, Moisés Fernandes' suggestions and references were centrally important and Ruth Rosengarten's revision

ACKNOWLEDGEMENTS

and comments significantly improved the quality of the manuscript. Göran Aijmer's friendly debate was a rich source of inspiration, for which I am grateful. Charles Stafford's encouragement and kindness as coordinator of the LSE series of Monographs in Social Anthropology were indispensable.

Finally, my personal and scholarly debt to my wife Mónica Chan is enormous. Her linguistic proficiency and anthropological scepticism were two constant pillars of support.

To Macao's *boon dei yan*

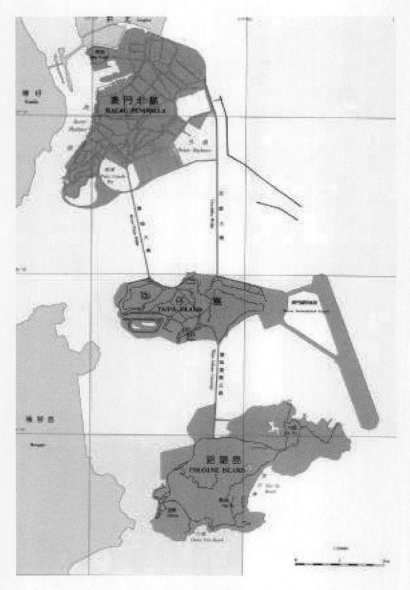

Figure 1 Map of Macao – 1997
(*Source:* Wang *et al.* 1997)

CHAPTER I

MACAO BAMBOO

> *Seagulls glide over a mirroring sea*
> *Sailing boats return over gentle waves*
> *In the morning, I buy fresh fish in the market*
> *Forgetting the perils of seafaring*
>
> Liang Peiyuan (1996 [1968])

Since its foundation in the second half of the sixteenth century Macao has been one of the few permanent points of contact between China and Europe, managing to weather all of the often stormy clashes between two of the greatest and most distinct civilizations and political conglomerates in history. Macao's longevity is without doubt surprising, if we take into account its troubled history.

Its capacity for survival is directly related to its fragility. It was always impossible to protect the city in military and commercial terms, as it is situated at the tip of a minuscule peninsula surrounded by hilly islands in the Delta of the Pearl River – the coastal hinterlands of the wealthy Chinese province of Guangdong. Originally slightly over 3 km^2, the peninsula grew and, at the time of the handover in 1999, it amounted to over 8 km^2 (cf. Wang *et al.* 1997).

China always was a continental power. Macao was China's sea gate where foreign merchants could settle because they did not thus upset the order of things by entering into China proper. The Empire's inner waters began at the Bogue (*Boca Tigris*), further up the Delta, half-way to the great city of Canton.

Thus, Macao was always at the mercy of the Chinese State. Today one can hardly guess at its existence, but for over three centuries there was a wall that cut across the middle part of the peninsula – on the sea side lived the Catholic subjects of the King of Portugal; on the inland side grew the Chinese bazaar. Inside this wall the Portuguese were protected from attack and could live their life as they wished; on the Chinese side the mandarins[1] ruled.

Further up, however, cutting across the minuscule isthmus, there was another wall or, rather, a set of gates – the *Portas do Cerco*, Gates of Siege – beyond which Europeans could not go without a special licence and which protected the Chinese from any sort of Portuguese whimsicality. The Chinese mandarins, with their headquarters at *Casa Branca* (White House), further upriver, only had to close these doors when they were dissatisfied with Portuguese activities. Within days, the foreign citadel invariably surrendered for lack of food, drinking water and goods for maintaining the commercial activities. For example, an American merchant who visited the city in the second half of the eighteenth century comments:

> at present it is much fallen from its ancient splendour, for though it is inhabited by Portuguese, and hath a Governor, nominated by the King of Portugal, yet it subsists merely by the sufferance of the Chinese, who can starve the place and dispossess the Portuguese, whenever they please. This obliges the Governor to behave with great circumspection, and carefully to avoid every circumstance that may give offence to the Chinese. (Yee 1989: 18)

In his evocative cosmogony of Macao, Father Benjamin Videira Pires S.J. identifies the two human forces responsible for the founding of this city: the boat people who, since time immemorial, permeated down from the tea-rich province of Fukien and who created and cared for the Temple of Ah-ma; and the Portuguese sailing merchants, who left behind the Japanese-inspired ruins of St Paul. They shared a common feature, he says: being subject to 'a kind of oceanic nomadism, which was, above all, spiritual' (1994: 6).

In these southern waters of the China Sea, navigation always carries a corollary – the impending typhoon (lit. in Cantonese, the big wind, *daai6 fung1*).[2] That is, to my mind, the import of our epigraph. The poet captures a sentiment that inevitably, even if only sporadically, assaults all who have lived in this city: the awareness that here the comforts of daily normality are charmed, for they depend on the forgetting of 'the perils of seafaring'.

In Macao, today as in the past, the typhoon is never very far away. And I do not speak merely of meteorology – like Father Videira Pires, I have in mind above all the more spiritual perils of cross-cultural nomadism.

In order to illustrate these, I have again chosen the words of a poet. Cai Yin Yuan, a literatus, was sent by the imperial authorities on an inspection tour of Macao in 1864. Whilst he was there, he met a number of Portuguese residents. He seems to have been well treated. In the notes to his poem 'Hearing music played by an European girl', he tells us: 'The foreign mistress of the house told her daughter to greet us and to play the organ. Gallantly dressed in silk as fine as a cicada's wings and ornamented with jewels, she plays lightly and graciously, and only stops when the visitors leave.'

One might have thought that he appreciated it. However, a little further on he comments:

> Foreign music is always characterized by its vigour, standing out for its harmfulness and violence, lacking gentleness and elegance; full of iron sounds, this music destroys the spirit and softens the will. There are the just sounds played in the Ming and Qing palaces, where mandarins are in authority and merchants are subjects. Let the Chinese literati appreciate the elegant classical music, preventing our people from being degraded by the foreign arts. (Quoted by Zhang Wenqin 1996: 58)

The cultural chasm between the two civilizations that met in Macao was such and their mutual sense of legitimation was so strong that we can safely consider that, in the majority of instances, what took place was more a mutual agreement to disagree than, properly speaking, a cross-cultural dialogue. For centuries there were, in theory, two cities: the Portuguese citadel and the Chinese bazaar, on either side of the city walls. You were either a Catholic subject of the King of Portugal or a subject of the Emperor, respectively – the two things were not compatible. And if you crossed this border of allegiance, you normally crossed it alone. Very seldom did such people keep anything like family relations on the other side, as we will see.

In fact this agreement of separation did not work fully and superimposition was always and constantly occurring, especially after the colonial period (1846–1967), when the two cities started physically to merge. It was not only legally and geographically that the borders of Macao were never fully agreed upon by the two States involved (see Chapter 3). People had to manage the discomforts that superimposition produced in all sorts of manners. In the pages that follow we will come across many instances where people came afoul of this Charybdis of intercultural navigation.

There is one fascinating manifestation of this still present in Macao's life today. When we visit the older section of the city, we discover that it is not only the toponymy that differs between Portuguese and Cantonese names (so that, for example, the 'Street of Pedro Nolasco da Silva' in Portuguese is called in Cantonese the 'Street of the White Horse', or the 'Hill of the Truths' in Portuguese is called in Cantonese 'Hill of the God Na Ja'); it is also the popular topography that does not correspond (so that a spot that is normally identified by the name of a square in Portuguese may well be identified by a street name in Cantonese).

PERIODS IN THE CITY'S HISTORY

I will now present the reader with a set of temporal referents for classification of the city's history so as to facilitate the comparison between the discussion of each of the various cases that will be analysed below. These are meant as nothing but rough guides to the more detailed analyses that will be undertaken later. The first period is far too large, but I have opted for leaving it thus vague, as we will seldom deal with it.

1557 to 1688 – Early period

Portuguese merchants and missionaries, mostly interested in the link with Japan, founded Macao roughly around 1557. As the Ming had broken commercial relations with Japan, the Portuguese found a window of opportunity (both commercial and religious) that worked particularly well for a few decades. By 1587, however, Shogun Hideyoshi banned Christianity in Japan and evicted the Portuguese. Nevertheless, the internal Asian trade continued to enrich the city. But after the Dutch took Malacca in 1641 and imposed a blockade on the Strait of Malacca, the vital link with Goa was broken and Macao lived through decades of great abandonment.

1688 to 1744 – Early Qing period

In 1688, the young Kangxi Emperor positioned a Chinese Customs office in Macao. This was the period when the Portuguese Jesuits living in Peking had great influence in court and Macao played an important role in terms of China's opening to the world. Commercially, it was the high period of the Canton trade in tea, when the British East India Company established its East Asian headquarters in the city.

1744 to 1846 – Late Canton Trade period

This was the period when the opium trade became more important and the 'country traders' started increasing their importance. In Macao, these were dark times, when Qing intransigence with foreigners increased, as their problems with pirates also mounted. During the second half of the period, Portugal underwent a particularly difficult stage of civil war and social upheaval in the wake of the Napoleonic invasions.

1846 to 1967 – Colonial period

Hong Kong was founded in 1843 in the midst of the Opium Wars and, shortly after that, the principal British and Chinese merchants abandoned Macao. Faced with immediate crisis Macao attempted to renegotiate its position *vis-à-vis* the Chinese State, which was then in the middle of a great internal crisis.[3] This period was launched by the actions of Governor Ferreira do Amaral, of whom we will hear more in Chapter 3. By the time the Chinese Communist Party (CCP) assumed full control over Mainland China (1949), this situation of colonial independence had to come to an end, as it eventually did in the throes of the Great Proletarian Cultural Revolution (3 December 1966 uprising).

1967 to 1987 – Post-colonial period

Contrary to what they expected, Portuguese authorities discovered that the Chinese leadership in Canton and Peking did not want to recover the administration of the city. Rather, they wanted to keep Macao under Portuguese administration but in such a manner that they could dictate the terms of the local policies. Such a situation continued until roughly 1987 when the Joint Declaration was signed that established the terms of the transition. This period can be further sub-divided. The period up to the Portuguese Democratic Revolution (1974) and Mao's death (1976) were years of relative hardship and abandonment. After that, however, Macao entered a cycle of prosperity and development such as it had not seen before in modern times.

1987 to 1999 – Transition period

The Luso-Chinese Joint Declaration concerning Macao's future was signed on 13 April 1987. From then onwards, the Portuguese and Chinese authorities started collaborating closely to organize a smooth transition. Following Hong Kong by a few years, Macao became a Special Administrative Region of the People's Republic of China (PRC) on 20 December 1999. Its relative autonomy has allowed life to continue without great upheavals during the transition and after. This is not the end of Macao's history and it is not even the end of the structural contradictions that have characterized Macao's history, as will be argued in the last chapter.

Although this book is in no way an ethnographic monograph in the traditional sense – as each of the examples discussed is followed through in its separate temporal development – the conception of the work does correspond to a temporal conjuncture. I carried out fieldwork in Macao at the expenses of the Cultural Institute of Macao between 1990 and 1995 in order to write an ethnographic monograph about the *Macanese* – the Eurasian community of Macao.[4] During that period I stayed in Macao annually for three to four months. I was initially accompanied by a sociologist colleague, Nelson Lourenço.

Thus, my arguments and my sensitivity concerning the Territory are definitely marked by that temporal perspective (cf. Pina-Cabral 2000b) quite as much as by the facts that I am Portuguese and that, in the middle of fieldwork, I got married to a Macao-born Chinese.

THE *INCIDENTES* – INSTABILITY AND PERMANENCE

When I first arrived in Macao, I discovered that the Cultural Institute had drawn up a list of 'privileged informants' that I was supposed to interview. They even organized transport for me to these interviews in official cars. One of the first people on the list was Carlos D'Assumpção, the most prestigious political figure in the Territory at the time. A Eurasian, he had studied Law at Coimbra, where he had already distinguished himself as a student leader in the camp of the dictatorship. In 1961, at a relatively young age, he played an important political role as lawyer to Stanley Ho, when the latter collaborated with the Governor in wrenching the gambling monopoly away from the old syndicate. This benefited the Territory greatly, as the new owners paid considerably more taxes into the coffers of the Administration, which allowed an important set of public works that launched the modernization of the city's infrastructures to be undertaken.

When we met, shortly before he died, he had the bearing of a distinguished senior politician. He called my attention to the fact that Macao's longevity was not based on continuous peace but on regular crises. I asked him to explain further and, smiling, he said:

> We, the Macanese, are not like the iron that breaks; we are like the bamboo that bends. The typhoon comes and we are thrown to the ground. But then we straighten up again and spread our branches.[5]

This image of the *Macao bamboo* is perhaps one of the best points of entry in order to understand Macao's social construction. As we will see later, the secret of Macao's survival was its capacity to bend with the winds of history, its acceptance of its own weakness. We are reminded of Confucius' saying, which may well be the historical ancestor of this particular founding myth. When his disciple asked Confucius whether it was necessary to execute those who contravene the Way, he answered: 'Is it really necessary to kill in order to rule? If you choose goodness the people will improve. The virtue of the noble man is powerful like the wind; the virtue of the small man is like the grass that, under the wind, folds and lies down.'[6]

Thus, Macao's virtue was that of the small man and, to that extent, Macao lived under the permanent threat of higher powers. The risk of annihilation was always in the air. When we look through the literature that has been written about Macao, we inevitably come across sentences that announce the death of 'Macao as we know it' in the near future or the imminent disappearance of the Macanese – the Eurasians – that part of the population most directly associated with the city's history. This prophecy of doom is associated to an image of abandonment locally called 'the Macanese Diaspora'.

For example, a certain author tells us, 'in the period that followed on the leaving of the Japanese [at the end of the Second World War], the native Macanese, eager to find better living conditions, started a flow of massive emigration – a Diaspora that, in fact, is still continuing today' (Leal Vilarinho in Silva 1991). But then, when we read the Macanese historian Montalto de Jesus, who wrote in the 1920s, we come across a number of similar predictions – for example, for the period of the 1840s immediately after the founding of Hong Kong (1990 [1926]: 252). The same author quotes from a disdainful report of the Chinese Customs Service, written in the 1920s by a British official: 'Each change of governor or each new round of gossip brings its quota of emmigrants, whose only wish is to leave the place where they were before' (ibid.: 306).

It was not only in written formulations that I encountered this fear of abandonment. In numberless interviews I came across expressions of this nature. For example, I was told that the Second World War was 'the end of Macanese life as such'. The social and economic morass of the 1950s was seen in the same light ('Macao's tragedy in the Fifties was the haemorrhage of young people. Whole families disappeared. The boys that went abroad to study, never returned.'). Later still, during the Cultural Revolution, 'it became obvious', I was told, 'that Macao had its days counted'. In 1993, people were telling me again that, after the 1999 handover, 'no one will be left behind'. They said, 'Now, with the Agreement, it is going to be emigration. In 1995 or 1996 everyone will go, except for the Chinese'. Finally, when I went back in 1999 to participate in the handover celebrations, I was assured that this would be it, everybody would now go. But in 2001, they are again celebrating a reunion of the Macanese Diaspora in Macao.

The Macanese dilemma is as follows. Due to their historical association with the citadel's history, they always possessed greater capacity to exercise their *rights of citizenship* in the city than did their ethnic opponents, the Chinese. They did this through their privileged access to the middle ranges of the Administration during the colonial period and their control of the *Leal Senado* (the Municipal Council) during pre-colonial days when it had considerable powers. Notwithstanding, they lacked ultimate *rights of sovereignty* over this territory that was their birthplace for over four centuries. Repeatedly, the Chinese reminded them of this by means of yet another experience of siege.

Thus, on the one hand, their condition as subjects of the King of Portugal (and later the Republic) shielded them from the worst insecurities that befell the population of south China throughout the chaotic political events of the past two centuries. Their administrative independence has been a great privilege. But, on the other hand, the Cantonese that surround them have always been certain of holding the ultimate rights of sovereignty over this land and of letting them know that. The Macanese have always had to face up to great insecurity at the hands of the local representatives of the Chinese State.

The Chinese in the city have suffered from the contrary syndrome: they hold ultimate rights of sovereignty over the land, but they suffer from considerably diminished conditions of citizenship[7] – due, not least, to the transitoriness that has historically marked their individual presence in the Territory (what Albert Yee called the *stepping-stone syndrome* – cf. 1989). This was particularly the case during the colonial period.

The grievances of the Chinese middle class that fed the public manifestation of collective anger at the time of the Cultural Revolution have been slowly addressed during the transition period (1987–99). Nevertheless, as will be argued in the last chapter of this book, the basic contradiction between sovereignty and citizenship that has been Macao's bane for four and a half centuries did not terminate with the handover to the PRC in 1999. There are signs that the ground merely shifted.

This contradiction means that Macao is a land subject to social typhoons: an insecure land where every now and then a rupture in legitimacy brings everything to the brink of disaster. Curiously, this is even codified in local lore by a characteristically numerological saying. A Macanese informant told me:

> The Chinese are fond of saying that, here in Macao, there are six years . . . six years for things to run smoothly. Then comes a short period in which the economic situation, or rather . . . for various reasons the situation does not progress – the city stagnates. Then comes again economic progress. Then, six years pass again, and another similar sort of thing occurs that makes the economy go back into crisis. This is something they already expect to happen. Any person in the street here, or rather, let us say, the futurists [the soothsayers] always have this. Every six years there is a period when Macao collapses, some sort of scandal. [. . .] This is a barrel of gunpowder.

The word used in Macao to describe these recurrent crises is *incidentes*. In Hong Kong, where they also occur (only, perhaps, in a less devastating fashion) they are known as 'troubles'. These are processes of liberation of the energy that has accumulated over periods of apparent peace and prosperity during which the central contradiction continues to operate but in a repressed fashion. The accumulated tension explodes regularly, or so the Chinese soothsayers insist. As the accumulated tension explodes, it allows for an adjustment of accounts at various levels. As we shall see, the contradiction manifests itself in all sorts of different areas.

The contradiction has been present ever since the Portuguese had a presence in China, finding its roots in the very ambiguity of the process of institutionalization of Macao during the Ming Dynasty. The citizens of the Christian citadel had the right to govern themselves and were subject to the King of Portugal, but the Chinese that cohabited with them were strictly dependent upon Chinese magistrates. If it had been possible to keep a strict separation between the two populations this system would have worked, but in fact that would have countered the very benefits that justified Macao's existence. For the system to function, the local magistrates, quite as much as the local representatives of the King of Portugal, had to pretend they did not notice the inconsistencies that necessarily arose. K. C. Fok calls this 'the Macao Formula'.

> Trade relations were [. . .] made possible through the connivance of the provincial officials. The exchange was voluntary. Its continuance depended on the goodwill of the Portuguese to honour their obligations

to the local officials and the willingness of the Chinese officials to run the risk of being censured by Peking. In realistic terms it depended on whether both sides had any compelling needs for the profits that could be derived from such an exchange. But the workability of the formula, above all, had to largely rely on the compliance and tranquillity of the Portuguese in Macao. (1991: 343)

On the one hand, the mandarins of the Canton region were always interested in the presence of this small and controllable Portuguese factory. On the other hand, the local Portuguese were always interested in keeping it alive for commercial and missionary reasons at first, and later simply because Portugal was a long way away and they had become a semi-independent Creole elite. Thus, although it was always subject to this central ambiguity, Macao achieved unexpected permanence.

The size of the territory, the distance from the central power in Goa, and later in Lisbon, and the very weakness of the Portuguese State meant that the Macanese lived in permanent confrontation with an alternative cultural universe that imposed itself daily on them as ultimately more powerful. In 1777, the bishop-governor D. Alexandre da Silva Pedrosa Guimarães wrote that:

> We have been accepted in this precarious land two hundred and twenty two years ago, living in good Harmony and with subjection in crimes to the Emperor's justice whenever a homicide is practised on a Chinese person. . . .

He further states,

> [. . .] we have no means of forcefully resisting any order that we might wish to disobey, because the Chinese that live in the City are nearing twenty two thousand and all the Christians (young and old alike, black and white and of both sexes) do not reach six thousand and are very weak: and the Emperor will bring in an instant into this City so many Chinese men that, if each one of them were to throw one shoe into the river, the flow would stop, as he himself stated concerning the inhabitants of Macao, when someone attempted to turn him against them. . . . (Silva Rego 1995: 11)

Its very weakness before the Chinese Empire was the secret that has allowed the city's survival over the centuries, as was clearly shown in the 1809 crisis that resulted from an attempt on the part of the British to land troops in Macao. As Portugal was being governed by a British Military Junta, as a result of the Napoleonic Invasions during the

Peninsular War, the British decided it was time to take over Macao peaceably. The Chinese State, however, reacted violently, showing that they were perfectly conscious that it was far easier to negotiate with the Portuguese than with the British, due to their military and economic might (Guimarães 1996).

This state of affairs meant that the Portuguese of the city were obliged to play the duplicitous game implicit in the 'Macao Formula', reproducing the essential ambiguity. For example, in a letter to a local official written in 1837, the Portuguese Procurator evokes the Qing legislation concerning the boat people – *tancares*[8] – that forbade them from living on dry land. He was afraid of the disorders that might result from the activities of prostitution that they engaged in with 'soldiers, youngsters and blacks'. Foreseeing that, sooner or later, trouble would flare up, he wanted to warn that it was the mandarin's responsibility should 'any disastrous event thus occur' (Isabel Nunes 1991: 103). This document clearly exemplifies the potential for conflict that existed in such a situation of superimposed administration.

As the Qing Dynasty weakened, particularly after the Opium Wars, the situation in Macao changed radically. In 1840, Captain Elliot took over the island of Hong Kong on the other side of the Pearl River Delta. Soon after, in 1846, the Portuguese evicted the resident Chinese officials from Macao, starting the 'colonial period'. The *incidente* that took place that same year with the owners of transport boats who attempted to charge the Fortress and the one that occurred at the time of the Governor's death were in some ways unique (cf. Chapter 3). Notwithstanding, they carried the central characteristics of the *incidentes* that preceded them and those that were to follow with similar regularity.

Two aspects in particular deserve our attention due to their systematic occurrence and their structural importance. In the first place, in each case Chinese merchants strictly followed the orders they received from Chinese officials to close all shops and stop providing the market with foodstuffs. This siege technique is an integral part of the Formula. In the second place, once the crisis was declared in all of its violence, the Eurasians that previously were a part of the processes that led to the opening of the conflict started to adopt strategies of mediation and crisis resolution, resorting to their personal networks of friendship among the local Chinese elite.

Victor Turner's notion of the *social drama* inevitably comes to mind (1957: 91–3). For Turner, society is in constant flux. Social order is not an acquired fact, for it is necessarily based upon contradictions and conflicts of interest. Thus, the reproduction of social structure is not a continuous and consensual phenomenon. On the contrary, it takes place by means of processes of rupture and reparation, schism and continuity. Whilst studying a matrilineal Central African society, Turner discovered that this process does not occur in a random fashion. Rather, it possesses a clear diachronical structure characterized by recurrences and regularities.

Thus, he postulates a fourfold processual structure for the social drama. In the first moment – the moment of *rupture* – it is observed that certain social actors do not undertake the sort of behaviour that others expect of them. A public breach occurs in the rules that normally would have applied. If the process is not interrupted at this point by means of mediation, it gives rise to a second moment – the *crisis* – by means of a progressive expansion of the conflict. At this point the camps are clearly separated into two opposing factions.[9] Immediately, however, a third moment begins – the *reparation* – in which mediation generally takes place, normally at the hands of the more prestigious people. These initiatives of reparation may be more or less successful. Depending on their success, the fourth moment may be one of *reintegration* or of *recognition of schism*.

Macao's *incidentes* are textbook cases of social dramas. The trouble is always anteceded by a period of growing conflict and mutual acrimony. The intensity of the accusations mounts and smaller *incidentes* occur that are resolved with increasing difficulty. Sooner or later, however, the crisis manifests itself and Macao divides itself into the 'dominant cleavage in the widest set of relevant social relations' (Turner 1957: 91): Portuguese subjects to one side; Chinese subjects to the other. If prior to this there was margin for manoeuvre, during the explosion of the crisis the Chinese are to one side and the Macanese and Portuguese to the other.

Amidst the confusion and aggression that follow, old personal relations start to manifest themselves timidly. Typically these are seen as acts of great personal worth and courage. The Macanese I interviewed were keen to cite examples of old Chinese friends or old family servants that, in the middle of the night, against all odds, came out to drop food parcels at the back gate of their Macanese friend's house. In time, new chances for mediation always emerge. A period of reparation is initiated which may at times be rather lengthy. At the end of it all, there is a renewed sense of peace and prosperity. In the words of an old Portuguese resident of Macao, 'to grow presupposes that one must undergo crises. Once these are overcome, they are like our familiar typhoon – they clear the air!' (Basto da Silva 1988: 88).

It must be noted that, in the course of the *incidentes*, the contradiction that is at the centre of Macao's social structure manifests itself at all levels for each of the four types of agents involved: the Portuguese, the Macanese, the Chinese of Macao and the Chinese officials.

The Portuguese authorities feel obliged to reiterate their rights of sovereignty, knowing full well that they cannot exercise them against Chinese wishes. The Macanese are 'born of the land', the only ones that can truly exercise rights of citizenship, but they have no rights of sovereignty whatsoever. The local Chinese fully own up to their ethnic and national identity but, notwithstanding, feel that Macao's autonomy is a source of security that they cherish – they know that their citizenship in the city may be denied at any moment.[10] Finally, the Chinese authorities, fully aware of their rights of territorial sovereignty, also know that if they exercise them to the full, they will destroy the city – one of the principal economic and social assets of Guangdong Province.

Thus, right up until the handover in 1999, the Chinese authorities felt that they had a right to intervene in the running of Macao, but lacked the institutional means of doing so without casting out the Portuguese and jeopardizing the survival of the city. The Chinese of Macao felt that their rights as citizens were being diminished, but did not have the means to demand them. When the two met or clashed, an *incidente* flared up. Then, characteristically, the Portuguese and Macanese were left without food and water – and everyone was forced to find a compromise.

The opposition I am making between *rights of citizenship* and *rights of sovereignty* may arguably be contested on the basis that the word 'citizen' is most often applied to people who owe allegiance to a government in which the sovereign power is exercised by the people, whilst the concept of 'subject' is more applicable to situations where allegiance is owed to a personal sovereign. I can only counterargue by pointing out that the ambiguity in definitions is precisely the point. The Chinese Emperor (or his Republican elected successors) has always been, in theory and in practice, sovereign of Macao in the sense of being the ultimate power, the supreme ruler of the land. Up until 1999, however, the Macanese had always been more fully citizens of Macao than the Chinese, for it was they who exercised full rights in the city by virtue of their birth.

Thus, one of the interesting characteristics of the history of Macao is the colourful figures of political mediators that it regularly produces. Men who, in the course of undertaking the most contorted processes of negotiation, end up accumulating considerable personal power, wealth and prestige. Ouvidor Arriaga was one such complex character, who acted as central mediator during the period of the Napoleonic Wars when Britain tried to occupy Macao and when the pirate fleet of Chang Pao surrendered to the Qing (cf. Guimarães 1996 and Murray 1987: 138). Austin Coates says of him that he was 'one of those able, devious and cunning men, of whom Macao has experienced a number, whose commercial and personal ties with the Chinese have been so extensive that in emergencies they have been capable of serving political ends' (1978: 67).

In the twentieth century, Macao produced a number of such complex and ambiguous personalities whose role in the resolution of apparently insurmountable conflicts was often brilliant and whose personal fortunes interpenetrated with their political activities. One such man was the gangster music-lover Pedro José Lobo who negotiated the terms with the Japanese during the Pacific War. Others were Carlos D'Assumpção in the decades that followed the Cultural Revolution, and Ho Yin, who functioned as intermediary between Portugal's right-wing rulers and the CCP during the same period.[11]

Since the beginning of the colonial period, the city's life has been punctuated by the flaring up of *incidentes*, of both major and minor proportions. The most serious, although they have been regular, have not been too frequent. Shortly after the colonial reforms, the killing of the Governor led to one of these processes in 1849/50; in 1900, there were serious disturbances associated with the Boxer Rebellion; in 1922, the events of *Rua da Felicidade* took place in association with the problems that Sun Yat-Sen's regime was having in Canton (cf. Montalto de Jesus 1990: 295–6, Guedes 1991: 87–94); in 1952, during the Korean War, there were important border struggles at the Portas do Cerco (cf. Morbey 1990: 50–1; Fernandes 2000b: 109–15); in 1966/7, the Cultural Revolution came to Macao's streets in what is now called the *123 incidente*. Finally, in 1997/9, the Triad Wars exploded in preparation for the handover. In June of 2000, another minor *incidente* occurred, suggesting that the contradiction that has ruled Macao's existence might not have simply vanished with the handover but merely changed its aspect, namely in ethnic terms.

The major *incidentes* always take place as the result of the unfortunate conjunction of internal and external causes. Thus, on the one hand, they signal the collapse of the balance of power between the Territory's Administration and the Chinese authorities. This collapse tends to be contemporaneous with the occurrence of deep alterations within the Chinese political *status quo*. On the other hand, they are often signs that the interests of the Chinese community in the Territory are not being sufficiently protected by the Administration. They always come about as the result of a slow process of deterioration in the informal links between the Chinese local elite and the principal Macanese figures.

It is worth noting, furthermore, that the more serious crises often coincide with phenomena of population mobility in Guangdong Province. At times of drastic political change in China, vast movements of refugees have occurred. Macao, a territory which is unmoved by the surrounding political upheavals (such as the early Republican struggles, the Civil War, the Maoist Purges or the Cultural Revolution), is a natural *stepping stone* for such political or economic refugees.

Characteristically, after the internal political crisis has been resolved and, as a result, institutional peace has been re-established in China, the refugees merge into the general population or pass on to other destinies of emigration. Then it is the Macanese that enter into crisis. The trauma that they have just undergone functions as a reminder of past traumas and the *fear of abandonment* raises its head. They ask themselves: if we only managed to avoid major disaster by a hair's breadth, will we manage to do so in the next crisis, in six years time or so? Typically this gives rise to another diasporic haemorrhage, as happened after the *incidentes* in the 1920s, after the end of the Pacific War, after the events at the time of the Korean War or after the Cultural Revolution. Over a period of time, the benefits of staying behind outweigh those of leaving the Territory and another period of normality declares itself when, as the poet says, people go about their daily tasks 'forgetting the perils of seafaring'.

The post-colonial period (1967–87) brought about a change in this process, due to the fact that the CCP definitively established its leadership over the Territory's Chinese population. This allowed the CCP to successfully install a shadow government, which continuously and directly oversaw the activities of the Portuguese Administration. Using the neighbourhood associations (*gaai1 fong1 wooi2*) as its foundation in the Territory and the Chinese newspapers as its mouthpiece, the CCP managed to keep reasonable control over Macao's Chinese population, as was all too clear at the time of the elections for the Legislative Assembly in September 1992. In many ways this was only a return to the pre-colonial system of superimposed administration then personified by the figure of the *tso-tang* (*joh2 tong4*) mandarin (cf. Chapter 3). It is perhaps worth noting that the activities of the neighbourhood associations were integrally subsidized by the Administration, out of its annual budget.

This shadow government initially had its headquarters in *Nam Kwong*, the holding firm that, in the 1950s and 1960s, functioned as China's main agent in the clandestine trade that broke the United Nations embargo and made Macao so indispensable to the PRC. During the transition period, after the signing of the Joint Declaration in 1987, the responsibility of the shadow government was handed over to the New China News Agency (*Xinhua*).

It is worth noting that the CCP probably had planned to install a similar system of shadow government in Hong Kong but failed to do so due to the different way in which the British authorities dealt with the Cultural Revolution crisis. As the then Governor of Hong Kong, Sir David Trench, stated, 'Their aim is to Macao us' (Scott 1989: 87).

It would be too simplistic to presume that Macao's contradiction would resolve itself once it was handed over to the PRC. In fact the CCP and the Portuguese government are not the only important agents in this unstable equilibrium. Local forces are of prime importance – both the Macanese and the local Chinese have a say in how the Territory is run, and their opinions seldom coincide. Thus, life in Macao is continually marked by small mutinies, street demonstrations, boycotts by professional groups and politically motivated crimes. For example, in 1989 the migrants without personal documents staged a siege of the Government Palace and, as soon as this was over, the police (PSP, Polícia de Segurança Pública) organized an illegal demonstration in retaliation. These eruptions are an incontestable sign of the tragic lack of institutional means of negotiation that existed in the Territory. Macao's residents (of all ethnic groups) suffer from a serious democratic deficit (cf. Morbey 1990), enhanced by the basic contradiction outlined above. Judging from the Basic Law, which plays the role of a sort of constitution for the post-transition period, this will continue to be the case for the forseeable future. A clear sign of this are the small social dramas that started occurring in the Special Administrative Region in 2000.

This contradiction, which lies at the heart of Macao, has always remained unresolved. The Chinese elites of Guangdong Province have never been persuaded to abdicate from their ultimate rights of sovereignty over Macao but they never wanted to integrate Macao into the Mainland system. The 1999 handover may well not have altered this. On the one hand, the absence of the Portuguese takes away one of the traditional actors but, on the other, the new political system does not resolve the essence of the problem. Three factors subsist: (a) the lack of internal democracy; (b) the attribution of enhanced rights of citizenship to the *boon2 dei6 yan4* (Macao's local people); (c) the essential ambiguity between the interests of the commercial elite of a self-governing territory and the interests of the elite in central control of the Chinese State.

ABOUT THIS BOOK

An anthropologist who writes about Macao and who wants to undertake historically inspired research is constantly faced with a problem of sources. As it happens, the dilemma of failed communication that has always characterized the history of the city permeates all that is written about it. The different interlocutors do not acknowledge that they dialogue with each other. Thus yet another version of the 'negotiated separation' that characterizes the city's ethnic relations is created.

Portuguese-speaking writers tend to focus with unabashed pride or indignant despair on the older history of the city and to write as if China began on the other side of the *Portas do Cerco*. English-speaking writers are systematically unsympathetic to the constraints that led Portuguese historical agents to make their choices. Journalists and commentators on contemporary affairs, in particular, are prone to interpret events in Macao in the light of the Hong Kong experience, often seriously distorting events as a result. The 'thinly veiled snobbery' that Peter Fry identifies in Anglo-American historical and sociological analyses of Portuguese African colonialism is equally found by relation to the Far East (Fry 2000: 121–2). Chinese writers seldom have the political freedom to distance themselves from official policy.[12]

Over the past two decades, the appearance of Macao has been radically altered – its past, its hills, its quarters, its occupants were hidden beneath layers and layers of concrete; its characteristic coastal outline was dramatically changed by landfills; the majority of its population are recent arrivals; the terms of ethnic differentiation have been completely redrawn; the class composition of the city has also changed. In this book I have chosen to focus on specific situations, following them from the present to the past with the hope that, in this way, we can constitute a more fleshed-out context for the events studied.

In a city where changes are so drastic and so sudden, it is impossible not to adopt a historicist perspective. Not least because we ourselves are inevitably part of the processes we describe. I started working on Macao because, together with Nelson Lourenço, I was approached by the Cultural Institute of Macao and invited to write a study of the Macanese. Thus, my very arrival at the Territory was caused by the locally felt need for a monograph about the Eurasian population. Whilst carrying out fieldwork, I was systematically encouraged to give public presentations of my work at which the major cultural representatives of the Macanese as a community were always present. I have always made an effort to steer the course that I feel is most correct. Nevertheless, I do not deny that this reflexive dialogue was a contributing factor in the shaping of my ideas.

Having published a more traditional ethnography of the Eurasian population of Macao, I felt free in the present book to explore different techniques of exposition. Although the book is not an ethnographic monograph, the majority of the discussions are related in one way or another to actual experiences that I had whilst carrying out fieldwork. As Macao's history is so unexpected and so long, I found that in order to make sense of the anecdotes that challenged me intellectually I had to go back into the past and, at times, I had to reflect on the future.

Thus, the strategy I adopted for writing the papers that ultimately gave rise to the present book was to choose an event that seemed to merit clarification. Then, I tried to develop it until I was satisfied that I had somehow made sense of it. This makes for an anecdotal structure and for a temporal disposition of the argument that does not follow the linear chronological arrangements characteristic of most anthropological studies.

The obvious benefit is that, in this way, each case enabled me to explore one or more theoretical problems that seemed to arise out of the cases studied. Going back and forth in temporal terms around each particular quandary, I aimed at setting it within an explanatory framework. The obvious drawback, of course, is that the reader who opts for reading the book from beginning to end will be confronted with a temporal oscillation that may, at times, be confusing. I have attempted to prevent that by being quite systematic about the characterization of the periods of Macao's long history. As the book unfolds, the reader will begin to re-encounter periods and events. Hopefully this will make for a sense of increased familiarity with a social and cultural context that, at best, is rather exceptional.

Chapter 2 deals with the social characterization of the city in the 1990s. It aims to provide a reasonably holistic framework of Macao's social composition. Chapter 3 focuses on the story of the statue of the governor that started the colonial period. By drawing out a biography of his statue, I tried to identify the various forces that moved through it.

Considering that gambling has shaped the city's economy over the past 150 years, Chapter 4 is an essay on gambling and on the history of the first gambling monopoly. It focuses on the issue of rationality and the paradoxes of human action. Chapter 5 occupies itself with the interrelation between person, culture and emotion – one of the central concerns of the book as a whole. I have chosen to study this by reference to the story of a little boy who, at the turn of the twentieth century, was stolen from his home in order to be adopted.

Chapter 6 evolves around another statue. This time one that did not survive but whose absence was repeatedly noted. It is a study of organized amnesia and of the interrelation between memory and trauma in an ethnically divided city. Chapter 7 is about the relation between naming and ethnicity. I look into the way in which Eurasians use naming and explore the differences that are implicit in the two systems of personal naming that have coexisted historically in the Territory – the Portuguese and the Chinese – and which differ in such fundamental ways. Chapter 8 is about gender and its relation to ethnic differentiation and dis-crimination. I draw my principal examples from Eurasian strategies of marriage.

Chapter 9 aims to prove that China's cultural revolutions in the twentieth century gave birth to a modern condition that, in many ways, is unexpectedly continuous with the past. I discuss the way in which the change in gender relations associated with the entry of women into paid employment has dialogued constructively with the Confucian tradition of filial piety, creating new but continuous forms of family life. The final chapter is an attempt to show how the contradiction that we have discussed in this introductory chapter is manifesting itself now that the handover has occurred and that the political and ethnic map of the Territory has been redrawn.

CHAPTER 2

THE CITY'S PROFILE

This chapter introduces the reader to the major traits of the social organization of the Territory in the decade before the handover in December 1999. I carried out fieldwork in the city during annual visits of three to four months from 1990 to 1995. This was followed by shorter visits during the second half of the decade. Therefore, even though the present book is not an ethnographic monograph and the examples discussed here are contextualized in historic terms, the main temporal referent of the research is the transition period (1987–99).[13]

During that period, Macao was a unique place in many respects: the city's population was in constant flux; its economy was dominated by gambling; its political life was marked by a considerable ambiguity of power between the Portuguese and the Chinese State; and its cultural life polarized around a major linguistic and religious faultline. So, after a brief historical incursion into the origins of the ethnic composition of Macao, these various aspects will be discussed. Finally, I will attempt to characterize the three principal ethnic categories that structured the Territory's everyday life: the Portuguese, the Macanese and the Chinese.[14]

THE HISTORICAL ORIGINS OF MACAO'S ETHNIC COMPOSITION

The subjects of the King of Portugal that settled in Macau in the 1550s formed a Christian community that spoke some form of maritime Portuguese which included elements of the most diverse origins, from everywhere in the Asian seafaring world. In time, a local Creole culture came into existence that, having its roots in the Portuguese cultural world, evinced distinctive features.

Thus came into existence the Macanese: a group of Eurasians who have played a central role in the four and a half centuries of the city's history. The Cantonese refer to them as *to2 saang1* (lit. 'land born') – which is quite apposite, considering that they are the only group that can properly lay claim to being of this land. In its everyday usage in the Territory this category is still ethnically restrictive, excluding the Chinese.

A Chinese person living in the city describes him or herself as *O3 Moon4 yan4* (lit. Macao person) and not as *to2 saang1* (Port. *Macaense*). Technically, in the pre-colonial periods, the Chinese resided outside the walls of the Catholic citadel and could not be considered as belonging to it. This explains why you could still hear in the 1990s older Chinese people responding to the question 'where do you live?' with the expression *O3 Moon4 Gaai1* (lit. Macao road). For the Ming and Qing authorities, Macao did not have a separate existence. It was subject to the military mandarin at Casa Branca (Mand. *Qinshan*) and was part of the district of Heungsan (today Mand. *Zhongshan*).

In order to understand Macao, we have to grasp the history of this 'negotiated separation'. To one side of the wall, there were the Chinese folk who, although living here, were identical to the remainder of the subjects of the Chinese Emperor. To the other side, there was a local Creole population who distinguished themselves from the former by two main features: being Catholic and being subjects of the King of Portugal – these two features were, in fact, rarely distinguishable.

To cut a long story short, it can be said that this Creole community integrated people coming from other groups by means of one of two processes: marriage (or concubinage) and conversion. In the first instance, all evidence suggests that, as elsewhere in the Portuguese overseas expansion, children born of local women were often recognized as offspring by their Portuguese or Eurasian fathers – even when such relations were temporary or not legitimized by religious marriage.

The contrary, for example, was the case with the British. For this reason it is still important today to draw a clear distinction between ethnic relations in Hong Kong and in Macao. An older Macanese man, who still remembers the unpleasant treatment he received in Hong Kong in the 1940s, told me: 'A Portuguese *mestiço* was called Portuguese. An English *mestiço* was called *half-caste*.' This explains why up to the 1970s, it was common in Hong Kong to distinguish clearly between *Europeans*, *Eurasians* and *Portuguese*. The latter category comprised mainly the offspring of Macanese families and resulted from centuries of cross-ethnic intermarriage.

The second way in which the Macanese community integrated people was through conversion to Catholicism[15] – particularly if these people were young and had been brought up as Portuguese speakers. Up until 1841, the Qing forbade any of their subjects from converting to Christianity. That meant that all the persons who converted lost their Chinese ethnic identity, cut their long plait (which symbolized their condition as subjects of the Manchu emperors), started wearing Western clothing, adopted a Portuguese name and were integrated into the Macanese community in one way or another.[16]

For most of the city's history, Chinese residents felt rather jaundiced about Christian conversion. It was considered a sort of treachery, not only towards one's Chinese identity but specially towards one's ancestors. From the late eighteenth century to the mid-nineteenth century, the Catholic Church did not allow converts to continue to celebrate the Confucian rites of respect for the ancestors and encouraged converts to change their name. In the eyes of traditional neo-Confucian opinion this was highly deplorable.

The 'personal parish' (missionary) of Saint Lazarus was founded just outside the walls of the old city in 1846 precisely in order to respond to the needs of the growing number of Chinese Catholics after the Opium Wars, when the Qing were forced to allow conversion of their subjects. Nevertheless, this Confucian prejudice did not disappear until the 1960s. Chinese Catholics told me that in their childhood in the 1930s they were subject to humiliation by their fellow Chinese (cf. Chapter 7). Today, conversion no longer brings a conflict in ethnic identity.

PEOPLE IN MOTION

From the outset, when it received people from the four quarters of the Portuguese commercial empire in South and East Asia, Macao was a point of passage. This became the case increasingly once the Chinese started emigrating. At the end of the Qing period, Macao became notorious as one of the principal points of departure for the Chinese Diaspora: Macao was the point of departure for the majority of coolies – indentured labourers destined for the plantations and mines of the Caribbean, Southeast Asia and South America.

The first cargo of coolies left from Amoy (Mand. *Xiamen*, in Fukien province) and arrived in Cuba in 1847. The export of coolies from Macao started in 1851 (cf. Teixeira 1976: 77). After the foundation of Hong Kong, Macao's economy was seriously debilitated, so this activity was welcomed at first by local residents as a possible source of revenue. The export trade expanded rapidly, largely due to the fact that there was a large increase in the number of people wishing to emigrate from southern China in the decades that followed the social disorder and devastation caused by the Taiping Revolution and its suppression (1850–64 – cf. Hsü 1990: 221–58). The activity was prohibited in Hong Kong, but the shipping of emigrants from Macao was mostly subsidized by British and Chinese capital.

All too soon evidence of abuse of the emigrants became apparent. Such abuse was taking place all along the way: in the manner men were engaged inside China; in the way they were quartered, chosen and shipped in Macao; in the conditions to which they were subjected in these ships, which often led to a high percentage of deaths; and, finally, in the horribly brutal destiny that awaited them at the end of the trip. Eça de Queiroz, the famous Portuguese novelist, who was at the time consul in Habana, was one of the principal personalities who pressed the Portuguese government to forbid this commerce by insisting on the brutality and lack of freedom that coolies faced in Cuba (cf. Teixeira 1976: 50–69).

In Macao, the first legislation attempting to control the export of labourers dates from 1853. Many other acts aiming at a 'moralization' of procedures immediately followed it: in 1855, 1859, 1860, 1868, 1871, 1872 and 1873 – all to no avail. Finally, due to international humanitarian pressure, the transport of coolies from Macao was forbidden in December 1873.

To give an idea of the size of the tragedy involved, it is worth citing an official report of May 1872. It admits that crimes were indeed committed but it attempts to free the Territory's Administration from responsibility by stressing the efficacy of its policing. As proof, it states that 57 883 men left for the Americas between 1868 and 1872. But it declares that, as a result of its activities of policing, a further 15 138 men did not go and were freed because they declared they did not wish to go! The question remains, if they did not wish to go, how come they arrived in Macao, all 15 138 of them?

The role of Macao as a stepping-stone for the Chinese Diaspora, however, was not limited to the coolie trade and continues to the present day. Many intellectuals passed through Macao on their way out of China during the troubled years of the collapse of the Qing regime. Famous among them are the figures of Kang Yu-Wei (Lo 1967) and

Sun Yat-Sen. The latter had a lasting relationship with the city (cf. Guedes 1991).

Later still, the civil war that followed the end of the Pacific War and the first decade of the Communist regime saw large numbers of people passing through the Territory. Those who felt dissatisfied with the new Chinese regime were often able to escape via Macao due to the relative informality of the administrative arrangements.[17] Between 1949 and 1976, there was a steady flow of migrants, many of them political refugees who arrived at the Territory in the direst conditions.

In the 1950s, however, many people made the inverse trajectory. Ethnic Chinese of Southeast Asia, who were being subjected to political and ethnic persecution in Indonesia, Malaysia and Burma, returned to China via Macao. Some even came back from further afield. An old Eurasian man I met had arrived in Macao when he was a child. His father was the son of coolies in Peru and had decided to return to his father's native village. He brought with him his young son and his Peruvian wife of Hispanic origin. He died soon after arriving at his ancestral village. His wife, the old man's mother, lost in the midst of a people she could not communicate with, fled with her son to Macao, where he was raised and lived his whole life as a Macanese.

Those migrants who came from Southeast Asia constituted an important sub-group of the Territory's Chinese elite in the 1980s and 1990s. The story of a friend of mine is characteristic. His father decided to return from Indonesia, where he was persecuted for his left-wing views in the early 1960s. He brought with him a considerable fortune, which he handed over to the Party. Some years later, the whole family was subjected to persecution in China for their capitalist past and was classified as belonging to one of the sadly famous Maoist 'black classes'. After much suffering he managed to bring his family to Macao, where he died soon after. His courageous wife raised their four children in the Territory, but none of them now live there, having emigrated to Canada and the United States.

After the political changes associated with Deng Xiaoping, the numbers increased but then most migrants were motivated by economic considerations. This is not to say that many did not suffer considerably in order to make their escape. In the 1990s, the Territory's Administration was still returning 6 000 clandestine migrants to China annually, which gives only a vague idea of the movement of people involved.

The Eurasians too have a long history of migration. Every time the city undergoes one of its major *incidentes*, families start preparing to leave in order to search for a more secure abode. Considering how small the Territory is, there are surprisingly large communities of Macanese emigrants in São Paulo, Lisbon, Sydney, Toronto and San Francisco.

THE POPULATION OF MACAO IN THE TRANSITION PERIOD

The Territory's population has been increasing since the beginning of the twentieth century. In 1936, for example, it was thought to have reached 120 000 inhabitants. During the Pacific War, Macao was not formally occupied by the Japanese, as Portugal was a neutral country, so it functioned as a refuge. With the result that, in 1940, a reasonable estimate points to the presence of 400 000 persons in the Territory (cf. Chan and Tan 1990: 219).[18] The city was filled with refugees. The supply of basic foods was very limited and many people lived a tragic existence (cf. Silva 1991).

Immediately after Japan's defeat (1945), a large number of the refugees returned to their places of origin or emigrated further afield. One of the largest surges of Macanese emigration occurred at this time. Thus, in 1960, official estimates report the resident population as amounting to 169 299 inhabitants (Chan and Tan 1990: 219). In 1970, due to the refugees that fled from the PRC at the time of the Cultural Revolution, it was estimated to have increased to 248 636 (Macau 1979–88). The process of economic and political migration associated with the Chinese Communist regime had started. At this time the migrants were mostly men and they usually arrived in the Territory in a desperate state.

During the 1970s, Macao experienced a period of great demographic growth. This was intensified after 1976, when Deng Xiaoping started his 'Four Modernisations Reform' which eventually liberalized the circulation of persons and goods in the PRC. At the same time, the fast economic development of the Pacific Rim benefited the Territory, with the result that many more migrants decided to remain here. The official population figure for 1981 was 261 806, but the real number was probably much higher. During the following decade the rate of growth continued.

The figures in Table 1 are official estimates. It has to be stated, however, that many sectors of opinion have declared that they are grossly under-evaluated.

THE CITY'S PROFILE

Table 1 Population for 1991 and 1996

	1991 Census	1996 Intercensus
Population total	403 038	454 607
Resident	355 693	414 128
Present Mobile	47 345	40 476

Source: Macau 1997a

In 1989, Alice Delarue de Matos declared that,

If the trends in migratory movement and natural population growth registered between 1970 and 1988 are kept constant, Macao's population would double in 21 years, that is it would reach 887 000 persons by the year 2010. The continuation of migratory movements of the order registered during that period would raise very serious problems of social order, so much so that the population density of the Territory already represents one of the highest values in international terms (25 500 inhabitants per km^2). (1989: 448)

The rapid growth of the Chinese economy and the liberalization of the social system of the Mainland in the late 1980s and 1990s means that these predictions were not confirmed.

The official figures allow us to evaluate the nature of the flow of immigration (cf. Macau 1993; Macau 1997a). In 1996, 56 per cent of the population of Macao had been born outside the city. Moreover, only 20 per cent of these had been in the Territory in 1976. People born and previously residing in the PRC constituted 80 per cent and 81.3 per cent (respectively in 1991 and 1996) of the resident population that had been born outside Macao. If we look at the first year of residence in the Territory of these people, we can get an idea of the periods of greater immigration.

These figures suggest that the years 1977–81 were years of particularly intensive immigration, especially by comparison with the five previous years. During the 1980s, immigration was stabilized at a slightly lower level, corresponding to more or less half of the flow. During the first half of the 1990s, the trend was maintained at roughly the same level.

Furthermore, we can observe that, once the 1976–82 migratory climax was over, immigration from the PRC assumed different characteristics. When we consider the male/female ratio among migrants, we observe that before 1982 there was more than one man for each woman. After that date the tendency is for the female component to increase until it

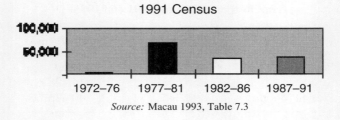

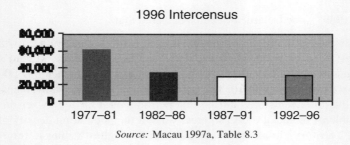

Figure 2 Year of entry of residents in Macao born in the PRC

reaches a level of nearly two women for each man (cf. Macau 1993, Table 7.3 and Macau 1997a, Table 8.3). These figures are distorted by two factors. On the one hand, male clandestine labour (usually in construction) is far more visible and subject to policing (as female clandestine labour tends to be domestic or associated to prostitution). On the other hand, there is a greater male drive to re-emigrate to economically more attractive destinies.

Finally, the immigrational flux is mainly composed of young people – in 1984, 82 per cent of the immigrants were in the age groups between 5 and 34 years old (cf. Macau 1984). What this means is that, by the 1990s, Macao had a population with very high levels of economically active members: 'The Dependency Ratio in 1985 (39.0) was the lowest among the 129 countries whose statistics were published by the World Bank' (Tse 1990: 79).

MAIN ECONOMIC ACTIVITIES

By the 1870s it was consensual in the city that the administration of the Territory would not be possible were it not for the taxes produced by the opium and gambling concessions (*O Independente*, 11/02/1875, p. 2). The monopoly that started Macao's long history of gambling concessions is that of the curious lottery that was played on the basis of the family names of the candidates that passed the imperial examinations – the *vaeseng,* which is described in Chapter 4.

In 1910, the Governor's report to Macao's representative in the Portuguese Parliament stated that 70 per cent of the Administration's income resulted from taxes raised from the opium and gambling monopolies and only 30 per cent from the remaining taxes (quoted in *A Verdade*, 31/03/1910, p. 3). To a greater or lesser extent this tendency is still valid today. The opium concessions terminated immediately after the Pacific War – the opium houses were burnt in 1945. However a new profitable business appeared: gold. Portugal's neutrality during the Pacific War meant that it was not one of the signatories of the Bretton Woods Agreements that founded the International Monetary Fund. This meant that Macao was not subject to the controls over the commerce in gold imposed on other countries.

The Western blockade of the PRC, particularly during and after the Korean War, also meant that it needed a safe haven for the purchase of international goods. Right up until 1970, the gold commerce brought fabulous profits to the Territory's concessionaires – the principal members of this syndicate being Pedro José Lobo and later Y.C. Liang and Ho Yin. The taxes raised from this activity by the Administration constituted 15 per cent to 22 per cent of its annual income. Only after that date does the gambling concession become the principal source of public funding of the Territory's administration (cf. Fernandes 2000a).

Other commercial activities (often clandestine) were of major importance to Macao's survival during the second half of the twentieth century. For example, in October 1997, as a result of a shootout with the police, two Chinese men from Macao involved in arms and drugs dealing were caught in Phnom Pehn, Cambodia (*Reuters*, 20/10/97). In Macao, a spokesman for the Undersecretary for Security told the press that it would be reasonable to suppose that, if there were Macao people dealing in arms in Cambodia, it was because the border between China and Macao had become temporarily less permeable due to the recent collaboration between the authorities as a result of the conflicts concerning the Triads (*South China Morning Post*, 22/10/97). There was nothing new about this trade, as Macao had been an important stepping-stone for the armament business during the Korean and Vietnam Wars.

In the 1980s and 1990s the main economic activity of the Territory was gambling. The first modern concession, integrating various types of games, was made to *Companhia Tai Hing* in June 1934.[19] Everything points to the fact that the principal members of this syndicate – Fu Tak-Iam and Kou Ho-Neng – derived immense wealth from it, but very little found its way back to the Administration. In 1961, after the death of the original concessionaires, Governor Jaime Silvério Marques managed to negotiate new terms for a gambling contract with STDM (*Sociedade de Turismo e Diversões de Macao*). This society's figurehead was Stanley Ho – a member of a distinguished Hong Kong Eurasian family. However, the principal shareholder has always been Henry Fok, a 'red capitalist' of humble origin, who played an important role in the transition of Hong Kong to Chinese rule in 1997. This new gambling contract with the STDM obliged the gambling company to undertake a number of public works. These were carried out in the 1970s and early 1980s and came to constitute the basis for the future prosperity of Macao in the 1980s.

Subsequent renegotiations of the gambling contract have been of central importance to the development of Macao. The additional income obtained from the 1983 negotiation allowed for the modernization and expansion of the Administration that took place under Governor Almeida e Costa. The 1986 agreement and the added benefits it brought allowed for the major public works conceived by Governor Carlos Melancia and carried out by his successors before the 1999 handover – the New Taipa Bridge, the recent landfills, the airport.

During the 1980s, the textile industry developed due to the advantageous conditions Macao had in the GATT Agreement. New sectors of industrial activity also made their appearance: toys, leather articles and electrical products. At that time, the Province of Guangdong entered into a process of accelerated economic growth. The formal and informal interpenetration between Macao and its surrounding region is determinant. The 1990s saw great development in the building industry, but the decade ended with a near collapse of this sector.

In spite of all this, Macao's economy is solidly based on the 'leisure industries', particularly those activities that are associated with gambling as practised in casinos. Approximately one-third of the declared legal profits of STDM are paid to the government as taxes, constituting around 40 per cent of the income of the Administration and 27 per cent of the Gross Domestic Product (GDP).

In this respect, very little has changed over the last two decades of growth. In 1984, a government report stated that the activities associated with gambling 'represent around 25% of GDP' (Macau 1984: 27). It went on to say that the income from the concession of exclusive rights to gambling constituted 56 per cent of the Administration's income (ibid.: 142).

In turn, it has been estimated that roughly three-quarters of the tourist industry is geared to serving gamblers. The number of entries and exits from Macao is considerable: for example, in the first six months of 1997, nearly four million people passed through the Territory, a figure corresponding to a large majority of the inhabitants of Hong Kong. In previous years the figures had been higher (Macau 1997b), which was due to the Triad War that was going on at the time (see Chapter 9). The traditional flow of tourists from Thailand, Taiwan and Japan remained stable throughout the 1990s, whilst the number of visitors from the PRC increased annually, according to the increase in prosperity of the province of Guangdong.

A curious essay published by the office of the Inspector of the Games' Contracts states that, 'Gambling and its associated activities (hotels, restaurants, bars, shows, transports, etc.) are a sector of intensive labour use; for example, at each casino table there are normally four employees (aside from the numerous inspection personnel) who work in shifts of four to six hours. In a casino that operates for twenty-four hours, therefore, there will be a minimum of 20 people per table (16 dealers + 4 inspectors)' (Macau 1985a: 55). In 1984, an official publication further specified that 'gambling employs directly around 3% of the active population of the Territory, and the group of gambling-related activities reaches 10% of total employment' (Macau 1984: 85).

This is doubtlessly still an underestimation. The numbers of people involved in activities associated with gambling must be very large. Experience of random street interviewing in Macao indicates that a considerable number of the men who are asked to fill in sociological questionnaires reply that it is not 'convenient' to specify their employment (cf. Brito 1994: 79).

All of this means that, during the 1980s and early 1990s, the city had very low rates of unemployment, even in official terms. In 1996, the Census Office estimated that only 3 per cent of the population of over 14 years of age was unemployed; of these, 7.5 per cent were students and 15 per cent were domestics (Macau 1997a, Table 5.1). However, as a result of the Asian economic crisis in the late 1990s, unemployment has become a serious problem in the post-transition period.

BROAD LINES OF CULTURAL DIFFERENTIATION

In its broadest perspective, social life in Macao in the transition period structured itself around two linguistic universes: the Cantonese and the Portuguese. A large majority of the population (97 per cent in 1991) spoke one of the Chinese languages – in turn, 89 per cent of these were Cantonese speakers (Macao 1993, Table 4.6). Portuguese was important as a language of administration, not as a home language, since the largest number of Eurasians spoke Cantonese as their home language. English, which is in all likelihood everyone's second language, does not constitute a source of cultural self-identification in the Territory.

Each of the two linguistic universes had its own media – both on television and in the press, where the linguistic split was absolute. Although they corresponded to some feelings of personal identification, these linguistic universes will not be considered here as ethnic communities. Rather, they constitute the background upon which ethnic identity builds itself. I will start by qualifying two of the institutional fields within which these factors of cultural differentiation are played: formal education and religion.

Formal education

1985 will be taken as an example. By then the effects of the considerable investment that the Administration had made in the quality of the educational system in the early 1980s were beginning to be felt.

The Administration directly controlled ten official schools, of which six taught exclusively in Portuguese and three were Luso-Chinese (cf. Macau 1985b). There were still three semi-official schools (two were religious and the other was ethnically specific, the Macanese school). There were sixty-five private schools. Among these, fifty-seven taught exclusively in Chinese; five exclusively in English; and two were Anglo-English (one of these, a night school, also had a Portuguese variant). The great majority, 92.9 per cent, of all the students in the Territory studied in private schools.

As can be seen in Figure 3, only 83 per cent of the students followed an exclusively Chinese curriculum, 8 per cent followed an English curriculum and 4 per cent mixed language curricula (Portuguese-Chinese or English-Chinese). Therefore, we can say that 95 per cent of the student population corresponded *latu sensu* to the linguistic community of Chinese language speakers in the Territory. This again corroborates the notion that Macao's population is a population in flux, one whose horizons lay in further migration: in the mid-1980s, Macao and Hong Kong were *stepping-stones* between China and the world (Yee 1989).

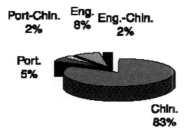

Source: Macau 1985b: 79–82

Figure 3 Language of schooling – Macao 1985

The repeated attempts to develop integrated schooling curricula were always thwarted by the fact that the Chinese middle class that controlled the schools and the Administration did not share the same cultural referents and had widely divergent socio-political perspectives. For example, only in the late 1990s did it become possible to teach the history of Macao in the Chinese and Anglo-Chinese schools. Informal interviews with a significant sample of the Territory's Chinese secondary-school history teachers showed that they were not clearly conscious that the city's foundation had been part of a larger movement of commercial and political expansion that had carried the Portuguese State to many other parts of the world![20]

As for higher education and professional training, concerted and expensive efforts were undertaken in the 1990s to provide the city with a modernized infrastructure. These were not as successful as might have been hoped, due to the lack of informed and systematic policies on the part of the Administration, but it is reasonable to hope that the post-transition period will see a consolidation of the institutions that are presently in the Territory.

As often happens with Chinese Diasporic communities, migrants that arrived in the city after the late 1970s went to great lengths to improve their education. Between 1991 and 1996, the percentage of the population that lacked all forms of schooling dropped from 15.2 per cent to 14 per cent. The percentage of those who only attained a primary school education dropped from 47.7 per cent to 45.9 per cent. On the other hand, the percentage of the population with some form of secondary schooling increased from 31 per cent to 34.7 per cent and those who had undergone higher education increased from 4.4 per cent to 5.5 per cent (Macau 1993, Table 4.5; Macau 1997a, Table 4.8).

Religious composition

I was surprised to discover that, in 1991, only 16.8 per cent of the resident population declared that they had a Buddhist religious affiliation. The only other religion with any statistic impact in the Territory was Catholicism – 6.7 per cent of the residents declared it. It should be remembered, however, that the majority of these would be included in the 5 per cent of the city's residents that claim not to have any Chinese ascendancy. Moreover, about 61 per cent of the residents declared that they had no religion (Macau 1993, Table 2.7).

These statistics could be interpreted to mean that the policies of militant atheism furthered by the Chinese Communist regime affected the population that arrived in the Territory after 1976. However, the available studies of religious practices concerning Macao and Hong Kong suggest that this was not the case (e.g. Peixoto 1988; Brito 1994; Lang and Ragvald 1993). The great majority of the population of these cities is regularly involved in one form or another of ritual and religious practice – in particular, the Buddhist/Taoist rituals that are characteristic of Chinese popular religion and that are such an integral part of the life of the Chinese population of these cities. In Sangren's words, 'much of Chinese ritual activity can be viewed in terms of various forms of exchange between people and categories of spirits. To put it rather crudely, one propitiates dangerous ghosts, provides for the material and spiritual needs of deceased kin, and bribes powerful gods' (Sangren 1987: 52).

We must, therefore, agree with Ana Brito (1994: 6 and 87–8), in the wake of an already long history of anthropological research on these matters, that what is at stake here is the very category 'religion'. This was not even a common concept in Chinese in the nineteenth century (cf. Feuchtwang 1991). Not only do the Chinese have a 'diffuse' experience of religion (Yang 1961), they even share a propensity to minimize the importance of religious behaviour (Brito 1994: 90 and J. Watson 1993). We conclude that those who declared themselves 'Buddhist' or 'Taoist' were declaring more than the simple generalized allegiance to a religious 'faith' and its life cycle rituals, of the kind that characterizes Portuguese Catholicism. On the contrary, we must read such declarations as implying a formal and intensive type of affiliation, generally associated to the sort of ground-level Buddhist and Taoist communities that were proliferating in Macao during the 1990s. These constituted small centres that were marginally associated to one or another of the large Buddhist monasteries and Taoist temples that were visited by the population on a regular basis.

Contrary to Hong Kong, Macao's Administration was never involved in the management of Chinese temples. The almost total association of the Administration and of the local Portuguese with Catholicism meant that strong efforts were always made to further the Catholic faith (cf. Brito 1994: 52). However, it was never possible to assume openly repressive attitudes towards Chinese religious practices as the authorities on the other side of the *Portas do Cerco* would never have allowed it.

Thus, the first time the Portuguese Administration got involved in Chinese religious matters was as part of the policy of preserving the city's historical sites that has been so successfully carried out since the mid-1980s. At the same time, during the 1970s and the 1980s, there was a decline in the importance of the role played by the temples as centres for the communal activities of the Chinese population of the city. This was the result of the new immigration and of the policies of informal control of the population carried out by the Mainland government. The management committees of the three wealthiest and most frequently visited temples are currently presided over by a single monk who has had solid connections with the PRC for a long time (Brito 1994: 58–63 and 74).

Before the changes that took place in the 1970s, there was a strong relationship between religious behaviour and ethnic belonging. This is no longer the case. The Catholic Church changed the way it ran its parishes in the mid-1960s. Previously, this was ethnically differentiated – there were parishes for Macanese that were territorial, as they are in Catholic Europe, and then there was a 'personal parish' for the Chinese (St Lazarus). As a result of the policies emerging from the II Vatican Council, this changed and the territorial system was applied to all Catholics. This meant that Chinese Catholics started using the old Macanese churches. At the same time, and for the same reasons, the number of Chinese clerics increased and started to have a more decisive impact on the running of the diocese. It wasn't until 1987 that a Chinese bishop was appointed – the first one in four and a half centuries. Being a strong advocate of the 'enculturation' of the Catholic religion, he put in train a programme to open up the Church to the Chinese community.

In the eighteenth century, Macao was the terrain where the famous 'Chinese Rites Controversy', which opposed the Jesuits to the Dominicans and Franciscans, was enacted. In 1742, the Jesuits finally lost the fight and the Pope decided in favour of forbidding Chinese Catholics from practising the Confucian rites of ancestor worship, considering them to be idolatrous. Ultimately, this led to the expulsion of the missionaries from China in 1770. There is something uncanny, therefore, about the fact that, today, Chinese Catholics in Macao have started to practise such rites again – even some of the most important clerical figures, as I chanced to witness whilst visiting a Catholic cemetery. In some of the parishes in the Territory, the Christian Day of All Souls is celebrated not on 1 November, but on the two days of the lunar calendar that the Chinese use to celebrate their dead (Brito 1994: 32).

Curiously, however, the privileged relationship between the Administration and the Catholic Church dating back to the *Padroado do Oriente* (instituted in the sixteenth century) has survived all of these changes. In the 1990s, the Administration subsidized annually the activities of the Church and Catholic priests continued to have the status of civil servants. Oddly enough, this is a survival of the nineteenth-century Liberal legislation. The Republican Law of Separation between the Church and the State (proclaimed in the early days of the Portuguese Republic, 20/04/1911) was never enforced in the Asian colonies, which were subject to the *Padroado*. This further explains the important role that was attributed to the Bishop during the process of drafting of the Basic Law of the Special Autonomous Region of Macao.

BROAD ETHNIC CATEGORIES

Macao's history is marked centrally by three broadly defined ethnic categories: the Chinese, the Macanese and the Portuguese. The relationships between these groups are not of the same type and the groups themselves are internally structured in divergent fashions. We will start with the smallest of them.

The Portuguese in Macao

According to the 1991 Census there were 4191 inhabitants born outside the Territory whose former residence was Portugal (Macau 1993, Table 7.2). In the 1996 Intercensus the figure for the same category was slightly higher – 4766 (Macau 1997a, Table 8.2).[21] The 1991 Census established that 321 of these people resided in the Territory before 1976. Such people, who arrived before the changes that took place in the late 1970s, are now an integral part of the Macanese community. The remainder, in particular those who arrived after the mid-1980s as part of the drive to modernize the Administration, developed a considerable identitary differentiation from the Macanese. In fact, in the Portuguese-language high school, there were regular conflicts in the early 1990s between the Portuguese children and the children of the Macanese.

Most of these stayed in Macao for short periods: in 1991, 75 per cent of the Portuguese residents had been there for less than six years (Macau 1993, Table 7.2). Some of these eventually developed closer links with the city's population and established permanent residence. Those who married Chinese or Macanese persons usually stayed in Macao and were integrated into the Macanese community.

The Macanese

It is impossible to know how many of the inhabitants of Macao consider themselves to be Macanese. The very nature of the Macanese as a community that occupied an intermediary area between the Chinese majority and the Portuguese administrative minority makes for many situations of uncertain definition.

A realistic estimate would suggest that, in the early 1990s, the Macanese ethnic community in the Territory numbered around 7000 (cf. Pina-Cabral and Lourenço 1993a).[22] It should be remembered that there are many Macanese living in Hong Kong and that there is a constant flux between the Territory and the areas where Diasporic communities have been formed (especially Portugal, Western Canada, the San Francisco Bay area and Australia). In all probability, the number of Macanese families living abroad is considerably higher than those living in Macao.

Over the centuries, a Creole culture developed in Macao in much the same way as it developed in other areas where Portuguese Eurasian communities were established – Malacca, Goa, Diu, for example. The word *creolo* was used in Macao until very recently to mean a Chinese person of servile status who was raised in a Portuguese home. In this book, however, I will use its English derivation 'Creole' in the sense that has become common usage in anthropological literature (e.g. Cohen 1981) to mean a socio-cultural community whose main historical elements derive from the cross-fertilization of historical traditions that are not only stronger than itself, but also continue to interrelate with it.

Right up to the mid-nineteenth century, the subjects of the King of Portugal that lived in Macao, integrated into their language, culture and life style a series of influences that reached them from the whole of the maritime world of Eastern Asia. Even though they remained Portuguese and Catholic, they created a life style that had its own distinctive identity and had an internal coherence. They developed distinctive styles of eating, dressing and domestic architecture, a dialect and a traditional outlook on the economic and social conditions that constituted their long-term environment.

All this was radically challenged during the 'the colonial period' (1846–1967). Soon after the foundation of Hong Kong, it was made clear to the Macanese that if they did not become more 'European' they would lose many of the privileges that justified their very continuation as a distinct community. Thus, their language first became a domestic language and then disappeared altogether in less than a century. Their cuisine, which survived only as a curiosity, was brought to light in the 1990s as a commercial tourist attraction. Their style of dressing was abandoned nearly overnight. Their domestic manners became increasingly European and modern.

For most of the twentieth century, right up to the late 1970s, the Macanese defined themselves as 'Portuguese of the Orient'. But, after this watershed – which is marked by the departure of Portuguese troops from Macao (December 1975) and the opening of China to an international style of economic development – the Macanese started looking for other ways of defining themselves. Ways that stressed their *intercultural condition*. The people I met with in the 1990s still felt strongly bound by their identity as Macanese and signalled this by means of a set of cultural referents, but their cultural dispositions no longer had the consistency that had characterized the Creole community in the precolonial period (before 1846). They shared in the cultural worlds of both the Chinese and the Portuguese.

Perhaps the best means of giving a sense of the main terms of self-identification of the Macanese of the transition period is to quote a passage from an interview carried out in 1992.

> Fundamentally, to be Macanese is to be born in Macao. But, in order to understand this community . . . the word means anyone who was born in Macao but has a Portuguese culture. [. . .]
>
> The Macanese is a trifle difficult; he is not an easy person. The fact of the matter is that, in order to reach a concrete definition, we know if someone is or is not Macanese because he shares some

features, a type of attitude, a certain way of speaking, of thinking, that identifies him totally as being Macanese [. . .].

To be a Macanese is fundamentally to be from Macao with Portuguese ancestors, but not necessarily to be of Sino-Portuguese descent. The local community was born from Portuguese men, [. . .] but in the beginning the woman was Goanese, Siamese, Indo-Chinese, Malay – they came to Macao in our boats. Sporadically it was a Chinese woman.

When we established ourselves here, the Chinese ostracized us. The Portuguese had their wives, then, that came from abroad, but they could have no contact with the Chinese women, except the fishing folk, the *tanka* women and the female slaves. Only the lowest class of Chinese contacted with the Portuguese in the first centuries. But later the strength of Christianization, of the priests, started to convince the Chinese to become Catholic. [. . .] But, when they started to be Catholics, they adopted Portuguese baptismal names and were ostracized by the Chinese Buddhists. So they joined the Portuguese community and their sons started having Portuguese education without a single drop of Portuguese blood.

Concretely, in the course of many interviews concerning 'Macanese identity', I came to identify three vectors of self-identification that were systematically used for the purposes of classifying themselves and others as being a member of the community.

The first vector is *language* – specifically, any form of association between a person or his or her family and the Portuguese language. The second is *religion* – some form of personal or familial identification with Catholicism. Finally, the third vector is *phenotypic appearance* – some type of Eurasian appearance. The order in which I presented the three vectors is not a statement of their relative importance.

Each of these vectors may constitute the basis for identification of a Macanese person, but it is not necessary for all or any of the three to be present in order for someone to identify him or herself, or be identified by others, as Macanese. In other words, it is possible for someone to be considered Macanese even when he or she does not possess one of the traits in question. For example, there are people today, who are generally considered to be Macanese, who do not have mixed European and Asian ancestry. Equally, there are persons who, while being regarded as full members of the community, do not speak Portuguese fluently. There is a certain element of personal option in this identity, since I could cite cases of people whose family background would suggest that they should be Macanese, but who have opted for a Chinese identity for personal reasons. The contrary may also happen – for example, people who were brought up in Portuguese schools and who took on the Macanese identity as a result of that.

It must be understood, however, that those persons and families who possess the three types of traits – particularly those who, in addition, achieve some sort of educational, political or financial distinction – constitute a nucleus of families around which Macanese identity constructs itself in association to a specific form of community life (cf. Pina-Cabral 2000a). These are the so-called *traditional families*.

The Portuguese inhabitants of Macao were always obliged to live in an intercultural condition. Their role as mediators and translators (the word used was *línguas*, meaning both tongue and language) is clearly expressed throughout the history of Macao and Hong Kong. During the colonial period there were many Macanese working in this manner in most Chinese port cities, such as Shanghai and Tianjin. Their linguistic dispositions are, therefore, a topic of considerable interest.

For roughly three centuries, the Territory's main language was *patuá* – a Creole dialect very close to the Portuguese maritime Creoles that were spoken in most parts of the Portuguese maritime empire, from Cape Verde to Timor. At the turn of the nineteenth century, Marques Pereira defined it thus:

> apart from the Malay influence, the *language of Macao* was influenced by the Indian *canarim* or language of Goa, due to the continued and ancient relations between Macao and Portuguese India, from which it was dependent. And the Chinese element. The greater part of the syntactic forms is of Chinese origin, which must not surprise, since there has been continuous contact between the Chinese and the Portuguese inhabitants. Furthermore, one should not forget the Spanish element, due to the proximity of relation with the Philippines and, more recently, the English element. (1984 [1889], I: 54)

These types of Portuguese Creoles were the principal commercial languages of Southeast Asia right up to the eighteenth century, giving way to the English *pidgin* in the early nineteenth century. Thus, at the beginning of the twentieth century, the intercultural condition of the Macanese meant that English had become an important language in the city. The same authority tells us, '. . . not so long ago, one rarely found a Macanese that did not speak English fairly correctly, with good grammar and pronunciation, whilst it was not easy to find anyone that could carry through a conversation in standard Portuguese [*portuguez legitimo*]' (1984 [1889], I: 55).

In those days, one could hear different versions of *patuá*, which is not surprising considering that it was a popular and commercial language that rarely found its way in to writing. The 'purest' *patuá*, we are told by Marques Pereira, had become a domestic and female language by the turn of the century, because formal education had made an impact upon the male population. But there were other versions of the language that were far more influenced by Cantonese and that were the principal commercial means of communication: the '*môdo de Vochom que fazê avano*' (the way of Vochom who makes fans), as the caricature of the time would have it (1984 [1889], I: 785).

Fifty years later, during the first decade of the Communist regime, no one in the city spoke *patuá* any more. The Macanese, now schooled in standard Portuguese, had abandoned the Creole dialect. Everyone spoke some form of English, but some of the upper-class Macanese were even poor speakers of Cantonese. The Chinese too, due to the repeated waves of immigration from China, no longer spoke the '*môdo de Vochom*'. In fact, even the Sekkei dialect was no longer the principal form of communication. Everyone spoke the language of the Hong Kong mass media, standard Cantonese.

When I arrived in Macao, at the beginning of the 1990s, there was an administrative elite, formed in Portugal in the 1970s, that spoke fluent Portuguese as well as Cantonese and English. But the home language then for most Macanese was Cantonese.

The late 1970s was a period of rapid change. The *123 incidente* (1966/7) had established the PRC's overlordship. When the city started prospering again, during Almeida e Costa's governorship (1981–6), it was obvious that the balance of forces had changed considerably. The Macanese started preparing themselves for living in a Territory run directly by the Mainland Chinese.

From the point of view of ethnic relations, the major change that took place was the abandonment of exclusionist attitudes against the Chinese on the part of the Macanese and a concomitant process of identitary demarcation from the Portuguese. This I call the *caesura of the 70s*. The new generation that came into power in the newly prosperous Macao abandoned the preoccupation that the older generation had with emphasizing its *capital of Portugueseness*. Rather, the new identitary discourse that one heard in speeches, in the new artistic manifestations and in the newspapers, emphasized a *capital of intercultural communication*.

This happened at the same time as the modern Chinese middle-class, which was finding its way in commerce, industry and the service sector, started to become an appealing partner to the administrative middle-class constituted by the Macanese. Some of the aspects of this convergence can be easily identified. First, finding themselves in similar situations concerning standards of living and educational levels, the people of the different ethnic groups started marrying each other (cf. Chapter 8). Between 1975 and 1990, in 64 per cent of the Catholic marriages that involved a Macanese partner the other partner was Chinese. Furthermore, the gender asymmetry characteristic of interethnic marriages during the colonial period – when the Chinese partner was almost always the wife – came to an end.

Second, the Chinese middle-class and the Macanese being equally subject to the impact of the Hong Kong mass media, their youth cultures became nearly identical in the 1990s, which made for greater affinities. Third, from a linguistic point of view, the improved Cantonese of the Macanese and the almost generalized use of English by the Chinese middle-class, meant that both groups had greater linguistic common ground.

These tendencies, however, should not be read in any way as signifying a weakening of a Macanese sense of ethnic self-identity. This did not happen until 1999. It is too soon to tell how the conditions in the post-transition period will affect the structure of ethnic relations in the city.

The Chinese in Macao

The greatest majority of Chinese residents in Macao have always been Han Chinese, which is the most numerous of the fifty-six ethnic identities that the PRC recognizes legally. There is a consensus among anthropologists working on China that these 'nationalities' (Mand. *minzu*, Cant. *man4 juk6*) are not sufficient to describe the complexity of the ethnic differentiation in this vast country. Within the broad group of Han Chinese many ethnic (or sub-ethnic) differentiations can be observed (cf. Honig 1992).

The authors who have written about Chinese ethnic identity insist that it must not be confused with national identity (e.g. Yee 1989 or Wang 1991). It has been argued that, among the Chinese, nationalism (political sovereignty within a common culture) is less characteristic than culturalism (attachment to a style of life and thought) (cf. Fairbank 1989: 69). There are a number of reasons for this. For example, the fact that the ruling dynasty has not been Han but Manchu, or the fact that over the past sixty years there have been two separate Chinese sovereign states, the Republic of China in Taiwan and the PRC.

This should be borne in mind when considering the existence of lively Chinese ethnic communities in Diasporic contexts. It is clear, both in the United States and Singapore, that the strong attachment to a cultural and ethnic tradition does not imply any sense of allegiance to the government of China.

Among the Han Chinese residents of Macao there is considerable diversity which structures itself according to three axes of differentiation: *origin*, *language* and *association to Macao*.

The oldest ethnic (or sub-ethnic) boundary in the Territory's residents is that which distinguishes the general Chinese population from the fishing folk (Cant. *daan6 ga1*, Port. *tancareiros*). The latter always constituted an important part of the Chinese population of the city. Living on boats, they had a parasitic relation with the Christian citadel. The few studies that have been carried out in Macao (cf. Peixoto 1988) indicate that the Tanka continue to exist as an ethnically self-identifying community. Most of them have stopped living on boats and have moved into apartments. The official census gives us some notion of how this process occurred. In the 1991 Census, the 'maritime population' numbered 2831 persons – 1691 men and 1140 women. The 1996 Inter-census provides with the figure of 2995 – 2273 men and only 722 women (Macau 1993, Table 2.1; Macau 1997a, Table 2.1)! This suggests that, contrary to their tradition, Tanka women have become terrestrial for their daily domestic existence. Eventually, if this movement is accompanied by a tendency to send children to school, the ethnic differentiation may tend to vanish in the near future.

In the past, the Chinese population of Macao included a significant component of Hokkien (or Min) speakers, originating in Fukien. The difference between them and the local people was felt to be significant. For example, when the Portuguese state finally wrote a legal code of the 'Ways and Customs of the Chins of Macao' for the use in Macao's courts (in 1909, cf. Chapter 4) it was only applicable to the people that originated in the Two Kwangs (the provinces of Guangdong and Guangxi). Over the past century, however, the descendants of these Fukinese folks have merged with the local Cantonese.

Macao's population is mostly composed of migrants from the region of the Pearl River Delta (in the 1996 Intercensus [1997a], these made up 78.5 per cent of the inhabitants that had been born in the PRC). There was still a small contingent from Fukien (13.8 per cent) and a yet smaller number of people from further north (7.7 per cent), especially from Jiangsu and Zhejiang (Woon 1987; Macau 1997a, Table 8.2).

In the 1990s, however, the principal line of differentiation that cut across the Chinese of the Territory related to the sentiment of belonging to the city or being an immigrant. This demarcation affected patterns of sociability and feelings of personal identity. The *incidente* that took place in the immediate post-transition period (June 2000) has shown how this gap may well assume more relevance in the future. The pertinent category is that of being a 'local person' (Cant. *boon2 dei6 yan4,* Mand. *bendiren*). It is an inclusive category that easily encompasses the various styles of life that coexist in the city – for example, it is inclusive of the Macanese (Cant. *to2 saang1*, Mand. *tushang*). One of its main markers is the ability to speak Cantonese in the way that it is spoken by the middle-classes of the city. Judging from personal conversations with many residents, the defining feature is not so much having been born in the city, but having undergone one's basic schooling in Macao. Moreover, it is a category that tends to be coterminous with having a middle-class condition.

There is no question that these people consider themselves to be Han Chinese. Nevertheless, they share strong feelings of differentiation *vis-à-vis* the recent immigrants from the PRC. Their personal and family histories, their education, the freedom of religious and political expression to which they have become accustomed, their relative cosmopolitanism, the fact that they often have some grasp of a foreign language (English or Portuguese), the fact that many of them have assumed a middle-class condition – all of these are strong factors of differentiation. Furthermore, many of them were Portuguese citizens from birth and their parents before them were Portuguese citizens. Some of them have family connections to the important figures in Macao's recent political history. Most of all, such people did not have to undergo the violent experiences of cultural manipulation associated with the Chinese Communist regime. They have a deeper sense of connectedness with China's past, which makes for a feeling of distinction.

The emergence of this category of identity as a relevant factor of social proximity is directly connected to the changes that took place in the second half of the 1970s (the caesura of the 1970s, cf. Chapter 8). The exponential growth of the population after 1976 and the rapid increase in standards of living in the 1980s led to a fading out of the neighbourhood communities that played such an important role in the life of the Chinese population of the colonial period. This 'village spirit' that is so vividly described, for example, in Henrique de Senna

Fernandes' book (1996) *A trança feiticeira*, gives way to a generalized Macao identity – 'local people', *boon2 dei6 yan4* – with distinct middle-class connotations. The way the population uses the Buddhist/ Taoist temples is a good indication of this. The small neighbourhood temples that were the centre of community life and that had neighbourhood committees associated to them have slowly lost their appeal. They are all impoverished and a number of them have simply closed their doors. The population now identifies itself with the larger temples that are associated with the history of Macao as a whole – in particular, the Taoist Temple of Ah Mah (Ma Kok Miu) and the Buddhist Monastery of Kun Yam (Kun Yam Tong). These temples have become tourist venues and have great media visibility (cf. Brito 1994: 77).

Many of these 'Macao Chinese' (*O3 Moon4 yan4*) have a foreign passport (Portuguese, Canadian or Australian) and are quite prepared to change residence in the event of social and political conditions in the city becoming untenable. Indeed, the old proneness to emigration (a kind of Diasporic propensity) that characterized the Macanese has now been passed on to the *boon2 dei6 yan4*. Their feeling of association to the city and to its history is quite deep – even though few of them have lived there for more than two generations. During the transition period, there were many who, having emigrated in order to ensure that they had an escape route, maintained their links with the city (both in professional and in family terms). As in Hong Kong, these people were called 'astronauts'.

By contrast with these *boon2 dei6 yan4* ('local people'), we may identify three further categories of Chinese people. In the first place, the *recent migrants*, most of them originating from the rural areas of Guangdong Province, who continue to arrive in the Territory by more or less clandestine means. The feelings of differentiation towards this category have a strong classist component – they are often people with a rural background, who did not have access in the PRC to the sort of schooling that is available in Hong Kong and Macao. They are depreciatingly called *Ah Chaan*. Often they have kinship links with older residents who consider themselves 'local people'. There is evidence, however, that these links seldom correspond to active forms of mutual support. Indeed, the sense of distance between the two groups is often stronger than the family connection.

In the second place, there are the Chinese who returned from the Diaspora (mainly from Southeast Asian countries). These are jointly known as *Naam4 Yeung4 Yan4*, 'people of the South Seas'. Most of them arrived in the 1960s, at a time when these newly independent countries (Burma, Indonesia, Malaysia) were carrying out policies that strongly discriminated against the Chinese. Although originally most of them were not Cantonese speakers (many were speakers of Hokkien and some didn't speak Chinese at all), today they all speak Cantonese. It is a very diverse group, whose relations with the local Cantonese no longer involve any conflict. Most of them have a middle-class profile and they tend to have levels of education that are frankly superior to the average resident.

In the third place, there are the Chinese from the north – speakers of one of the versions of the Northern Dialect. Historically, not many of these people came to Macao, except during the period of the Japanese Invasion and then the Civil War period that followed it (1930s and 1940s). After the Joint Declaration in 1987, when the PRC started getting ready to take over the city, many of them were sent to Macao. The response of the local people was one of deep suspicion and open irritation. Many of those who arrived in the late 1980s and 1990s were civil servants who had reasonably high levels of education but were far less familiar with international society than the local people. Furthermore, they shared a sense of real discomfort with the phonetic structure of the Cantonese language, treating it as a less sophisticated form of Chinese, and they often openly declared their dislike of the food styles that are such a central part of Cantonese sociability. As the decade drew to a close and the political handover approached, these feelings of mutual dislike did not improve.

In order to understand how these feelings of differentiation are structured in terms of collective action, it is necessary to describe briefly the way in which each of these groups is given coherence by means of an elite (cf. Pina-Cabral 2000a). It can be argued that three different types of people constituted the Chinese elite residing in the Territory in the 1990s.

First, the families that had been associated with the city for more than two generations. Many of these have considerable fortunes made in commerce and were represented in the main Chinese institutions that have given coherence over the years to a local Chinese leadership – the Chamber of Commerce primarily, but also the Tong Sin Tung (Hall of Charity) and the Keang Wu Hospital. This tends to be a conservative leadership, which is in direct succession to such informal leaders as Ho Yin in the 1960s and 1970s, Kou Ho-Neng in the 1940s and 1950s and Lou Lim-Ioc at the turn of the twentieth century. Their alliance with the CCP – the first signs of which date from the late 1950s – allowed them to control the evolution of the political situation throughout the transition period and to take over the government of the city after 1999. Their deeply rooted connection with the Territory's institutions meant that they were also in easy cohabitation with the world of the Triads (cf. Chapter 10). Many of the members of the generation presently in power studied in Anglophone countries and made personal fortunes in industry or banking.

Second, there are the people who arrived from the PRC in the 1980s. Those who made personal fortunes in a very brief period, mostly by involvement in clandestine activities, have achieved some form of leadership. Broken Tooth Kui, the leader of the 14K Triad whom the Portuguese imprisoned before they left the Territory, is perhaps the most notable member of this group. Not many of them have emerged as leaders, since they are neither identified with the city nor with the PRC.

Third, among the contingent of Chinese from Southeast Asia there is a small group of intellectuals and business people who played an important role over the years in the political and cultural life of Macao.

Other ethnic groups

There are other ethnic groups in Macao which, whilst not directly involved in the Territory's history, do have a significant presence: Indians, Pakistanis, Thais and Filipinos. Their presence tends to be less obvious, since most of them do not stay in the city for very long. In the case of the Indians and Pakistanis, there are families that have been in Macao for a number of generations. In some instances, they have even lost their original nationality, having become Portuguese citizens. Among these only the Thais and the Filipinos have any statistical significance.

Table 2 Thai and Filipino residents – 1991 and 1996

	Total residents	*Thais*	*Filipinos*
1991	355 693	726 (0.2%)	2170 (0.6%)
1996	384 995	577 (0.2%)	5190 (1.4%)

Source: Macau 1993, Table 2.3 and Macau 1997a, Table 2.3

It must be noted that, in both cases, we are dealing with immigration with very specific characteristics. These are essentially female migrants.

Table 3 Percentage of females among Thai and Filipino migrants – 1991 and 1996

	Percentage of women		
	Of all migrants	Of Thais	Of Filipinos
1991	51.5%	82%	70.5%
1996	52.3%	90.4%	52.3%

Source: Ibid.

In both cases we are dealing with economic migrants with contracts resulting in a short sojourn. Most of the Thai women were prostitutes on four-year contracts. The Filipino women were either prostitutes or domestic workers. In the case of the Filipinos there seems to have been a significant change in the early 1990s. The total population increased one hundred fold from 1991 to 1996 and the male–female imbalance seems to have altered. This would point to a more durable form of migration.

CONCLUSION

In December 1999 the Portuguese Administration of Macao came to an end and the Portuguese President Jorge Sampaio handed power over the Territory to General Secretary Jiang Zemin. Macao became a Special Administrative Region of the PRC and the First Chief Executive appointed, Edmund Ho (Ho Hau-Wah), was the son of the man who, in the late 1950s and 1960s, spearheaded the approximation of the city's traditional Chinese elite with the Communists. This political change has implications that extend well beyond the political and the economic spheres. The disappearance of the Portuguese State as an actor in this region significantly alters the way in which the ethnic groups in the Territory draw their frontiers.

Ever since Portugal became a democratic country in the mid-1970s, the Macanese have been aware that their previous proximity to Portuguese identity would have to alter should they wish to remain in China. At the same time, however, the economic modernization of China and its opening to the international arena meant that the Chinese middle class in the city has succeeded in redefining its boundaries with the outside world. The cultural misunderstandings and the prejudice that marked the boundaries between Chinese culture and European culture no longer make sense in the same way.

Furthermore, the cultural and economic world that confronts the Chinese who look outwards from Macao is no longer centrally dominated by European culture, as it was even fifty years ago. Taiwan, Singapore, Japan, Thailand, Indonesia and India provide strong examples of how an Asian society can be fully modern without losing its historical identity. The 4 May 1919 generation was confronted with a choice between 'tradition' and 'modernity'. They chose a 'cultural revolution', since they felt they had no other option. But now the question arises: 'did the Chinese really need a cultural revolution and do they need one now?' (Wang 1991: 230).

The heirs to the traditional Chinese commercial elite who are now running the city no longer see the Macanese as representatives of an oppres-sive power or of a stronger cultural force or even as a challenge to their power. The force of the various elites that control China (in particular the web of connections that branch out from Shanghai) is far more present as a challenge. We will return to this question again at the end of this book.

CHAPTER 3

HOLLERING IN BRONZE: MEMORY AND CONFLICT

In the park of a residential neighbourhood behind Lisbon airport, one comes across the bronze statue of a man on horseback. The horse is rearing and the man, with a fierce expression, has his left arm twisted across him in a fighting pose. The statue is far too grand for its locale.

At first, all you notice is the contrast between the grandeur of the statue and the tame domesticity of the environment – the fireman's lodge in front of it, the car park for used cars surrounded by wire netting to one side and the small council bungalows built in the 1950s to the other. The pedestal is low and unimpressive and, although the setting next to a roundabout would be theatrically appropriate, the obvious misplacing cannot escape anyone's notice.

In fact, when we asked the Monuments and Statues Service of Lisbon's City Hall where the statue was, we were treated to a bitter tirade about how the statue should not be positioned where it was, how they were not responsible for such a ridiculous decision and how 'the family' had exerted such irresistible and unacceptable pressure for it to be put up there. They knew that we understood what they meant. Everyone in Portugal is familiar with the name of the man on horseback. Not as that of a colonial governor and officer of the Opium Wars period, but as that of his great-great-grandson, the disputatious Minister of Public Works of the early 1990s, who was recently defeated in the Presidential elections.

The statue bears a plaque that reads:

> *João Maria Ferreira do Amaral*
> *(1803–1849)*
> *Illustrious soldier and Governor of Macao from 1843 to 1849*
> *Killed on 22 August 1849, near the gates of the Siege in Macao*
> *Made by Maximiliano Alves, the statue was unveiled on 24 June 1940*
> *and removed from Macao in November 1991*
> *It represents Ferreira do Amaral defending himself from his aggressors.*

Figure 4 Statue of Ferreira do Amaral in Lisbon

This inscription is full of elisions. It poses more questions than it answers: at what battle was the governor killed? What siege was this and why does the word have an initial capital? Why should it matter when the statue was erected in Macao (1940) and when it came to Portugal (1991)? How come it was brought here and why should it be put up here? Why is it important to explain that he is defending himself and not attacking? Who are these 'aggressors' whom he is so bravely beating down? If he is defending himself, how come he got killed?

But then, on closer inspection, there are other oddities about the statue. The man does not have his right arm and he is defending himself from his attackers with such theatrical grandeur merely by striking them with his riding-switch – an instrument rarely used when fighting for one's life, more usually connoted with the punishment of menials (*à la cravache*, as the French expression has it). Finally, all he beats down is the gigantic blades of grass beneath his rearing horse. Where are his enemies? When you look more closely you notice the bronze has been cut all around the bottom of the horse and you begin to suspect that the statue has been altered from the way it was originally cast.

Ferreira do Amaral's statue provides us with an interesting example of how memory enters into contextual dialogue with identity – how a governor who was disliked becomes a founding martyr, only to turn, later on, into somebody else's publicly forgotten ancestor. This discussion will prepare us for the story of the silenced statues to be analysed in Chapter 6.

In the 1940s and 1950s, Ferreira do Amaral took on the role of founding martyr for the Macanese, in their ethnic battle with the modernizing and nationalist Chinese middle classes. He represented their claims to sovereignty over Macao; whilst, for the generation of Chinese that emerged from the May 1919 Movement, he personified all that they most deplored and fought against in their history. This statue's grandiloquent presence in Macao – on top of its four-pillared, six-metre high stone pedestal – was a battle cry, a brutal assertion of rights.

By the end of the century, however, no one even noticed the statue in Macao, it had been completely drained of any significance save as a landmark on the urban horizon. In the end, its original meaning had been totally obliterated. To the people who now see it daily in that suburban park in Lisbon, whose knowledge of and interest in Macao is non-existent, it can only be a reminder of the lasting power of Portuguese political upper-class families.

In this chapter, I explore the way in which master narratives can be created and challenged and the way in which monuments can be instruments of political manoeuvre within an ever-changing terrain of contestation and ambiguity that is marked both by class and ethnic lines of identification.

THE *HOPPO* AND 'MACAO'S SUBJECTION'

To make sense of all this, we have to go back to the late seventeenth century and to the period in which the new Manchu dynasty – the Qing and their brilliant Kangxi Emperor (cf. Spence 1974) – implemented direct control over China's southern coastal borderlands.

In June 1582, shortly after the establishment of the citadel, the subjects of the King of Portugal (and Spain, at the time) living on the small peninsula of Macao, assembled and established a municipal form of government based on the prototype of that of the city of Évora in Portugal. In time, this became the *Leal Senado* (Boxer 1965: 44).

The existence of such a body complied with the traditional Chinese approach to foreign relations, which favoured controlling barbarians by means of other barbarians. However, there was a mandarin in the city, who was dependent on the mandarin of *Casa Branca*[23] and who taxed and dispensed justice to all Chinese inhabitants (cf. Russel-Wood 1998, II: 161). These Ming-period magistrates, furthermore, collected customs taxes and had something to say with regard to all construction in the city. The Leal Senado paid an annual ground tax to the Emperor for the right to reside on Chinese soil.

The late Ming, increasingly incapable of controlling the country and under pressure from the north, decided to impose a ban on foreign trade in the southern coastal regions – thus hoping to avoid Japanese piracy, increased European encroachment and official corruption. Had that ban been fully enforced, Macao would have ceased to exist. The policy, however, proved to be unrealistic and, as Weng Eang Cheong stresses, 'the vast expansion of foreign trade with active official collaboration reflects the cavalier attitude of local officials towards the closed door policy they were supposed to enforce' (1997: 192).

The Manchus entered Peking in 1644, but it was only after they defeated the satraps that had controlled in their stead the whole of southern China (Fukien, Guangdong and Yunnan) that they managed to impose new effective policies. In 1681, the still young Kangxi Emperor finally put down the Rebellion of the Three Feudatories. In late December 1683, the lifting of the ban on overseas navigation opened the gate to a whole new era in the commercial and political environment of the South China Sea (Weng 1997: 10).

In the meantime, Koxinga had expelled the Dutch from Formosa during the dynastic disputes and the Portuguese had lost their vital commercial link with Goa. Malacca fell to the Dutch in 1641[24] and their blockade of the Strait of Malacca did not ease off for a long time (cf. Bettencourt 1998, II: 366–9). Up till then, most European trade had been internal Asiatic trade carried out by the Dutch from Formosa, by the Portuguese from Macao and by the Spaniards from the Philippines. Two new actors, however, appeared on this commercial stage whose trade was very distinct from the carrying-trade of the earlier period. The French and, especially, the British were mostly interested in tea and developed 'bilateral trades, originating from Europe under almost free-trade conditions' (Weng 1997: 192).

Soon after the new appointment by the Kangxi Emperor of a Governor and a Viceroy for Canton, a Superintendent of Maritime Customs was also appointed (cf. ibid.: 195) whose role was to regulate trade and collect customs in the ports which had just been opened to foreign trade. He was originally appointed for one-year tenures from among the retainers of the Imperial clan, as it was judged to be a lucrative post and one for which a high level of trust was a necessity.

Known to foreigners as *hoppo*,[25] this official and his subordinates came to play an important role in Macao, as the city was used by the Chinese as a kind of touch point for entry into the Canton River. A portion of the port-charges that were gathered by the hoppo's men, for example, was paid to the pilots who led the boat from Macao inland and another one to the military officers who were stationed in Macao, *Casa Branca* (the headquarters of Macao's local officials) and the Bogue (Weng 1997: 241).

Foreigners were not allowed to reside permanently in Canton, being obliged to sojourn in Macao from June to December. Their wives and children also had to remain in the city. Only Portuguese subjects could be permanent property holders in Macao. As the Portuguese carrying-trade lost much of its significance in the late seventeenth and eighteenth centuries and the direct trade of the British, French and Americans increased, the Portuguese residents of Macao became increasingly dependent on salaries as merchants' clerks and on the payments they received from foreign merchants and their families for the renting of houses in the city. Even the East India Company's main building in Macao (today's *Casa Garden*) was nominally rented from a Macanese resident.

Thus, in the wake of bitter conflict in 1685 as a result of an attempt on the part of the Portuguese to prevent the landing of a Dutch trading ship, a hoppo's deputy was established in Macao in 1688. In this way, Macao became an integral link in what was known as 'the old China trade'. This is how Peter Ward Fay describes the progress of the foreign ships that approached Canton:

> Arriving at the Gulf of Canton, they stopped off Macao to obtain entry 'chops' or permits and take aboard pilots, at the Bogue to pay a variety of fees, then worked their way up to Whampoa. There 'chop boats' (lighters) with barrel hulls and mat sails came alongside to receive cargoes of woollens and lead from England; raw cotton from Bombay; tin, rattans, and fish maws from the Straits of Malacca; the balance in coin or silver with perhaps a few dozen Birmingham clocks and musical snuffboxes thrown in. Up the last dozen miles to Canton went the chop boats (. . .); until at last, forcing their way through river traffic as thick as a city street's, they reached the dock front of the appropriate warehouse and discharged. (1997 [1975]: 17)

In this first period after the Qing established imperial control of south China and right up to the early eighteenth century, the authorities adopted the view of the local commercial interests that, by reducing tariffs and taxes, imperial revenue could be increased and the population's living standards improved. In Macao, this was interpreted as a slackening of imperial control over the city and the Macanese and Portuguese inhabitants started to assume a certain amount of independence in the face of Chinese authorities. In Peking, the Jesuits played a decisive role in protecting Macao's situation before the Emperor, particularly during the long reign of Kangxi (which lasted until 1721). A constant stream of reproaches against the Leal Senado's unpatriotic subjection to Chinese authority flowed from Goa and Lisbon, but there seems to have been a reasonably mutual acceptance of a *modus vivendi* during this period.

However, all this started to change even before the emperor's death. European trade was becoming more important and the junk trade was on the wane from about 1716. In the following year, smuggling and piracy led to a ban on overseas navigation, but it does not seem to have affected European trade (Weng 1997: 37 and 325). The Jesuits' final defeat concerning the Chinese Rites Controversy (1742)[26] meant that their influence in Peking was cut short and Macao, as their bridgehead to China, saw its diplomatic importance reduced. In 1773 the Jesuit order was dismantled by Pope Clement XIV under pressure from the then dictator of Portugal, the Marquis of Pombal.

Furthermore, Qing attitudes were also changing. By the time the new Qianlong Emperor came to power, a new attitude to foreign relations was making its impact felt. This is how Weng Eang Cheong describes the change:

> The values and image of the traditional bureaucrat also seemed to be coming back into vogue: the withdrawal of officials from active trade and the successful impeachment of three out of the four Hoppos arraigned between 1727 and 1759 suggested a new concern for propriety and probity. The exceptional privilege, in practice for forty years, of allowing foreigners direct access to high local officials, became difficult by the 1740s, and hardened into the conventional denial of the right by 1759. The struggle between the Hoppo and the civil officials abated and died out after 1760; better relations and the crisis in the foreign trade in the 1750s forged an alliance among officials, and between them and merchants. This return to orthodoxy was consistent with the increased sinicization of the Manchus by the middle decades of the eighteenth century. (1997: 326)

In Macao, this attitude was sorely felt as one of increased official pressure and subsequent humiliation. As the interests and influence of the Portuguese State in the Far East waned – this was the heyday of the Second Empire in Brazil – the inhabitants of Macao were placed in the odd situation of living on the leftovers of the ever stronger British East India Company. Their subjection was harder to bear, both legally before the Chinese and economically before the British. The turning point that left a deep mark of humiliation on the inhabitants of the city for over a century was the 1744 incident. A Portuguese subject accused of having killed a Chinese man was judged by the mandarins and sentenced to be hanged publicly in the marketplace. This was considered to be deeply humiliating by the Portuguese of Macao and, although there were attempts to boycott the event, the Chinese magistrates and populace had their way in executing him there. From then on, all such executions took place in public in the marketplace (Montalto de Jesus 1990 [1926]: 135).

Lourenço da Conceição makes a list of the principal 'grievances' that accumulated against Chinese magistrates, of which I will detail a few. The Kangxi Emperor died in 1721, and the magistrates obliged the Leal Senado to carry out large public manifestations of bereavement. From then on, these public celebrations of joy and bereavement on major imperial occasions became obligatory. The same year the construction of boats was forbidden. Two years later, the Leal Senado was no longer allowed to grant or deny rights of stay to any foreign visitor. In 1725, a limit was imposed on the number of Portuguese-owned boats moored in the city (these had special customs dispensations). In 1732 a new office was established for the hoppos in Praia Grande, near the Governor's house, subject to the original 1688 office in Praia Pequena. In 1743 a sub-prefect whose task was the 'control of the barbarians in Macao' was placed in *Casa Branca*. Under his dependence, an adjunct district magistrate was created who was in charge of Macao. This *tso-tang* (Cant. *joh2 tong4,* Mand. *zhotang*) only came to reside in the city in the early nineteenth century.[27] In 1744, new penal laws were promulgated that applied to crimes practised by Europeans against the Chinese. In 1749 the construction of new houses was forbidden and the repair of old ones subject to licence from the *tso-tang* – considering the importance of the renting of houses to foreigners as one of the sources of income of the Portuguese residents, this was a heavily felt imposition. The same Vice-Regal edict extended to Macao the prohibition to Chinese citizens of practising the Christian religion. In 1836, the construction or repair of roads between the city and the isthmus to the Mainland was forbidden. In 1844, an attempt was made to fix the limits of the city to the old wall that cut the peninsula roughly in half and divided the Catholic town from the Chinese bazaar or 'road to Macao' (*O3 Moon4 Gaai1*), as it was then called.[28]

From the perspective of the Portuguese government in Lisbon, which considered itself in full possession of Macao since the sixteenth century, this was a list of tyrannical and illegitimate impositions. From the perspective of the Chinese authorities, who remained convinced the Portuguese lived in Macao, on Chinese soil, by special grant and through the payment of a ground rent, these were acts of official probity and administrative rationality. Thus, the sense of injustice on the part of the former and of irritation on the part of the latter was ever on the increase throughout the first half of the nineteenth century.

In effect, the Macanese and the Leal Senado were happy with neither view, for they were pig in the middle. Of all the actors, they were the ones who had the most to gain and the most to lose. So, whenever the Portuguese State attempted to force the situation, predictably, they rebelled. For the authorities in Lisbon, who were utterly distanced from the power conflict as it evolved on the ground, the Leal Senado's repeated concession to Chinese demands was proof of a culpable weakness. The Macanese Senators were even considered equal to convicted felons by the Minister of the Navy and Overseas Affairs on no other basis than that of their relative foreignness:

The Municipal Senate of that important dominion, composed mostly of convicted felons that found refuge there and other such like persons – all of them deeply ignorant of matters of government and without other horizons than the wish to find fortune by means of navigation and commerce – only concerns itself with reducing the cruelty of the Mandarins' tyranny. They accept servile humiliations and bear gifts, for all we know stolen from the Royal Treasury. They submit to whatever [the Mandarins] want, without any concern for the proper decorum of the Portuguese Nation, nor the incontestable Right of Sovereignty that the Portuguese Crown holds upon that dominion. . . . (Silva Rego 1995: 15)

In 1783, once again declaring its full rights of sovereignty over Macao, the Portuguese government reduced significantly the power of the Leal Senado by subjecting it to the Governor, who was now able to intervene in the city's management, was in charge of raising taxes and was granted a small military force to back his power. At the same time, and against the Leal Senado's protests, a Portuguese customs house was installed.

In the Portuguese Constitution of 1822, Macao was again presented as an integral part of Portugal's territory. In 1835, the government finally took away from the Leal Senado the remaining powers it had accumulated over the centuries, reducing it to the strict role of a municipal council. It always came as a shock to the people in Lisbon that all attempts to have the Chinese State confirm these claims systematically failed (cf. Gonçalves Pereira 1995: 29–32).

All of this came to a head when the British, finally certain of their power to impose their own decisions on the weakened Qing Dynasty, began the Opium Wars and, as a result, founded Hong Kong in 1843. This brought the Canton trade system to a sudden halt. At first, the Chinese merchants boycotted Hong Kong, and it looked as if it would not have any future. Soon, however, business started flowing there and Macao found itself confronted with the need to take some radical decisions concerning its status and system of functioning.

The Territory was then entering into a whole new era. Portugal's past glories had come to a miserable end, the country was undergoing the profoundly traumatic end of the Ancien Regime and had lost its Second Empire in Brazil. In the meantime, the world order had also changed. British colonialism was built on totally different foundations from those that characterized the earlier forms of European imperial expansion. Chinese officials negotiated with the British, the Germans and the Russians in terms of strength. They were forced to accept territorial claims that reduced their sovereignty. However, when negotiating with the Portuguese, they did not feel sufficiently pressed to be obliged to grant more definite rights of sovereignty over Macao. As the Portuguese saw it, this was an attitude of 'unacceptable arrogance', but in fact it reflected the international balance of power at the time.

Macao's ambiguous status, therefore, survived until 1999. Notwithstanding, at the time, the new world order – both in political and economic terms – demanded of the Portuguese State and of Macao's residents that considerable changes be made. Basing themselves on the usual panoply of arguments that then justified European colonialism, they attempted to impose a new colonial order in Macao.

Ferreira do Amaral, the man on top of the bronze horse, was the principal architect of these changes and he paid for it with his life.

THE GOVERNOR'S IMPOSSIBLE TASK

Briefly, the problem was that, after the foundation of Hong Kong as a free port, Macao's old system became economically unviable. Initially, the *hong* merchants refused to leave Macao, responding to pressure from the authorities in Canton, but English military and commercial might soon put a stop to this resistance. For Macao to be a free port in the same terms as Hong Kong, however, Portuguese sovereignty had to be enforced, otherwise the Chinese customs houses would continue to act as before.[29]

Soon after the signing of the Treaty of Nanking (1843) that terminated the First Opium War and granted the British rights over Hong Kong, Macao's Governor attempted to obtain from the Chinese a similar agreement to endorse the Portuguese official definition of the Territory's status. In April 1844, the Governor received a reply from the Imperial High Commissioner, who negotiated the Treaty of Nanking, stating that the Portuguese 'should not cherish vain hopes' of ever changing the previous understanding. He agreed to none of the Portuguese demands. On the contrary, he seemed to consider this to be a good occasion to impose further limitations. As it happens, the British backed him. The first statutes of Hong Kong state clearly that Macao was to be treated as one of the dominions of the Emperor of China. As far as the British were concerned, the control of the port of Macao by the Chinese Customs could only be a good thing as this meant that Macao would not compete with Hong Kong's future prosperity.

Distant as Macao was from the local situation, and although it was in the midst of great internal crises, the Portuguese government decided to act unilaterally in order to establish a new *modus vivendi* in Macao. The first of these decisions, taken in September 1844, was to separate the Territory from the *Estado da Índia* in Goa, in whose dependence it had always been, transforming it, together with Timor and Solor, into a separate Province of Portugal. The second – dating from November the following year – was to declare the city a free port, open to trade with all nations (with some minor limitations). Finally – in April 1846 – João Maria Ferreira do Amaral was appointed Governor with specific orders which stated that Macao 'is an establishment that must be refounded and entirely created anew' (cf. Oliveira 1998: 142).

When Ferreira do Amaral arrived in Macao, British military bravado was at its height, Macao was suffering a dire economic crisis and Portugal was in the midst of a civil war. But he was not a person to take half measures. On the contrary, this naval officer had already distinguished himself in service, showing that he was courageous to the point of excess. More than two decades earlier, he had lost his right arm whilst commanding a charge on the beach of Itaparica, near Bahia. He was fighting for the loyalist side which, in the north of Brazil, opposed D. Pedro's declaration of independence from Portugal.[30]

He focused his attention initially in Macao on taxation. He imposed a series of taxes applicable to all residents, Portuguese or Chinese. This immediately caused one of the more serious *incidentes* in the history of the Territory. Encouraged by the resident mandarin *tso-tang*, the owners of the fast transport boats (Port. *faitiões*, Cant. *faai3 teng5*) on whom the Governor had imposed a new tax, invaded the city and charged the fortifications using a cannon. Rapid action and the military support of the Macanese militia pushed them back and gave them a severe beating.

The Chinese authorities reacted in the usual way, by closing off the *Portas do Cerco* – the gates at the isthmus, connecting Macao to the mainland, through which all food and drink had to pass in order to feed the city. They further declared a shutdown of all the shops in the bazaar. This traditional method of siege had always worked very well in the past, and would work again in future situations of Sino-Portuguese disagreement, as a way of imposing Chinese decisions on the Macanese. For once, however, it did not work. The Governor relied on his fame as a rash and brutal man and declared that, if all the shops in the bazaar were not open on the following day, he would have the market blown to pieces by the cannons in the Fortress. This time the Chinese merchants believed him, and it is said that he personally insisted on riding through the market to see how well his bluff worked.

After this huge moral victory, the Governor started to receive all mandarins as foreign envoys and, being particularly punctilious, it is said that he went so far as to personally throw down the steps of his house a Chinese official who was insolent. He stopped paying the annual rent to the Chinese authorities; he occupied and fortified the Island of Taipa; he took away from the walls of the Leal Senado the stone inscriptions that had been placed there in the eighteenth century, where the Emperor declared the conditions under which the Portuguese could stay in Macao; he raised taxes; he subjected ethnically Chinese residents to Portuguese legal institutions. He attempted to impose restraint on British citizens, by imprisoning and subjecting to judgement a man who refused to take his hat off to a Catholic procession. This, however, led to a fatal loss of face, as the British simply landed troops from one of their boats and took the man away. It was perhaps a fatal error, as it demonstrated to the local Chinese authorities that the British were not backing the Portuguese decisions.

One of his most courageous and debatable decisions was to expel the *hoppo* (customs) officials from the city, to break their insignias, to raze their buildings to the ground, and to sell the land. This gesture deeply troubled the Macanese, for it implied that China would have to take some sort of action and because it seemed to them frankly illegitimate, whatever the Portuguese government had decreed.

A conflict exploded between the Macanese, represented by the Leal Senado, and the Governor, as so often happened shortly before one of these crisis in legitimacy that are characteristic of Macao's existence. The Leal Senado complained directly to the Portuguese government about Ferreira do Amaral's actions. The terms of this complaint are particularly interesting because they show the nature of the Macanese cultural dilemma at a time in which they had not yet opted for a fuller identification with Portuguese colonial interests.

> It is thus important to understand that, for the moment, we can only count on the usufruct [*domínio útil*] of this territory on the basis of the agreements that exist between ourselves and the Chinese; and attempting to transform it into absolute ownership [*domínio directo*] by means of force would be not only an effort vastly superior to our forces but also a most unfair and disloyal gesture, if we take into consideration the varied attentions we have always received from the Chinese. (Quoted in Gonçalves Pereira 1995: 36)

In fact, not only did the authorities in Portugal fail to be sensitive to their arguments, but the Governor, having been acquainted of this 'treachery', dissolved the Leal Senado and organized new elections.

Finally, he took steps to expand his control to the whole peninsula up to the *Portas do Cerco*. This involved building a road and imposing the new system of taxation on the people who resided there. Over the centuries many tombs had been erected in this area. He felt it to be necessary to destroy some of these.

When Amaral began implementing this latter policy, it was clear he had gone too far. Notices were posted on the walls of Canton, without any official opposition, offering a heavy price for his head. Perhaps in response to these, some men attacked him whilst he was out riding on 22 August 1849. They cut off his head and his remaining hand. In typical fashion, he seems to have been perfectly aware that he was risking his life by going out to ride near the Portas do Cerco with only his aide-de-camp at his side. It wasn't until January of the following year that the Viceroy of Canton returned his head and hand to the Portuguese in Macao.

In the meantime, something had happened that contributed decisively to establishing permanently the regime he had imposed. Three days after his death, the small armed forces stationed in the city marched out of the old city walls onto the Portas do Cerco to prevent any Chinese military attempt to occupy the peninsula. They were shot at from a fort in a small rise just past the isthmus, so they decided to make a surprise attack on the fort. This was led by a young officer, Vicente Nicolau de Mesquita, and a small group of armed men. Ill-trained as they were and perhaps unduly scared of European military might, Chinese troops immediately fled from the fort. This meant that, for the only time in its history, Macao managed to impose by force its independence from the Chinese State.

Coronel Mesquita, as he came to be known, became the hero who redeemed Ferreira do Amaral's martyrdom. Later on, the two men came to play a central role as legendary figures in the Macanese pantheon, even though in their respective times they were both equally disliked by the city's Eurasian residents. Much like the dead Governor, Mesquita seems to have been a person given to emotional excess, who came to a sad end after having killed his wife and daughter in a fit of jealous rage.

Ferreira do Amaral's statue in Lisbon once had a companion that has now disappeared, the statue of Coronel Mesquita. The two were made by the same artist and erected at the same time. Both statues had troubled lives, their different trajectories will be described in due course.

A NEW *MODUS VIVENDI*

After Coronel Mesquita had managed to prevent Chinese military intervention and the Bishop, as head of the interim Governing Council, had succeeded in negotiating with the Viceroy of Canton for the return of the martyr's relics, Macao entered a new era – one where the Portuguese administration, headed by the Governor, had all the formal qualifications that were, at the time, normal for a colonial government. The Leal Senado had been transformed into a municipal council and the Chinese authorities into foreign powers, at least in principle.

This gave rise to a major renegotiation of positions between the three main actors: the Eurasian Macanese residents; the Portuguese officials; and the Chinese local merchants and officials (as the active intervenors in Macao's life rarely went above the level of the Guangdong Province authorities). Up until then the Macanese Eurasians had lived in a situation of double servitude. They were subjects of the King of Portugal (at this period, it was actually Queen Maria II), but they lived under the authority of the Emperor of China – which awarded them the privilege of ruling themselves autonomously through the Leal Senado. Thus they were indebted to the Chinese.

As far as the Portuguese were concerned, however, as in fact Ferreira do Amaral is said to have explained to the mandarin of *Casa Branca* after the incident with the fast boats, Macao was theirs. The fact that the Chinese were annually compensated for their loss of this land in no way made the Portuguese obliged to them. Amaral was no more obligated to the mandarins than he was to the men from whom he bought his shoes, his hat or his food. Once the goods were paid for, the obligation was cancelled out.

The Chinese considered this an absurd response. The Chinese were not selling their land annually, nor was the ground rent seen as a term of binary reciprocity. On the contrary, the Portuguese were receiving a favour from the Emperor and it was only natural that they should demonstrate their gratitude and allegiance by offering an annual sum of money. This was all under a system of redistributive reciprocity in which the Emperor stood at the hierarchical apex – much as Chinese children, following the neo-Confucian logic that still pertains today, are supposed to hand back to their parents a portion of their earnings on commemorative occasions.

Once again, there are three distinct ways of understanding what took place: for the Portuguese all exchanges with China were part of a reciprocity between equals; for the Chinese they were part of a form of redistributive reciprocity, which meant they were a sign of submission; for the Macanese the lack of fit in the two earlier understandings was clearly visible, so they felt they owed gratitude to the individual local Chinese mandarins and merchants who turned a blind eye to the obvious lack of fit.

For the Portuguese, Ferreira do Amaral became an instant hero – he had managed to shift the balance of power in such a way that the scales tilted in favour of the Portuguese control of Macao. It should be understood that, in economic terms, this was nearly insignificant for metropolitan Portugal. Macao's importance in those days was measured in terms of the competition for prestige among European nations in the face of the growing British Empire.

Thus, he instantaneously assumed the allure of a martyr. Upon his arrival in Macao, and before his burial, a Portuguese traveller describes his contact with the Governor's remains:

> I had that naked skull in my own hands, and I could well see the vestiges of the blows of barbarity and treachery upon it, they were indelible as surely they must remain in Portuguese designs [*ânimos*]. (. . .) You could read in the faces of those present the intimate sentiments of longing and respect for that righteous citizen; the martyr to the fatherland, who sealed with his blood the improvements and the truly national character that he bestowed upon Macao. (Caldeira 1997 [1852/3]: 119–20)

The new *modus vivendi*, however, was by no means free of the ambiguities in sovereignty that so troubled the Governor and his besieged generation. Indeed, it could be said that the situation was never clarified until 1987, when the two states finally agreed on the terms of the handover of Macao to direct Chinese administration.

By the mid-nineteenth century, the European model of the territorial nation–state had become internationally dominant and colonial forms of sovereignty had become common. The situation of an ethnically divided sovereignty that had characterized Macao before Ferreira do Amaral was not sustainable. The Qing model of foreign relations was coming to a bitter end in the midst of a series of external humiliations and internal revolts. China was obliged to accept the model of bilateral relations with foreign powers and lay aside the tributary system that considered the Emperor to be universal overlord. The *Zongli Yamen*, a sort of Foreign Office in Peking, was founded in 1861 in the wake of the negotiations that culminated in the Treaty of Tientsin (1858) – signed with English forces at the doorstep of the capital and ratified one year later when these forces actually entered Peking and burned the Summer Palace.

In 1868, the Chinese Customs Service, then under British administration, established a string of customs houses on the beaches of the islands surrounding Macao, in this way abolishing, to all intents and purposes, the city's status as a free port and forcing the local government into a situation of dependence upon a set of expedients that were later to establish the economic future of the Territory – as we will see in the next chapter.

Finally, in 1887, a treaty was signed in Lisbon between the Minister of Foreign Affairs and a duly mandated British employee of the Chinese Customs Services. Later ratified in Peking, this treaty temporarily resolved the position of Macao. But it did so in an unsatisfactory manner, as it never established the borders of the Territory and obliged the Portuguese Administration to cooperate with the Chinese Customs in gathering dues on the opium trade. Another treaty, signed in 1902, only served to stress this obligation further by granting the Chinese Customs the right to open an office in Macao and continuing to leave the matter of the territorial limits undecided. This time, it was the Portuguese Parliament who refused to ratify it.

After such a pained and contorted process, the territorial limits of the possession remained unclear and the *hoppo*, now dressed in British clothes, had managed to re-enter the Territory. Macao's Portuguese sovereignty continued to be debatable, if not on paper, at least in practical terms, obliging its governors to look for expedient means of obtaining the funds to run the Territory's administration and leaving the Macanese and resident Portuguese with an uncomfortable sense that their rights to the land were not indeed all that secure.

THE COLONIAL PERIOD

This new *modus vivendi* that took form in the wake of Ferreira do Amaral's actions gave rise to important changes in local ethnic relations and, in particular, in the ethnic self-identification of the Macanese. They were forced to adapt to a world order where colonialism was dominant and where racism was becoming increasingly fierce. Their Eurasian appearance and their Creole language and manners were fast becoming major drawbacks and negative assets in the negotiation of their individual and collective life conditions.

As Macao was economically dormant and impoverished, the Macanese became dependent on serving as local interpreters and intermediaries for British commercial interests. Many emigrated to Hong Kong, where they managed to secure a safe niche as clerks in the major financial institutions and in the colonial administration. This meant that they became increasingly dependent on their association with Portugal and Europe in order to mark out a territory of relative privilege that saved them from merging with the impoverished Chinese masses.

We should not forget the general evolution that characterized race relations in the British empire and its zone of influence during the second half of the nineteenth century. In Leo Spitzer's formulation, 1870–1945 was

> a period when a new, biologically based racism began to challenge the prevailing assimilationist ideology and its various 'successful products'. Within the dominant realm, this was a time when pseudo-scientific ideas connecting 'race' and 'cultural potential' served as a basis for the resurgence of old exclusionary practices and new patterns of discrimination and persecution. (1989: 14–15)

In China – as in Africa, Europe or Brazil – attitudes of discrimination affected people in their very personal identity and, concomitantly, also in their economic and political horizons. 'Anathema, then, to British colonialism from the turn of the [twentieth] century onwards were people of mixed race, "pseudo-Europeans" and "Europeans gone native". Stepping out of the cultural attributes associated with race or nation constituted a logical and moral scandal' (Fry 2000: 125).

Thus, Macanese Eurasians found their position increasingly challenged. They were forced to rely on what I have called their *capital of Portugueseness* (cf. Pina-Cabral 2000a). To an extent, the distinct values prevalent in the Portuguese-speaking world towards racial mixing, allowed them to claim a greater association with Europeanness than it did to local British Eurasians. They were in a better position to defend their 'assimilation'.

Defining themselves as 'Portuguese of the Orient' they gained the benefits of distinction that allowed them to preserve their relative colonial privilege, but the price they had to pay was to lose their age-old Creole specificity. In this way, as we have seen, their language (the *patuá*) first became a domestic female language and then vanished totally in favour of Portuguese or English; their special manner of dressing was abandoned; and they started practising forms of marriage and of selective genealogical memory that emphasized Europeanness.

At the time of the Japanese Invasion and the Pacific War, this distinction played a central role in saving many of these Portuguese-descendants who were scattered throughout China and who flooded back to their ancestors' city of origin. Many of them did not even speak Portuguese or *patuá* any longer, having become completely immersed in the English-speaking environments of Shanghai and Hong Kong. For these people, Macao provided a safe haven during the War. They were given a survival stipend by the Administration of the Territory on the basis that they were Portuguese citizens under duress and were provided with rice by the services then directed by the boss-type Director of Finances of the period – Pedro José Lobo (cf. Teixeira 1986).[31] The Chinese that arrived in the city – refugees and beggars alike – were allowed to stay and were even accepted into charitable institutions, but many died of hunger in the streets or were forced to engage in practices that they would never have thought possible, in order to survive at a moment of such tragedy. So, for the Macanese of the period, their Portugueseness was a palpable asset. Very few who lived through that period would forget that. This ethnic barrier would only start to be breached by their children and granchildren in the 1970s and 1980s.

At the time of the Pacific War, Portugal was struggling to emerge from the terrible political upheaval of the Republican years and, in particular, the dire economic crisis that followed the First World War. By the time the new dictatorship of Salazar consolidated its power – in the 1930s – Portugal found a need to reaffirm itself as a colonial power. The 1930s and 1940s witnessed a plethora of congresses and exhibitions which were aimed at reformulating Portugal's wounded sense of incomplete modernization in a newly affirmative light. In this perspective, and even if the territory remained economically irrelevant to the metropolis, Macao played an important symbolic role in the Portuguese Empire.

It is against this background that Ferreira do Amaral, the martyr, and Coronel Mesquita, his redeeming hero, make their reappearance in the form of statues. They arrived in the Territory in 1940 as blatant affirmations of colonial pride – as forms of *hollering in bronze*. Their presence shouted Portugueseness and aims to 'prove' to the Chinese what actual diplomatic negotiations had never managed to do: that Macao was an inalienable part of Portugal (to use the Salazarist turn of phrase characteristic of the period).

Now that the Governor's statue is no longer on top of its six-metre-high four-pillared pedestal rising above a large platform, but on a simple two-metre-high stand, we can easily read the sculptor's signature and dating: M. Alves 1935. Why should it have taken so long for the statues to find a home? I am not at the moment in possession of any information concerning this, but we should be attentive to these dates, as is suggested by the inscription in the new Lisbon pedestal.

At the time, China was deep in war – both civil war and war against Japan. To give some points of reference: Manchuria was occupied by the Japanese army in 1931; the Long March took place between 1934 and 1935; the Marco Polo Bridge incident that started the Sino-Japanese War occurred in July 1937. Canton was occupied by the Japanese in October 1938; Swatow and Hainan in 1939; and Hong Kong finally in 1941.[32] Macao was never formally occupied, as Portugal was a neutral nation during the Second World War. In effect, however, the collaboration with the Japanese was very close and the Japanese had a headquarters within the city.

In short, when the statues were erected, the Japanese canons were firing just on the other side of the Portas do Cerco, and there were absolutely no Chinese authorities who could possibly complain. Even so, we know that the decision as to where to place them was marred by complaints on the part of the Chinese residents. The erection of the statues was part of an aggressive process of affirmation of ethnic identity on the part of the Macanese of the city – who, during this period, and contrary to what would happen later, were undergoing a process of ethnic approximation to the Portuguese.

The original idea was to put Coronel Mesquita next to the Portas do Cerco, in order to remind (or to convince?) the Chinese that never could they cross the threshold. He is represented stepping forth into Chinese territory in brave pose, drawing out his long sword with bravado. The notion of placing him there, however, was so patently odious to the city's Chinese residents that, even at such a time, they managed to deter the Portuguese authorities. Instead, he was placed in the central square, in front of the Leal Senado's building, in what had become the city's main commercial thoroughfare.[33]

In turn, Ferreira do Amaral's statue was placed in a much grander setting in the middle of a then new square that jutted into the ocean next to an important landfill. Two decades later, the bridge that connected the peninsula to the Island of Taipa was constructed next to it. The control over the Island of Taipa was one of Ferreira do Amaral's policies that the Chinese most opposed. Ironically, however, the characteristic profile of this bridge made its way into the flag of the Special Administrative Region of Macao after 1999. In the early 1960s, furthermore, Macao's casino, the flagship of the magnate Stanley Ho's empire, was raised in all of its kitsch magnificence in front of Ferreira do Amaral's statue. Later still, in the 1980s, Macao's tallest building, the Bank of China, a symbolic representation of China's new capitalist might, that is supposed to have altered the *fengshui* of the city, was built just behind the statue.

There can be no doubt, therefore, that the placing of these statues was carefully chosen so as to leave a central symbolic mark of Portugueseness on the Territory. At any other time, this would have been thoroughly impossible, and even during China's darkest hour, the original jingoistic feelings of the statue's proponents could not be fully implemented. Coronel Mesquita's statue could not be placed at the Portas do Cerco and Ferreira do Amaral's statue had to be altered, so as to soften its message.

Presently, the statue represents the Governor on horseback, twisting down towards the left as he attempts to repel his enemies by beating them with a riding-switch held in his left hand. Originally, however, it contained the figures of two Chinese men, represented in a smaller scale, just as they were being thrown to the ground by the Governor's spirited response.

In fact, this representation was not only odious to the Chinese in the way it depicted them, but also it did not correspond to the reports given by the Governor's aide-de-camp of what actually had taken place. It would seem that, as they were passing through the Portas do Cerco, which he had arrogantly crossed, Ferreira do Amaral was hit on the face with a cane by a boy. Before he could react, and even though he was armed with a pistol, he was pulled down from his horse and killed by armed men (Montalto de Jesus 1990 [1926]: 233).

We know from a telegram that a governor of the 1960s sent to the Overseas Minister in Lisbon[34] that the statue had to be altered to make it less offensive. The little Chinese men at the feet of the horse were taken away sometime during the 1950s. That is, immediately after the Japanese Invasion ended, Chinese voices in the city started insisting on being heard again.

We must consider who were the people who, at mid-century, stood on the other side of the ethnic divide from the Macanese and Portuguese. Contrary to Ferreira do Amaral's opponents, who were Qing traditionalists, by the 1930s we are dealing with the generation that came out of the May 4th (1919) Movement. Chow Tse-Tung, a famous writer on the subject, defines their ideals in the following way:

> [The leaders of the] May Fourth period proposed science and democracy; proposed the revaluation of everything; proposed the

liberation of the individual; the revolution of the family and creating the new woman; proposed critiques of the old ethics and morality, the overthrow of Confucian monopoly, thus causing the popularisation of vernacular language and the questioning of old history, introducing all kinds of new thought and having young people publish several hundred little magazines. The influence [of May Fourth] is long-term and basic. . . . (Quoted in Wang 1991: 242)

As Wang Gungwu has stressed, at mid-century the Chinese had to decide between two alternative paths to modernity – the Russian or the American – but ultimately all the Chinese shared the same dream of modernization (1991: 239–40). Furthermore, it should be understood that the Chinese people whom the Macanese were challenging by putting up these statues were both modernists and nationalists – the two things were inseparable. Their passion for modernity was a burning desire to find a way to save their nation. The ideals of nationhood were deeply embedded in the modern ideals of science and democracy (the two consensual ideas which Sun Yat-Sen represented, cf. Wang 1991: 241).

The then new middle class that later came into power in China, Taiwan, Hong Kong and Macao were modern *because* they were nationalist. The sort of identitary complexity that characterized Eurasians did not appeal to them. The stage was set for the sort of confrontation that would soon arise involving these statues.

A MARTYR AND A HERO

Let us consider how the statues operated from a symbolical point of view. We can easily understand that what is at stake here is the affirmation of domination over a territory and control over the privileges this territory provides, by means of claims of identity. The Macanese, whose very existence is connected to the city's century-old presence as a commercial post in China, feel that they are 'born of the land' (as their Cantonese designation implies – *to2 saang1jai2*). This identification, however, is challenged constantly by the Chinese, who claim ultimate rights over the land. This is another formulation of Macao's central contradiction that we identified in the previous chapters and it begs for a symbolic mediation. The statues aimed at doing just that.

All identities are processually built on instances of identification. Thus, the bearers of these identities will feel threatened when the central identifications on which their identities are built are challenged. The exception to this, however, is when this break somehow can be made to provide an axis for a new polarization and a consequent new differentiation in identity. Then, identities are legitimated further – the challenge turns out to have functioned as a consolidation.

This new polarization (what Lévi-Strauss called 'helicoïdal mediation') cannot result merely from a symbolic process. Associated to it, there has to be a factual vindication of power. A substantive confirmation must exist if such a break in identification is to function not as a denial of identity but as a legitimation of a new set of identitary referents.

Thus, if a factual vindication of power can be shown to have occurred, that which might have been a traumatic memory – dangerous because it collapses identity and, to that extent, unrememberable – may turn out to become a redeeming memory.

We may then look at the story of Ferreira do Amaral and Coronel Mesquita not as a set of factual events but as a symbolically constructed narrative and see them as agents of mediation. Ferreira do Amaral was *par excellence* the person that made Macao Portuguese, whilst the Chinese mandarins tried to prevent that from happening. Ferreira do Amaral was killed by the Chinese (and the Macanese finger is always pointed at the Viceroy of Canton who, as it happens, later had a long and sad official career, marred by the Taiping disasters). When that happened, Macao was left without Portuguese authority. All attempts to gain control over Macao might well have collapsed.

In fact, what actually happened was just the opposite. Due to Coronel Mesquita's courage, Ferreira do Amaral's actions as Governor were confirmed and Portuguese Macao managed to expel from its border the power of the Chinese State. What allows for this helicoïdal twist at the end is the substantive vindication of power that occurred during the fight at Portas do Cerco. It did not cancel out Ferreira do Amaral's death at the hand of the Chinese. It did something better, because it definitely altered the terms of the situation. By means of the hero's victory, Ferreira do Amaral's demise turned into martyrdom, the trauma became redemption. Or, so hoped the Macanese of the time. In fact the subsequent history of the statues would show that their hopes were at least partially unrealistic.

MESQUITA DURING THE CULTURAL REVOLUTION

The first statue to be taken down was Coronel Mesquita's. Indeed, it was not only the most accessible – as its pedestal was lower and it was very near the central market – it was also the more offensive. Once the small figures of Chinese men at the feet of the Governor's horse were removed, if one chose not to know too much about the character's political opinions, Ferreira do Amaral's statue might even receive a reasonably neutral reading. Coronel Mesquita's, standing at arms length right in front of the Leal Senado[35] was a clear offence to the Chinese people that passed by, who felt their ethnic rights as 'owners' of the land daily challenged by 'Macanese arrogance'.

This is not the moment to analyse in any depth the *incidente* that came to be called the *123* (because it occurred on the third day of December 1966, cf. Fernandes 2000b). An event of such magnitude can never be said to have one single cause. Various factors contributed to this explosion. On the one hand, the Communist Party needed to find an occasion to further establish its informal hold over the Chinese population of Macao now that the Kuomintang presence in the city had sufficiently weakened (they had left the Chinese mainland in 1949). On the other hand, the small nucleus of Chinese magnates, which controlled the incredibly profitable gold trade, felt that their monopoly may be threatened as the casino's monopoly had been. Furthermore, they needed a good excuse to establish beyond doubt their allegiance with the new Communist overlords of China. Further still, the Macanese in control of the administration of the city were feeling increasingly threatened by the strengthening of the Chinese claims to control over the Territory, now that the Communist government was establishing its legitimacy internationally. The Chinese residents of the city felt that the time had come to put an end to the decidedly colonial tone of the Administration. Finally, the more extreme elements of the Chinese population, inflamed by sectors of the Red Guards, wanted to 'liberate' Macao or, at least, impose their ideology on this portion of China.

To cut a very long story short (cf. Fernandes 2000b: 235–97), incensed with the dilatory attitude of the Administration towards the opening of a Chinese school in Taipa, the population rose up in arms and took to the streets to march in the fashion characteristic of the Great Proletarian Cultural Revolution. One of their first actions was to attack the statue of Coronel Mesquita. They climbed up on it, tied ropes to it and physically pulled it down. Next to it, the archives of the Leal Senado were also sacked and the contents were thrown into the streets. Attempts were made to attack various other statues, such as that of Jorge Álvares, which lost the arm that was pointing at Portugal. The statue of Ferreira do Amaral, however, was positioned too high and it was too big to remove manually. Attempts were made to damage it, but removing it would have involved some planning and engineering equipment. These practical difficulties sufficed to cool the general anger and the statue survived.

At the height of the excitement, the *incidente* assumed a clearly ethnic profile. This was particularly the case when the Governor distributed arms to the European and Eurasian militia. It almost became reminiscent of Ferreira do Amaral's days, when the Macanese militia armed by the Governor fought off the attack of the boat men (cf. Fernandes 2000b: 248). Portuguese attitudes this time, however, were far more conciliatory. Gradually, as always seems to happen in Macao, cross-ethnic allegiances led to a cooling of spirits. Moreover, it soon became clear that the Chinese army, which had posted itself at the Portas do Cerco, and the navy, which had surrounded the city, were not attacking it but were, on the contrary, engaged in violent armed struggle against groups of armed Red Guards who wanted to 'liberate' the city. Rightly or wrongly, the newly arrived Governor conceded to all the demands that were made of him.[36]

The aim of the Chinese authorities slowly became clear. They did not want to take over Macao, all they wanted was to put an end to the balance of power that had been in force since Ferreira do Amaral's reforms. The internationally besieged Communist regime deemed it useful to maintain the Portuguese presence in the city. Furthermore, now that the Chinese authorities had finally cleared the Territory of Kuomintang influences, they had secured as much control over the situation as they thought necessary. They instituted a system of neighbourhood associations (*gaai1 fong1*) which was ethnically specific to the Chinese, providing welfare services and controlling most of the population; they managed to assume indirect control of most of the Buddhist establishments in the city (cf. Brito 1994); they controlled the principal trade unions, the Chinese hospital, an important number of schools and the main Chinese-language newspapers; they established a semi-official representation in the business firm *Nam Kwong*; they saw to it that Macao's principal business leaders were members of the party and played a public role as *red patriot capitalists*.

The balance of power had been reset in a clearly post-colonial tone. It cannot be said that it ran against the Macanese and the Portuguese. Rather, the sense of national humiliation and subjugation that had irritated the Chinese authorities and the principal Chinese residents during the colonial period now eased off. The overlordship of the Chinese was again clearly established. The role of the main mediator of the *123 incidente* in the city was symptomatic – Ho Yin, the magnate who controlled the gold trade, became a sort of Chinese counterpart to the Governor and was publicly recognized as such, as was quite openly stated at his burial celebrations. Even Stanley Ho, the Hong Kong Eurasian who controlled the casinos, started presenting himself as Chinese and assumed an equidistant attitude towards the Portuguese and Chinese authorities.

The Macanese soon started adapting themselves to this new situation by decreasing their reliance on their capital of Portugueseness and beginning a new process of ethnic reformulation that brought them closer to the Cantonese local residents – the *boon2 dei6 yan4* (cf. Pina-Cabral and Lourenço 1993b).

SOME GUY ON A HORSE

Until Mao's death in 1976, the future of the whole of China remained highly uncertain. After the emergence of Deng Xiaoping as a national leader, the situation evolved more rapidly. Emigration from China increased again and the city entered into a process of very fast development that brought considerable wealth to many of its residents. During the early post-colonial period (from 1967 to 1974/6), ethnic tension had slowly been easing off and there had been an increased approximation between the Macanese administrative middle class and the Chinese middle class that was now in control of all private sectors of the economy.

The Governor's statue lost its political connotations. It became known to all Cantonese residents as *tung4 ma5 jeung6* (lit. bronze horse statue). It was a leisure area where people went to breathe the fresh air during the stuffy summer evenings and play in the merry-go-round next to it; where visitors were taken to remember their visit to the city or groups of friends memorialized their friendship through photographs. Marriage photographs were also taken there, as the steps of the platform on top of which the pedestal was raised were conducive to good poses.

In fact, Cantonese people who came of age in the 1970s and 1980s, and to whom I have posed this question, stated that they were not even sure that the man on top of the horse was Portuguese. They were never told anything about the statue, as indeed they were not about most aspects of their city's fascinating history. One of the curious effects of the sort of equilibrium of forces that prevailed throughout the post-colonial period was that the curriculum of Chinese-language schools was not determined in any way by the Portuguese administration and it systematically excluded all references to the city's long history.

So everyone was very surprised when, on 28 June 1990, the Vice-Director of the PRC State Council's Office for Hong Kong and Macao Affairs, Lu Ping, made some acerbic declarations, among which there was a sentence stating that, in the future, Ferreira do Amaral's statue would have to be brought down as it was 'an excessively colonialist symbol' (Fernandes 2000b: 461). At that time, the negotiations for the Basic Law of the future Special Administrative Region of Macao were well underway. The sort of hard talk in which Lu Ping engaged did not have a very positive effect on the Portuguese authorities. In statements to the press, the Governor used the occasion as an example of the sort of useless intervention in the Territory's life that was thoroughly undesirable. However, the comments must have gone down well among the elites of the Chinese Communist Party, as Lu Ping was promoted to the role of Director the following November.

Although the Chinese residents of Hong Kong and Macao felt reasonably comfortable with the situation, the older members of the Peking establishment still felt deeply troubled by the symbols of a colonialist past that, in these territories, had lost most of its meaning. Furthermore, it must have come as a real surprise to Lu Ping and his comrades to discover how distant the Portuguese felt from the more jingoistic excesses of the Salazarist regime. For the Portuguese of the early 1990s, the sort of colonialist bravado that characterized a figure such as Ferreira do Amaral was on the whole distasteful. A few months later, a Portuguese member of the Macao government made a statement to the Lisbon press to the effect that he understood perfectly well that the Chinese did not want to lose face and that they would need to prepare the Territory for their future control by altering a few symbols (cf. Fernandes 2000b: 464).

On 28 October 1992, the statue was taken down, wrapped up and quietly and quickly sent to Portugal. The local press gave considerable attention to the event, but no one seemed to care about it very much either way. Some younger Chinese journalists complained that the city's historical heritage was being taken away. A young American anthropologist quotes the comments of one of her local Chinese informants:

> He was just a guy on a horse, right, I bet if you took a poll of all the people who used to play in that park, that almost no one would know or care about its history. So in some ways there was no reason to tear it down. But when they dismantled it, they dismantled part of my childhood with it. They dismantled part of my feeling for Macao. . . . (Clayton 1999: 99–100)

CONCLUSION

The rapid removal of the statue might not have taken place were it not for the fact that, as luck would have it, the Portuguese Minister for Public Works at the time was the great-great-grandson of Ferreira do Amaral. It was perhaps out of consideration for his feelings that the government of Macao was so prompt in resolving the matter.

The Minister and his family felt that they had to salvage their family's moral heritage. They had a problem, however, as a statue of such a scale and import is not easily hidden. So they had to find somewhere for it to stand. After the Democratic Revolution of 1974, Macao was dependent directly on the President of the Republic and not on the government of Portugal. Coincidentally, the Mayor of Lisbon was the son of the then President of the Republic. In short, in spite of all the opposition from the technical personnel of the City Hall, who felt that such a statue was not deserving of their parks, the Minister and his family prevailed, and the Mayor found a location for the statue.

Coronel Mesquita's statue did not have the same luck. Today, no one is the least bit interested where the broken parts of his statue landed. He is best forgotten. For many years, the space where he had stood was left empty. Later, a little decorative fountain was placed there. Later still, shortly before the handover in 1999, a large armillary sphere was placed over the fountain, representing the universalizing achievements of the 'Portuguese Discoveries' (the same that is found in the Portuguese coat of arms). Again, most Chinese residents are ignorant of the symbolic meaning of the decoration of that little fountain. How long will it remain there?

CHAPTER 4

PARADOXES: GAMBLING AND THE IMPERIAL CIVIL SERVICE EXAMINATION[37]

In collaboration with Mónica Chan

As you enter the main hall of Macao's *Casino Lisboa*, you will read a notice which, roughly translated from Chinese, reads:

> There is no certainty that you will win if you gamble (*do2*). Placing small bets can be fun. Playing (*waan2*) with spare money keeps it a form of entertainment.[38]

Everyone in those rooms knows that the odds are loaded in favour of the casino; how else could the building be so lavish, the owners so fabulously rich? And yet, the hall is full of people 24 hours a day; in the upstairs VIP rooms, fortunes exchange hands in less time than it takes to count them; loansharks, with their telltale waist pockets, move freely among the clients. One night in November 1994, as we came back to the hotel from our nightly round of the casinos, the television was reporting that yet another young woman had been found dead on the beach of Coloane, apparently drowned. In her coat pockets she had a Hong Kong ID card and some pawnshop tickets. . . .

As one moves among the tables, time and again one is confronted with the age-old 'gambler's paradox': in Olmstead's formulation, 'why do otherwise rational people continue to gamble?' (1962). But it does not end there. For when one speaks to people, one finds that the terms they use to describe their actions also seem ambivalent. Take a look back at the notice translated above: two distinct words are used to describe what people do in casinos – *waan2* and *do2*,[39] their implications are totally distinct, as we will see later. At the same time as we were going round the casinos, we were digging in the archives to discover how gambling became so central to the city. We found out that the gambling monopoly that launched the city's career as a gambling haven was the now largely forgotten *vaeseng*[40] lottery, incongruously based on the results of the Qing Imperial Civil Service Examinations.

These findings struck us as paradoxical. That is to say, they seemed to conflict with common sense even though their factual basis was beyond reasonable doubt. Puzzled by them, we started collecting the material for the present chapter. As we proceeded, we came to agree with W.V. Quine that 'Of all the ways of paradoxes, perhaps the quaintest is their capacity on occasion to turn out to be so very much less frivolous than they look' (1966: 20). Increasingly, it seemed to us, examining these paradoxes forced us to challenge some firmly held ways of thinking, both of social scientists and of the Cantonese street folk that were our main subjects of study.

GAMBLING MONOPOLIES IN MACAO

Today, few people know anything else about Macao other than that it is a gambling haven on the South China coast. In fact this has only been the case for the past century and a half. After the foundation of Hong Kong, in the 1840s, the city lost its traditional commercial relevance almost overnight. Macao's Portuguese administrators were obliged to radically alter their *modus vivendi*. We have seen how the ill-fated Governor Ferreira do Amaral managed to change the traditional system of overlapping Chinese and Portuguese administration. He launched what we have called the 'colonial period' (1846–1967). Nevertheless, it has to be remembered that the wealthy Chinese men that locally controlled the economy and the Guangdong bureaucrats across the border maintained a much greater capacity to intervene in the city's life than one would normally associate with a colonial system.

Macao had to specialize in activities that Hong Kong and Canton could not offer. For a while, the coolie trade gave the Territory and its inhabitants some economic relief (cf. Chapter 2). However, the Portuguese Crown was soon obliged by public pressure to prohibit this and Macao returned to its economic morass.

Considering that, then as today, Portugal had very few economic interests in Macao, the survival of the local subjects of the Portuguese Crown and of the Portuguese administration depended on finding some internal sources of revenue. Many of the Macanese were obliged to move to Hong Kong in search of employment. The ones that remained behind – and, then as now, the majority were employees of the Administration – saw their livelihoods deeply threatened.

The granting of monopolies concerning just about any commercial activity that proved to be profitable was the strategy that the Administration used to survive. In 1859, for example, there were monopolies for the game of *fantan*, for Chinese lottery, for the sale of fish, for the sale of pork, for the sale of beef, for salt, for fishing oysters, for the sale of boiled opium (*Boletim Oficial*, 21/05/1859, n. 30, vol. V). Later on, monopolies were added of other things such as the collection of human manure, the sale of salted fish, oil, Chinese alcoholic beverages, etc.

From the point of view of the city's finances, however, the processing and sale of opium and the various gambling licences were by far the most important monopolies. From the 1860s to the 1900s the city progressively specialized in gambling and opium, the economic activities that seemed best to allow for the funding of its administration. By 1875 it was generally recognized that 'without the revenue derived from granting the exclusive [rights over the exploitation] of these heinous activities, the colony would collapse' (*O Independente*, 11/02/1875, p. 2). In 1910, the Governor, reporting to Macao's Deputy in the Portuguese Parliament, stated that 70 per cent of all income of the Administration came from the monopolies of gambling and opium and only 30 per cent from other sources of revenue.[41]

The aggregation of all forms of public gambling into one large monopoly, as is found today, was a solution that only came into existence after the founding of modern-style casinos, during the period between the two World Wars. Until then, gambling licences were given for different sorts of gambling to different persons, representing syndicates. Most often, the nominal owner of the rights was a Macanese – a Portuguese-named Eurasian – even though the owners of the capital and organizers of the activities were ethnic Chinese. The struggles, associations and swindles between the various Chinese magnates involved in these gambling syndicates, as well as the dealings with them during the regular negotiations of licences, were central concerns of the Administration.

The history of these activities has not been researched in any systematic way. Most of the governmental archival material previous to 1960 relating to gambling contracts seems to have mysteriously vanished.[42] Part of the veil can be lifted by gathering material from the local press of the period. In the pages that follow, therefore, we will focus on the *vaeseng* (Cant. *wai4 seng3*) lottery – the first gambling monopoly of any great importance in the history of the Territory. This lottery seemed particularly interesting since (a) it can tell us much about the process of political and economic integration of the whole Pearl River Delta at the end of the Qing Dynasty and (b) it provides us with a fascinating angle on the dying days of one of the most ambitious scholarly ideals ever conceived, the Chinese Imperial examination system. The period that we will attempt to cover is that which goes from the foundation of Hong Kong in 1843 to the onset of the two republican regimes, the Portuguese one in October 1910 and the Chinese one in October 1911.

WAAN2 OR DO2?

Before doing this, however, an important matter has to be addressed. How do the Chinese classify the gaming activities which are the subject-matter of this chapter? In the English language, all games of chance played for money fall under the general category of 'gambling'; a concept that heavily connotes righteous criticism. In Portuguese and French, such is not the case. There is no exclusive term that specifies gambling activities, even though moral judgements on the evils of gambling are quite as widespread. The general verb *jogar/jouer* applies to all forms of play activity (*activités ludiques*), be they children's games or games of chance played for money (*jogos de fortuna ou azar*, literally games of fortune or bad luck, as Macao's legal texts euphemistically call them).

In Cantonese, as in the other Chinese languages, the conceptual classification is different. One might choose to describe the same gaming activities as *waan2* or *do2*. When asked, people will probably tell you that *waan2* refers to 'healthy', recreational games played in sociable contexts. The fact that they may involve chance and money is considered an added stimulus for excitement. The term emphasizes the sociable and playful character of the activity and is applied to all forms of games. The term *do2*, on the other hand, describes compulsive gaming involving money and chance: that which is practised sacrificing reason and financial equilibrium, beyond self-control, supposedly involving addiction, high risk and anti-social behaviour.

At first glance, this distinction seems to coincide to some extent with that made by Otto Newman in his interesting analysis of British gambling. He defines gambling as 'either betting on a future event or series of events, whose outcome is uncertain and beyond the direct power or control of the bettor, or the placing of stakes in money, or in tokens passing as money, on a future chance event . . .'. Newman then proceeds to exclude from his definition 'the large field of private gambling where money circulates exclusively among the participants' (1972: 1). In the Chinese case, however, this differentiation is not satisfactory. As we will see later, the criteria are multiple. Distinguishing between 'public' and 'private' would draw a rather artificial line between activities which, at times, not only involve the same games but also produce the same social consequences that the Chinese regard as important differentiating criteria between *waan2* and *do2*. Moreover, the extent of private extra-casino gambling in Chinese society no doubt contributes to the socialization of future gamblers, not to mention the considerable size of the sums involved.

Let us analyse further these two concepts. We have seen that, in both cases, money and chance may be involved. Furthermore, the same games can be played inside and outside the casino, in both private and public contexts, e.g. *mahjong* and *paicau*. There are games that can be found exclusively in casinos. However, so long as one engages in them in a spirit of 'play', then it is *waan2*. The same applies to location. A group of women may spend a pleasant afternoon in a casino or a group of male friends may play mahjong for high stakes in a private room at a restaurant. As long as this is carried out among friends for the purposes of pleasure, it is considered *waan2*. Whether or not the money remains within a closed circle does not really matter. The key distinction seems to lie in the 'spirit'. When does the pleasant *waan2* spirit degenerate into the addictive *do2* spirit? More precisely, since the majority of people prefer to describe their own activities as *waan2*, when is one judged by others to be engaged in *do2* instead of *waan2*?

One notion which is particularly associated with *do2* is that of addiction (*cham4 mai4*), which can be measured by the frequency of practice: the more often one engages in the activity, the more likely it is that it will be classified as *do2*. W*aan2* is supposed to be that which is practised by people who engage in pleasure-seeking without falling prey to uncontrollable desire.

In point of fact, it could be argued that many people are quite addicted to this form of 'pleasure-seeking'. Mahjong is the daily activity of many housewives while their husbands are at work and the children at school, whereas many men play mahjong, cards or paicau during their spare time, with variable frequency. As a result, regular practice alone is not sufficient to qualify someone as *laan6 do2 gwai2* (literally, fellow rotten with *do2*). However, if the person practises the game with such frequency as to neglect his or her duties, e.g. a housewife leaving her children and daily obligations unattended, then he or she has definitely crossed the threshold to *do2*.

Similarly, the high stakes only begin to matter when they exceed the financial capacity of the players, putting in danger their own well-being and that of their families (like borrowing from loan-sharks). Normally one plays with people of similar socio-economic status, who can afford to run the same risks.[43] The higher the bets, the better-off one is – or the better-off one is announcing oneself to be. For this very reason, there are always people who are willing to risk more than they actually can comfortably afford, trying to simulate superior status or seeking to be promoted into a higher social circle. Therefore, the relative size of the stakes stimulates excitement and is simultaneously an indicator of status: rich people may *waan2* at high stakes; whilst poor folk may well *do2* at rather low stakes.

To conclude, it only matters to a limited extent what games are played, where and with whom. The real distinction lies somewhere between ir/rationality, compulsiveness/self-control, self-destruction/self-preservation. And since everyone would prefer to be on the 'correct' side of the threshold, most people would refuse to describe what they do as *do2*, referring to their own gaming activities, however frequent, as *waan2*.

By choosing one term or the other, the speaker is making an assessment of the subjective intentions of the gambler (whether it is him or herself or another) on the basis of a supposed personal and/or financial equilibrium. Between *waan2* and *do2*, therefore, there is a continuum, each implying a different degree of personal engagement, with a fluctuating borderline between them, liable to manipulation which is often purely judgemental and rhetorical.

Of particular relevance in this respect is the generalized, almost obligatory gambling which goes on at the time of Chinese New Year and which means that everyone in the population is perfectly familiarized with the rules of most gambling games. New Year is an auspicious period *par excellence*. The spirit under which people engage massively in gambling at that time is that of *waan2*, as it is supposed to be pure entertainment. This requirement is an integral part of Chinese New Year. Speaking of 'occasions of the domestic calendar when the prospective continuity of the household receives special attention' in Taiwan, Stephan Feuchtwang claims that

> Both the weeks of the New Year season and the weeks around the Autumn Festival are thought to be good times for weddings. They are times for making arrangements, divining the prospects of the household, or completing arrangements for new households, a wedding and the installation of a domestic altar. Furthermore, both the New Year season and the Autumn Festival are times of increased licence. Gambling is sanctioned by custom if not by law. And the evenings of the Lantern Festival and the Autumn Festival are spent by both men and women out of doors, the autumn viewing in particular being a time for courting. (1992: 104)

PARADOXES

This form of gambling is *waan2* in that it functions as a means of connecting people and celebrating their well-being. It strengthens the bonds of family and friendship, contrary to *do2*, which is a major source of family disruption and social marginalization. For example, on New Year's Day, Stanley Ho, the gambling magnate who has been of late the figurehead of the syndicate that controls Macao's casinos, has the custom of visiting his main casino – the baroque *Hotel Lisboa*. There he holds a private celebratory meal to which he invites his close relatives and his closest associates. After the meal, the entire company pool their resources in order to make up a reasonable sum of money which they hand over to one of the more junior members (usually a younger woman) who is sent down to the casino to place a bet on a table of *taisai*.[44] She does this at a time when the casinos are overflowing, when vast sums of money are rolling across the tables, when pawn shops are doing brisk business, when loan-sharks are at their busiest, when many people are desperately hoping that, it being New Year, they may have that breakthrough that they had never achieved before. This young emissary is seen to be celebrating a notion of gambling as *waan2*; a positive, socially constructive entertainment activity, in the midst of people who, to her eyes, are in all likelihood engaging in *do2*.

On one point, however, there was absolute consensus among the people whom we interviewed in Macao about gambling: games which do not involve some form of monetary transfer do not have the same intrinsic interest as those which do. They lack the essential factor of being 'real'. In fact, our own reluctance to gamble placed us more than once in uncomfortable situations when playing mahjong in the homes of our Cantonese friends. When we lost, they politely insisted that no money should be paid. But when we won they politely insisted that the game was not interesting if no money was paid.

In the light of all this, it is surprising to observe that there has always been, among the Chinese of the Delta, a systematic opposition to gambling and a generalized espousal of repressive attitudes towards gambling. In fact, in Hong Kong, the repeated claims that the best way to curb clandestine gambling would be to open legalized casinos have met regularly with opposition from the more prestigious sectors of the Chinese establishment (*Report* . . . 1965: 15–16).

Such attitudes do not seem to be specific to the Cantonese. Speaking of shrines to the unknown dead, Feuchtwang says that in Taiwan 'they are intermediate, with some people despising and fearing and some people helped by having placed offerings at them'. Often 'they were shrines to gamblers, robbers, or gangsters killed in action. These too were feared and despised or admired as robbers of the rich and defendants of the poor. Or else they simply became objects of request for success in gambling or seduction, and other favours of a less than upright nature' (1992: 48).

A similarly ambivalent attitude is reported by Lang and Ragvald in their study of the Hong Kong popular deity Wong Tai Sin. Believers were known to ask the deity for gambling tips, but others reported that this was wrong, as it demeaned Wong Tai Sin, and thus might result in the God taking vindictive action (1993: 104). This is nothing recent either. For example, in his study of the capital city of the Song Dynasty Jacques Gernet claims that 'Gambling games with cash coins sometimes used as chips, were the favourite amusements of the lower classes, in spite of official prohibitions' (1962: 226–7).

Even gambling magnates were prone to dwell on this paradox. Kou Ho Neng[45] was a major influential figure in Macao in the 1930s, 1940s and 1950s. He was the second partner in the gambling syndicate that held the monopoly of casino gambling in Macao before Stanley Ho's syndicate prised it out of their hands in 1961. Someone who was close to him over a long period of time reported to me that he was very uncomfortable about his involvement in gambling and tried to cleanse himself of what he felt to be a serious stain by means of religious deeds. Being a devout Buddhist, he is said to have believed that his involvement with gambling was likely to reduce his kharma and thus he refused to have any direct contact with the gambling activities, apart from receiving the profits of his investment. We were told that he left all managerial tasks to his partner, Fu Tak-Iam, even going so far as to refuse to inspect the account books.

The fact that there is something paradoxical in the prevailing attitudes towards gambling in the Chinese culture emerges clearly in the protests of the Portuguese editor of the newspaper *O Independente*. He complains that no one should be surprised that the youth of Macao were so prone to gambling, considering that they were introduced to it at an early age in their own homes (26/12/1891, n. 26, p. 2). At New Year the whole family went to the fantan dens to gamble small amounts of money. At the same time, it was customary for the households of wealthier people to call into their house an ambulant organizer of taisai (the game was then known to the Portuguese speakers of the city as *clú-clú*).

Indeed, gambling is still perhaps the major form of communal activity in which relatives engage at the time of family gatherings. Mahjong tables are an integral part of most meetings of friends and relatives. Whether the stakes are high or low, the activity is a major form of recreation and confirmation of friendship links between people. Anyone strolling through the popular quarters of Macao at the end of a summer day will find card games and mahjong games being played in every alley and every square. Anyone visiting the restaurants where the Chinese middle class does most of its socializing can peer into the private rooms filled with friends and relatives of all age groups playing mahjong, from which peels of laughter and loud chatter regularly permeate the restaurant.

In short, the *waan2/do2* paradox is that although gambling is such a central part of Cantonese social relations, it is also perceived as a potential source of social disruption and thus there is an outward consensus of the need for measures of prohibition.

This cycle of fascination and rejection continues today. In late 1994, when we were visiting the hinterland of Canton, the province was in the throes of yet another of the regular and always short-lived campaigns against gambling. On TV, a few exemplary small-time organizers of gambling were shown being judged and given drastic sentences; in the streets, we saw a number of small informal casinos being hastily 're-modelled' in order to become 'music bars'; in the homes, people were telling us how then, and for the duration of the Canton International Trade Fair, it was not safe to play gambling games in the streets at the end of day, as was their customary practice.

The *waan2/do2* paradox still continues in full force. In fact, it seems to increase precisely where and when gambling is forbidden due to the contrary fear of its perceived antisocial implications. By the mid-1990s, as a result of Deng Xiaoping's policies of economic liberalization, the customers of Macao's casinos were largely Chinese from the Mainland, supplanting the traditional Hong Kongese clientele in number and in volume of money involved. In a way history was repeating itself. Macao was once again taking advantage of the prohibition of gambling in mainland China for the purposes of its own prosperity. But fortune is fickle. In 1996, with the approaching return of Hong Kong to Chinese sovereignty, a war for the control of gambling profits burst out among triads which led to a considerable decrease in gambling revenue. At the same time, in 1996/7, the Chinese authorities slowed down their anti-gambling campaign and were once again less repressive towards gambling.

POPULAR GAMBLING GAMES

Gambling is a common activity almost anywhere (cf. Kusyszyn 1977, Newman 1972, Olmstead 1962), and certainly it plays a major role in

Chinese culture (cf. Price 1972: 163; Culin 1958 [1891]). Some forms of gambling have always been practised in Canton and Hong Kong. On the whole, however, two important forms of gambling that had an immense appeal to the Chinese population were regularly prohibited in these cities: these were a table game known as *fantan* and a number of Chinese forms of lottery. It is these games that are primarily responsible for the launching of Macao as a gambling enclave, particularly as the late nineteenth century witnessed a surge of anti-gambling feeling on the part of Chinese authorities (Price 1972: 173). As John Price has emphasized, the foundation of gambling enclaves like Macao is a function of the Chinese authorities' opposition to gambling (ibid.: 177).

> *Fán t'án* is a game usually played upon a mat-covered table, with a quantity of Chinese coins or other small objects which are covered with a cup. The players guess what remainder will be left when the pile is divided by four, and bet upon the result. The name means 'repeatedly spreading out,' and refers to the manner in which the coins or other objects are spread out upon the table. (Culin 1958 [1891]: 1)[46]

This game was also very important in the rest of the Delta. In Hong Kong, for example, gambling was only prohibited in 1843. Later on, in 1867, realizing that the prohibition was not effective, the colonial government granted a gambling licence, but this was withdrawn in 1871 for a number of complex reasons, one of which was the opposition to gambling of prestigious Chinese figures (Lu 1978: 1).

In spite of the prohibition, however, the game continued to be played widely in Hong Kong – we encountered repeated references to illegal fantan rings being broken. In one case the organizers of the gambling were associated with the police (*Echo Macaense*, 08/08/1897, n. 56). Furthermore, the game was officially allowed during the horse race meetings in grounds near the Happy Valley racetrack on Hong Kong Island (*Echo Macaense*, 26/02/1899, p. 3). In Kowloon Village, the small enclave that was not administered by the British in Kowloon, there were fantan houses that were so popular with both Europeans and Chinese that the Administration felt the need to threaten any public servant found gambling there with immediate dismissal (*O Macaense*, 22/11/1890, n. 47, p. 3). In Macao, too, this injunction came to be established[47] and it is still enforced today, except on the five days of the Chinese Lunar New Year. In Canton the official prohibition was stricter, even if we can safely presume that its enforcement was less effective.

In Macao, fantan was practised in special gambling houses, most of them situated in the neighbourhood of the Chinese bazaar around what is now the *Rua das Estalagens*. As is the case with modern casinos, these houses were hardly elite establishments (the Portuguese called them *as espeluncas do fantan*, 'the dens of fantan'). They were open to all and sundry and offered their activities at all hours. For example, when in August 1888 the Administration attempted to enforce a temporary ban on boat people disembarking during the night, in an attempt to control some of the acts of vandalism that had been occurring, the gambling magnates protested vigorously and refused to place offers for the renewal of their licence unless the Administration allowed these people, who were at the bottom of the local social scale, to enter their fantan houses in the middle of the night.[48]

The other form of gambling that was important in keeping Macao's administration afloat during the second half of the twentieth century were the lotteries. There were a number of these and it is not certain that we have an exhaustive list of all of them. The least important was the Portuguese one, organized by the *Santa Casa da Misericórdia* – a Church-run charity that has the exclusive for all lotteries in Portugal. Judging from the figures involved in its accounts, it is to be supposed that the tickets were bought by everyone and not just the Portuguese population (e.g. *Echo Macaense*, 30/10/1898, pp. 1–2). Then there were the *pacapiu*, the *sanpiu* and the *poupiu*. There is at present no evidence that *jifá*, another form of lottery that was very popular in the middle of the nineteenth century in Canton and later on in Hong Kong, was ever run in Macao.[49]

By far the most important in financial terms as well as in terms of its significance for the relations between Macao and the Qing state during this period was *vaeseng*,[50] the annual lottery that was run on the basis of the family names of the candidates that passed the Chinese imperial examinations. Robert Douglas, writing about Chinese society in 1894, tells us that 'Quail-fighting, cricket-fighting, and public events are also made subjects for wagering, and the expected appearance of the names of the successful candidates at the local examinations is a fruitful source of desperate gambling' (quoted in Price 1972: 173).

Contrary to the impression that may have been given by these comments, however, by the 1860s this form of betting was not an informal, disorganized affair. Rather, it involved an extensive financial and scholarly organization.

THE *VAESENG* LOTTERY

The imperial examination system was definitively instituted during the Song Dynasty (960–1279) although its mature form was reached during the Tang Dynasty (618–907) (cf. Billeter 1977; Elman 1994; Franke 1960; Miyazaki 1981 [1963]). From then, until its final demise in 1905, during the pre-republican years (Miyazaki 1981 [1963]:10), it was a major component of the Chinese State and of the Imperial conception of the world that ruled it. It was on the basis of these examinations that, in principle, the administrators of the empire were chosen; it was the impartiality and rationality of the examinations that, in principle, ensured that the Chinese were ruled by a meritocracy. Finally, again in principle, all learned subjects of the Emperor could apply to sit these exams and be received, with the exception of the members of a few polluted classes (actors, prostitutes, boat people, etc.).

In fact, things were rather more complex. The acquisition of the necessary knowledge and the participation in the exams involved an educational and financial capital that was definitely not within the reach of the majority of the Emperor's subjects. Years of solid learning and enormous costs were involved in sitting a Palace examination. Stories of amazing success by candidates with very humble origins were avidly consumed by the people and openly diffused by the Administration, but they were definitely not the norm. It has been cogently argued by a number of authors that, behind the apparent façade of an open examination system aimed at deciding anyone's scholarly prowess, there was the reproduction of a landholding gentry (Fei 1953: 32; Billeter 1977). In fact, during the Qing Dynasty, it has been estimated that 63.4 per cent of all successful candidates had official connections in their immediate families (Hook 1991: 111). As we shall see, the examination system which legitimated the rule of the scholar–gentry was open to all sorts of contradictions and manipulations.

A man wishing to become a scholar had to start by passing a series of entrance examinations at different institutional levels, after which he had to sit for a qualifying examination at the prefectural capital.[51] Candidates passing this exam could, in principle, take part in the provincial level examination which took place every three years (the years of the rat, hare, horse and cock) in the eighth lunar month. But, as there were too many potential candidates, they had to sit a pre-selection test. According to Lu Jin, during the 1860s, only 400 candidates from Guangdong Province were allowed to attend this exam and only ninety candidates were allowed to qualify, receiving an academic title (1994).

The candidates had to stay in the examination compound in an isolated cell for three days and two nights. The results were usually announced between the 5th and the 25th day of the ninth month.

In Canton city there were a number of academies where the candidates for these exams studied and resided. These were organized by local associations and/or lineage (name) associations. For example, the Chan's association had a large and beautiful building that is still one of the touristic highlights of the city.

The year after the provincial examination was held, another one was organized at the nation's capital. This triennial exam took place in Peking and involved three parts. The first of these started on the 9th day of the third lunar month. Candidates had to write three essays on the Classics. The second part was on the 12th day of the same month and dealt with History topics. The third part took place on the 15th day and its content changed during the Qing Dynasty. During Qianglong's reign, for example, it consisted of one poetic composition and five critical essays. The results were published within the fifteen days that followed the end of the examination.

The final examination took place within the Forbidden City itself, during the fourth lunar month of the same year. The candidates entered the Examination Halls on the eve of the 26th day of the fourth lunar month and the results were published on the first day of the fifth lunar month.

There were, therefore, three main levels of examination: the prefectural level, the provincial level and the metropolitan level (including the capital and the Palace examinations). We are unsure as to whether the vaeseng lottery functioned at all of these levels.

According to Lu Jin,[52] the lottery system used for provincial and for metropolitan examinations was distinct. For the provincial level lottery, the players bet on the family name of the top candidate or on combinations of the family names of the top three candidates. The rate of gain of each name varied according to the frequency of appearance of that name among the candidates. Here it is important to clarify that Chinese patronymics are limited in number (cf. Alleton 1993; Chapter 7) and that, therefore, the chance of candidates with the same name appearing was rather high. What this meant was that, if a candidate with a less common name were to win, the people who bet on his name would have a higher rate of gain. It was incumbent on the lottery company to pay these variable rates of gain independently of the overall revenue resulting from the sale of tickets that year. This implied that the company ran a relatively high risk but also that the profits could be considerable. Thus, the temptation to tamper with the results was very strong.

Both the organizers of the game and the gamblers depended on very elaborate systems of information gathering about the candidates and their chances of winning. This meant that organized channels of information were established and that there were periodic publications relating to the candidates and their relative abilities and credentials. It was, for example, important to know whether potential candidates had entered into periods of formal mourning that prevented them from participating in the exams or whether it was suspected that they had provided false personal information that might disqualify them at the last minute. Finally, a brisk trade in substitutes appears to have existed, although of course this was strictly illegal. There were customary norms for the dealings between candidates and their substitutes.

Accusations of bribery to the examiners were also common. For example, at the first drawing after the 1884 re-legalization of vaeseng in Canton, the Portuguese newspapers of Macao reported that:

> One of the examiners bought a large number of tickets, in which he chose the name of a certain student. Obviously this man received the prize [of the lottery] and, in fact, he was the only one to receive a prize, so as to avoid having to share it. This 'honoured' professor received over 900 000 patacas with which he is said to have moved to America to further improve his science. (*O Independente*, 09/04/1885, n. 288, p. 4)

According to Lu Jin, at the capital level examination, because there were too many candidates coming from all over the country and because it was hard for the lottery organizers to collect precise information on all of them, the system was run differently. At this level, the company took a fixed rate of commission[53] of the total amount of money staked and the remainder was distributed among the various winners.

We are not certain, however, about the accuracy of this information. In fact, it could well be that the system underwent changes during the complex history of the game. In Macao, we even find that Lou Lim-Ioc, the son of Lou Gao, the main gambling magnate involved in vaeseng, was still adjudicating from the Administration the right to organize this lottery four years after the imperial examination system was terminated (*A Verdade*, 09/12/1909, n. 56, p. 3). This seems to indicate that, by then, the lottery was being run independently of the actual exam results, much like pacapiu, which still goes on even though pigeon racing stopped being of any relevance whatsoever long ago.

Lou and Wang provide us with slightly different indications of how vaeseng was organized (1992: 61ff.). Ticket buyers had to choose twenty names out of a list of patronymics published by the organizers (who excluded the more common patronymics). The stakes were variable. All tickets of the same stake value were grouped into 'volumes' of 1000 tickets. Within each 'volume' the person who had guessed the largest number of correct names received the first prize, which corresponded to 30 per cent of all the money of the volume. Within each 'volume', there were also prizes for second place (receiving 20 per cent) and third place (receiving 10 per cent). The house received 20 per cent and the remaining 20 per cent was paid as tax. This system appears to have been the same as was used for the poupiu lottery (Lou and Wang 1992: 66ff.).

In conclusion, we feel that much research still needs to be done on the internal system of organization of the lottery, as the authors consulted do not provide us with sufficiently conclusive information and archival material is scarce in Macao. Similarly, the origins of the game remain hazy. It is only when it became a major source of concern for the Portuguese administration of Macao that we started to find more reliable reports.

THE HISTORY OF THE GAMBLING SYNDICATES

Informal gambling on the names of successful candidates is probably something that has always existed. These kinds of informal gambling games are still an integral part of Cantonese street culture about which, for example, Portuguese schoolteachers in Macao report with a mixture of surprise and reprehension. For instance, it is common for schoolboys to bet small objects or small amounts of money on the winners of sporting competitions during their physical training classes. Groups of adolescents entertain themselves by betting on the number of pips that are to be found in tangerines. This seems to be an old custom as, in 1890, a newspaper of Macao, berating the brutal behaviour of the Chinese agents of the 'secret police', reports that

> with the pretext of preventing street gambling, [a certain policeman] beat up a boy that went around asking people if they could guess the number of pips contained within an orange he carried in his hand. Such was the beating, that they took this Chinese boy to the hospital, where he proceeded to die. (*O Macaense*, 18/01/1890, n. 3, p. 2)

The first report that we found of organized gambling in the manner of a vaeseng lottery dates back to the time of the Taiping Revolution.

According to this report, the Examination Halls of Canton were destroyed by fire during the fighting and, in 1861, a number of scholars suggested to the provincial government that the best way to obtain money to rebuild them would be by organizing a lottery. The government granted a licence for two years (cf. Lou and Wang, 1992: 53). Another author reports that, by 1863, the game was very popular in Guangdong Province (Lu Yan 1978: 34). In fact, in 1870, Lou Gao, who later moved to Macao, and his associate at the time, Lei Gang-chun, obtained a new licence to run it. Still according to the same author, the lottery was prohibited by Imperial Decree in July 1876 (ibid.) because there so many complaints that it was having a detrimental effect on the examination system.

It must be understood that we are dealing with a period in the history of China in which the values that held up the neo-Confucian establishment were beginning to come under serious strain. Joseph Levenson, for example, argues the point saying that:

> In the eighteen-sixties, after the Taiping Revolution (1850–1864) had been put down, when the classical examinations were reinstituted in the Shanghai region, troubled Chinese observers noted that candidates were inordinately few. [. . .] Thus, new roads to power for Chinese, roads smoothed by Western knowledge, had come to be seen. A challenge was offered to the usefulness of Chinese thought, and when the question of its usefulness could be raised, the question of its truth came alive. Chinese thought, all schools of it, had a genuine, serious Western rival. (1965: I, 65)

By the time vaeseng was again prohibited in Canton, the granting of gambling licences had become an indispensable source of revenue for the Macao government. The first licence for the game of fantan was granted in 1849 (*Boletim Oficial*, 21/05/1859, n. 30, vol. V). In 1851 we find reference to the granting of a licence for organizing a 'China lottery', which may have been either vaeseng or pacapiu (ibid.).

The dates are clearly important. At this time, on the one hand, Macao's government was desperate to find new forms of revenue in the face of the continued commercial collapse resulting from the competition of Hong Kong. On the other hand, the measures for greater administrative independence from China instituted by the ill-fated Governor Ferreira do Amaral were taking effect and it was starting to be possible for the Administration to authorize practices that the Qing government attempted to repress.

A newspaper reports that, in 1875, there had been a failed attempt to grant a monopoly for the organization of vaeseng in the islands adjoining

Macao (Taipa and Coloane). Considering that these islands were largely uninhabited and that the game was being organized in Canton at the time, it is not surprising that no one was interested. However, this information suggests that a monopoly for Macao itself had already been granted (*O Independente*, 11/03/1975, p. 3).

In 1876 another licence for the exclusive rights to the organization of fantan were granted in the name of Ho Lok-Gwai, and it is stated that he had a number of partners (*O Independente*, 26/08/1876, n. 131, p. 1). This is, in fact, characteristic of the financial practices of the period. The names of the main capitalists involved in gambling in Macao during the latter half of the nineteenth century are encountered time and again in a complex network of associations, competitions and back stabbings. The principal figures of the period are, on the one hand, Ho Lok-Gwai and his son Ho Lin-Vong and, on the other hand, Lou Gao and his son Lou Lim-Ioc. The latter had moved from Canton to Macao, having been the principal partners in the organization of vaeseng in that city.

By this time it had already become common practice, in Macao, to use Eurasians, and particularly civil servants, as figureheads for government contracts. The practice has continued to this day. When he obtained his first gambling contract (in 1961) Stanley Ho, the present-day magnate, was classified as Eurasian, being a nephew of Sir Robert Ho Tung and married to the daughter of a locally important Eurasian family (the Leitão family). Moreover, he was a figurehead for a syndicate in which he held only a minor share. Since then he has altered his importance within the syndicate as well as his favoured ethnic self-definition, insisting now on being considered Chinese.

During the second half of the nineteenth century the most important of these Eurasians were also a father–son duo, the Baron Senna Fernandes and his son, first Viscount, then Count, then Baron. In contrast with all the other Eurasians that were involved in gambling contracts at the time, the Senna Fernandes duo succeeded in playing a more than subsidiary role in the financial networks of the period. Often associated to Lou Gao, Senna Fernandes' son acquired a particularly bad reputation in Macao, due to his more than shady financial activities.[54] In his dealings with the Chinese, the Baron adopted the name San Sam-Ki (*Echo Macaense*, 9/04/1899, p. 2).[55] Such was his reputation that, when his descendants became involved in the legal profession in the 1930s and 1940s, they found it necessary to adopt a different Chinese patronymic so as not to be persecuted by the ill-fame of their ancestor.

It would seem that the same magnates that were involved in gaming activities in Canton also operated in Macao, progressively moving there in order to circumvent the prohibitions to gambling in Guangdong. This was certainly the case with Lou Gao and his partner Lei. In fact, Lu Jin gives us a rather appealing and fantastical account of the reason why they moved to Macao. This was supposed to be because all the good geomantic sites (*fung1 sui2*) in Canton had already been occupied and that in order to find a good site for their 'yang' residence,[56] where they could find good fortune leading, for example, to their sons passing the imperial examinations, they had to move to a place like Macao, which was full of good spots. As foreigners were ignorant of what was good for them, many such places were left unoccupied. In this way, Lei chose his house on Rua Central, close to what is now the Headquarters of the Judicial Police and Lou chose the field that is now Macao's only Chinese-style garden, the famous Lou Lim-Ioc Garden.

Although Lei never became very important in Macao, it would seem that he was the more fortunate of the two partners, as his son was the only resident of Macao who ever qualified in the Palace examination. Lou's main heir, Lou Lim-Ioc failed the examination, having committed some sort of error of etiquette. His younger brothers, however, qualified at the provincial level. Perhaps that is the origin of the dispute over inheritance between the brothers and explains why no agreement was ever reached about the division of the garden. The land, therefore, remained in the name of their dead father. Local lore reports that this was the main reason why the garden was never sold for property development like most other Chinese mansions in the city and why it has survived to this day.

Another of the financial figures who moved between Canton and Macao was Ian Min-Chi. This man was accused by the newspapers of Macao of being responsible for promoting the memorial to the Emperor that led to the reopening of the vaeseng lottery in Canton in 1884 (*O Macaense*, 24/08/1889, n. 5, p. 1) and to the increased persecution by the Qing police of anyone who carried or sold Macao lottery tickets. This was a major tragedy for Macao at the time.

From about 1880, the vaeseng lottery in Macao was in the hands of a society called Chiong-On of which the main partners were the Hos and two other persons, Chan Lok and Fong Heng-Seng.[57] At the time they were granted the licence, the society had deposited in the Hong Kong and Shanghai Bank of Hong Kong a large sum (100 000 *patacas* of the time) as security that they would pay the government of Macao the promised regular payments which would have amounted, over the whole period of four years, to 640 000 *patacas* (*O Independente*, 22/08/1883, n. 203, pp. 2–3). Meanwhile the vaeseng in Canton was being strictly persecuted by the Qing officials but Macao's lottery was making vast profits and alone constituted the greater part of the income of the Administration (*O Independente*, 13/11/1884, n. 267, p. 1).

At the time, the Canton authorities were being plagued by a serious shortage of funds primarily caused by the need to pay for military expenses incurred by the Sino-French War over Annam (1884–5, cf. Hsü 1990: 325–30). This led the Viceroy Li Hung-Chang to accept the proposal for the reinstatement of the lottery, promoted by Lou's partners, in spite of his stated belief that the game was harmful to the country in the long run (*O Independente*, 23/10/1884, n. 264, p. 4). The agreement with the Canton government established that the syndicate would pay the sum total of 3 800 000 patacas over six years (*O Independente*, 13/11/1884, n. 267, p. 1). The launching of the game in Canton, added to the increased persecution of the traffic in Qing territory of tickets for the Macao lottery, led to a rapid collapse of the Macao company. By March 1885, they had stopped paying the prizes for the winning tickets and the government was led to declare the gambling contract null and void (*O Independente*, 05/03/1885, n. 283, p. 3). The government desperately attempted to hand the contract to other people, but no one was interested. In April the syndicate attempted to withdraw the money that had been left as security in Hong Kong. The Macao government succeeded in preventing this but the funds were frozen by the British courts in a series of legal manoeuvres that might have had politically strategic motives but which eventually led to the freeing of the money and its handing over to the Macao Administration.[59] This was a major source of relief to the authorities who would not otherwise have had the money to pay the civil servants' salaries.

In the meantime, in Canton, an ugly fight had occurred between Lou Gao and his associates and the members of the old Chiong-On syndicate. One of the latter, Chan Lok, was foolish enough to go to Canton in order to compete for the monopoly. Unfortunately for him his opponents conspired with the authorities to imprison him under the accusation of being an organizer of illegal gambling. The Portuguese newspapers report that he was forced to pay the Qing government 400 000 patacas and that this directly led to his death, but we are not told how (*O Macaense*, 24/08/1889, n. 5, p. 1).

Things did not go well for the Canton vaeseng. As we have seen, the very first extraction was accompanied by a major act of corruption on the part of one of the examiners. The Canton authorities promptly used this opportunity to appropriate the remaining funds which were being held for paying the prizes (*O Independente*, 23/04/1884, n. 290, p. 4).

The following year, 1886, the authorities again attempted to extract from the Canton syndicate larger funds than those prescribed by the agreement.

In Macao, the old vaeseng syndicate collapsed as the Chiong-On Society declared bankruptcy (*O Independente*, 21/05/1885, n. 244, p. 2). Their Eurasian figurehead, Miguel Ayres da Silva,[60] was bailed out by his bosses from a bankruptcy process through a legal artifice (*O Independente*, 20/08/1885, n. 307, p. 3). In spite of the persecution of the holders of Macao tickets by the Qing police, it was becoming increasingly clear that the problems encountered by the Canton vaeseng left ample space for the relaunching of the lottery in Macao.

In October 1885, another Eurasian (Maximiano António dos Remédios), representing a syndicate including Lou Gao and Senna Fernandes, signed a contract for a new monopoly with the government, accepting to pay prize money to the ticket holders that the previous company had left unpaid (*O Independente*, 31/10/1885, n. 317, p. 2).[61] We are told by the newspapers that three-fifths of the capital of this syndicate was held by the same people who controlled the Canton vaeseng. It was also at this time that Lou Gao wrenched the Macao fantan monopoly from the Ho family. However, he did not manage to get rid of the Hos completely. They continued to be part of the Macao vaeseng syndicate in spite of his attempts to exclude them (*O Macaense*, 24/08/1889, n. 5, p. 1) and they managed to control the pacapiu lottery.[62]

By 1888, Lou Gao, in spite of his newly purchased scholarly title, was getting increasingly tired of dealing with the Cantonese authorities who continued to make excessive demands on his syndicate (*O Macaense*, 07/09/1889, n. 7, p. 3). Progressively, he based his activities in Macao. At this time he adopted Portuguese nationality and started dealing with the government directly under his own name (Basto da Silva 1986, I: 29).

In 1890, when the time came for the next gambling contract to be negotiated in Canton, the vaeseng syndicate was so dissatisfied that they allowed two outsiders to sign a contract with the Canton authorities.[63] At the same time, however, they organized a boycott on the activities of the new syndicate. For example, the old syndicate continued to pay the ticket house employees so that they would not work for the new company (*O Macaense*, 22/03/1890, n. 12, p. 3). Things got so bad that one month after the signature of the contract, the Viceroy himself was obliged to intervene, persuading the new syndicate to sell 50 per cent of the shares of the company to the members of the old syndicate (*O Macaense*, 05/04/1890, n. 14, p. 4).

Even so, by 1890, the lottery was not making enough money. Seeing that large sums of money were being paid to the Portuguese administration of Macao by the organizers of fantan, the Viceroy of the Two Guangs Li Hung-Chang was finally persuaded to grant a licence for the official organization of fantan (Lou and Wang 1992: 53).

The Macao vaeseng gradually regained some of its old vigour. One of the contributing factors to the recovery of the Macao vaeseng lottery was the fact that the organizers paid smaller amounts to the government than in Canton, which meant that, in the Portuguese enclave, they could sell the tickets at a lower price. In spite of rather desperate attempts on the part of the Canton authorities to prevent the traffic of Macao tickets in Guangdong Province, the fact is that these were bought widely and, in May, at the time of the decision of the exam results, the Macao shops were filled with people coming in and out (*O Macaense*, 10/05/1890, n. 19, p. 3).

In Macao too, the business was run with less than punctilious honesty. Repeated scandals involving more or less fictitious bankruptcies of ticket-shop owners, where Senna Fernandes and the Hos played a less than straightforward part, were common.[64]

Throughout this period the Imperial examinations were losing prestige and the lottery was becoming increasingly independent of them.

THE EXAMINATION PARADOX

In the vaeseng lottery we can detect a further paradox that may be termed the examination's paradox: vaeseng was dependent upon the neo-Confucian system of scholarship and yet it outwardly perverted its most dearly held values. The paradox which it fed on was the confrontation between an ideological representation of a meritocracy based on pure learning and disinterested service to one's fellow men and a reality of a class system based on economic inequality and its reproduction along familial lines. In this sense, vaeseng was a parasite that made its living out of the exploitation of this ageing giant, sticking to its underbelly and making a rich crop of its decaying parts.

The vaeseng organizers saw the exams and their inbuilt ambivalence as a window of opportunity. People had a deeply established disposition to associate the examination system with fairness and worthiness. The results of the exam were judged as being dependent on the individual merit of each candidate and, therefore, ultimately unpredictable and impossible to manipulate. As it happens, the key to success of vaeseng over other lotteries at the time was precisely this deeply held disposition to believe that the results were less dependent on the actions of the lottery organizers than in other systems of lottery and, consequently, likely to be fairer.

As a matter of fact, however, people's disposition to believe that this was the case went hand in hand with their knowledge that it was possible to predict the results to a considerable extent and even manipulate who was likely to win. If, in the course of the normal functioning of the system, it was mostly the sons of landowners that became scholars, then surely it was because other factors were at play beside mere scholarly disposition.

Some candidates had a greater chance of winning because, for example, they were better prepared, had the right connections among the specific panel of examiners, came from the right families, attended better schools, had more efficient (famous) teachers, had exposed themselves to the correct *fengshui* (geomantic environment), etc. Furthermore, during the period under consideration, everyone knew that the examiners could be corrupted and that substitutes could be hired.

If these factors improved one's chances of passing the exams, then each individual player could convince himself that, if he compounded those factors adequately, he was more likely to win than other players. So the other persons who bought tickets also bought the journals and paid the specialists who provided them with specialized information about the candidates who had better chances of success and were fully aware of the established routines for cheating. In fact, as Billeter argues, the examination system was built on an obsession with fraud (1977: 10). The belief in the ideology of meritocracy fully accompanied the knowledge of its being unattainable. This is the paradox of the examination.

It is, in effect, ironical that Lou Lim-Ioc, the son of the founder of the vaeseng lottery and certainly the principal heir to the fortune it spurned, should have run for the examinations and lost, not having managed to save his pride by one of the artifices upon which the success of his lottery depended.

CONCLUSION: THE THREE PARADOXES

In conclusion, this discussion should be set within a wider perspective. We have dealt with the paradoxical aspects of gambling in terms of the concepts of Cantonese everyday life and in terms of the gambling on the results of the Imperial examinations, but the fact is that most authors who have attempted to study the more general subject of gambling have had, sooner or later, to address what has come to be known as 'the gambler's paradox'.

In his interesting essay on the subject, Igor Kusyszyn formulates it thus: 'of all those who gamble, over 99% lose, yet almost all of these gamblers continue to gamble' (1977: 22). This statement might have been put in a way that would have been slightly less perplexing, for instance: 'almost 99% of all losing gamblers have, at one time or another, won, so they believe it is possible to win'. But even this formulation does not resolve the paradox with a simple solution.[65]

Whilst researching gambling in Macao, one is constantly reminded of this by the above-mentioned little gold-on-black notice, written in the most deadpan fashion, implying that, in the long run, the casino will get the larger profit. This clearly does not seem to have deterred a single person from gambling.

The various authors that have dealt with this issue have formulated diverse resolutions to this apparently paradoxical situation. Whether it is because gambling must be seen as a form of play or entertainment – as in Price's formulation (1972: 177; see also Smith and Abt 1984);[66] or because gambling responds to the need for self-assertion – as when Kusyszyn argues that 'the reality of stimulation-seeking may be taken as evidence for our need to confirm our existence' (1977: 28); or because gambling corresponds to a symbolical activity – as when Olmstead argues that such games are a form of dealing with unconscious symbolism (1962: 13); or because gambling is a 'safety valve' needed to reconcile the ideals of egalitarianism with those of capitalist competitiveness (Devereux 1949, quoted in Newman 1972: 9); or yet still because gambling is sound economic policy within the situational reality of the majority of working men – 'what point is there in saving?', explains Newman, 'when unpredictability and mysterious remote controls govern our life' (1972: 227–8).[67]

All of the above arguments seem perfectly satisfactory in their own way and help immensely in reconciling us with this 'antithetical passion' (cf. Kavanagh 1993: 61): an important human activity which, at first glimpse, appears to be plagued with irrationality. But if we consider the three paradoxes outlined above – the gambler's paradox, the *waan2/do2* paradox and the examination's paradox – as part of the same phenomenon, we will soon see that none of these answers is sufficient.

When they enter a casino the Cantonese resident of Macao believes that he or she is engaging in a rather harmless activity called *waan2*, whilst most of the other people present are engaging in an addiction called *do2*; the vaeseng bettor feels attracted by the ideal of fairness that is implicit in the Imperial examination system, while knowing full well that his or her very engagement in vaeseng contributes towards making it less fair; the gambler enters the casino in Macao and reads for the thousandth time the little notice explaining that, in time, he or she must expect to lose. All of these are perfectly rational human beings who are not aware that they are dealing with paradoxes. Indeed, the paradox is not to be found in the activity itself, but in the way we interpret that activity by confronting it with what we otherwise know about the world and presume to share with him or her.

Following Quine, we might say that these were paradoxes of the kind he calls 'antinomies': 'An antinomy produces a self-contradiction by accepted ways of reasoning. It establishes that some tacit and trusted pattern of reasoning must be made explicit and henceforward be avoided or revised' (1966: 7). If we are to avoid the anthropological fallacy of claiming that these people are irrational, then we need to change the basic presuppositions.

Thus, it is because we have set ideas about the world, where we consider economic motives to be incommensurable with symbolic motives of self-expression and cosmological construction and where we believe that economic well-being might better be achieved through long-term accumulation of small gains than through repeated risking of all gains, that the *gambler's paradox* arises. It is because we have set ideas about culture, in which we fail to understand that counter-hegemonic, repressed elements of signification are transmitted and reproduced quite as much as the more hegemonic formulations and in which we are reluctant to see these elements as integral parts of the cultural discourse, that the *waan2/do2 paradox* arises. And finally, it is because of the way in which the Imperial Chinese preferred to speak about their world and because of their attempt to repress the reality of a deep class differentiation underlying the neo-Confucian scholar–gentry system, that the *examination paradox* arises.

Finally, the paradoxicality of these activities may be seen as a function of our posture as external observers, with an ingrained disposition to reify culture, society and economy as finite, identifiable entities rather than seeing cultural, social and economic practices as deeply enmeshed in forms of evolving and always open-ended integration. Through the exercise of hegemony, some of these formulations assume greater visibility than others. The latter are repressed but are not abolished outright (cf. Pina-Cabral 1999b).[68] It is the confrontational relation between the more luminous and the more penumbral aspects of social and cultural life that gives rise to the paradoxicality of certain social

PARADOXES

attitudes and practices such as the three instances we have identified in this chapter.

But the refusal to see people's behaviour as irrational is not the same as to presume that socio-cultural life is rationally integrated. Indeed, as will be argued in the next chapter, all communication sits on an equilibrium between shared meaning and equivocation. That is what grants communication its dynamic, creative potential and prevents language and culture from turning into prisons.

To return to Quine, if we opted for looking at the three phenomena described in this chapter as paradoxical it is precisely because we chose to be challenged by them in order to acquire a fuller understanding of cultural and social life, one that is less constrained by the greater visibility of its hegemonic aspects. If there is any added intellectual value to the study of such a thoroughly interstitial place as Macao, it is precisely that.

CHAPTER 5

EQUIVOCAL COMPATIBILITIES: PERSON, CULTURE AND EMOTION[69]

It is a truism to say that situations of intercultural contact are fertile in the production of phenomena of misunderstanding and equivocal communication. Contrary to what may be thought, however, these phenomena may not necessarily lead to a break in contact or to situations of violent imposition of one set of definitions over the other, particularly when the political and military terms of the situation are such that no partner has the overwhelming strength. When that occurs, negotiation and adaptation often take place, even though the initial intercultural misunderstanding is maintained.

Contexts of this kind, it has to be stressed, are commonly unstable and prone to rapid flaring of open conflict. But they are not necessarily short-lived. Arrangements can be reached through which the needs of both parties in the exchange are satisfied, in spite of the fact that these needs may be defined on different terms. I have chosen to call these social contexts situations of *equivocal compatibility* because the acts of communication of the parties to such a contact situation are characterized by having a double meaning.

It might be argued that, strictly speaking, there is no equivocation, since each actor attributes only one meaning to each act of communication. This, however, is too simplistic an understanding of what goes on in such contexts. Through a process that I have elsewhere likened to Davidson's notion of interpretative charity (Pina-Cabral 1992; cf. Godlove Jr. 1989), partial agreements can be reached that allow for the continuation of an ongoing relation. Over time, actors become aware that there is a gap in understanding and they come to adapt to it in what could be called a perverse fashion, going so far as to consciously exploit it to their own ends.

Furthermore, it is characteristic of such contexts that agents of mediation become involved. Such persons or groups are, on the one hand, in the invidious position of dealing with two cultural contexts with which they are familiar but which they do not succeed in integrating into one overarching moral universe. Nevertheless, they may derive considerable benefits from exploiting the needs of the contacting parties. Notwithstanding the fact that they are indispensable for the survival of the arena of contact, they often bear the brunt of discrimination, as they are perceived by either group as being marginal.

In this chapter, I will show how Macao's history is permeated by this sort of cultural misunderstanding – the 'perils of intercultural navigation'. The example I will use is the notion of person. The Chinese civilizational world and the Western European world, which confront each other on either side of the city's ethnic divide, have different ways of formulating the notion of person. Such a difference allows for many *equivocal compatibilities* and the example of the exchange of rights over persons by means of money transfers provides us with a particularly interesting case study.

A CONFRONTATION OF HEGEMONIES

Whilst speaking here of Chinese and European cultures as if they were clearly identifiable units, I do so only because of the specific contextual nature of the material under scrutiny. It must be understood that, in a situation where Catholic Europe and Imperial China meet, we are faced with two of the most entrenched and forceful cultural hegemonies that ever existed.

In Macao, people confronted not only *actual* differences in cultural definitions, but also (and perhaps more to the point) the terrible force of legitimation that these definitions carried with them. In situations of this nature, one of the traditions in the confrontation might eventually have yielded to the other. In the China/Europe confrontation, however – and right up to the early twentieth century, when the Chinese decided to carry out a modernist cultural revolution (cf. Wang Gungwu 1991a: 230ff.) – neither of these traditions was ready to yield to the other.

The time-honoured way of the Chinese of dealing with foreign trade was to presume that their partners in the exchange were somehow in a vassal-type relation to them. In the words of Weng Eang Cheong, 'Acculturation affects all parties involved, but China's cultural and economic superiority made her always more of a giver than receiver of influence, and her values and ways of conducting relations became the established norm of frontier diplomacy' (1997: 2).

The Portuguese that were left in Macao after the fall of Malacca in 1641 only survived because they accepted to play the game by the Chinese rules. The *Leal Senado* (the city council) played the dangerous gambit of accepting the Chinese definitions and then renegotiating the terms of the contract for dealing with Europe. This was facilitated by Chinese approaches to foreigners which ultimately favoured a situation of *double entendre*. Again according to Weng, 'The ancient Chinese practice of relying on foreign headmen to manage their nationals under their own laws differed little from the later contentious extraterritoriality clause but unfortunately, from the mid-eighteenth century, these conditions were demanded by foreigners with increasing vigour as rights and, when not satisfied, were later taken by force' (1997: 3–4). We may safely presume that the author is referring to the British demands and to the ultimate Hong Kong solution.

Now, the reason why the Chinese used the Portuguese of Macao throughout the seventeenth, eighteenth and early nineteenth centuries as favoured brokers in this exchange with Europe is that they knew that the relative weakness of the Macanese made them more wieldy partners. After the Opium Wars, in the 1840s, they were forced to deal directly with far less pliable partners.

However, we must not be lured into thinking that the relative weakness of the Macanese and their *Leal Senado* meant that they would simply accept acculturation. This would be to misjudge in a very serious way the reach of the arms of the King and the Pope. Never, anywhere in the world, was there a Portuguese traveller who could afford to forget what might happen if he or she disregarded the basic tenets of Catholicism and of the King's rule. If such a traveller planned ever to come in contact again with any European – and particularly in a Catholic country – they would have to remember the sword of Damocles hovering over him or her.

When we read the log-books kept by the navigators who travelled between Portugal and India in the seventeenth century, it becomes apparent that the King's orders and the Church's rules were always to be followed. You might be lost in the middle of the Ocean or amidst the strangest folk and yet, should you happen to be saved, the King's gaols would continue to await and the Inquisition's fires would still be burning (cf. Pina-Cabral 1990 and Ataíde 1957 [1608–12]). Shusako Endo's novel *Silence*, where he deals with the condition of apostatic priests in Hideyoshi's Japan, is a perfect exemplification of this condition (1988).

So, the *Leal Senado* and each of its members knew full well that they were constantly crossing a tightrope of intercultural misunderstanding.

They were aware of the dangers that lay on both sides – the dangers of 'a kind of oceanic nomadism which was, above all, spiritual' (cf. Chapter 1, p. 2).

A CRITIQUE OF THE ISOMORPHIC MODEL OF SOCIAL REPRODUCTION

Macao's history provides us with a fascinating example of intercultural misunderstanding. The example in question is the practice of trading persons in exchange for money.

I am working on the assumption that, when trading a person in this way, the understanding of what a person is is of central importance. If then, as the bulk of anthropological opinion seems to indicate, cultures differ in their conceptions of personhood, the act of trading a person may have radically distinct implications if the actors in the exchange are operating within distinct cultural universes. The same physical object (in this case a 'body' – for the Cantonese term for the receipts for such purchases, *maai6 san1 kai3*, means 'sell body deed', cf. Watson 1980b: 234), then, is seen differently by each partner in the exchange. As we saw above, however, situations of prolonged intercultural contact often engender equivocal compatibilities. I believe that the case I will present in this chapter can only be understood in these terms.

For far too long, anthropologists have been working on the basis of a model of social reproduction that postulates the existence of an isomorphism between the processes of devolution of material patrimony, of devolution of genetic patrimony and of devolution of cultural patrimony.[70] What better example of this than Malinowski's and Mead's disquisitions on the topic of legitimacy which have been at the root of modern anthropological kinship theory? Both authors explain the supposed universality of paternity on the basis of the argument that, if males were not involved in the processes of social reproduction, cultural devolution could not occur.

The presupposition of isomorphism in social reproduction, however, although verifiable in many ethnographic instances, does not by any means cover all situations. In fact, more often than not, it functions as a hindrance to our understanding of the complexity of social situations of devolution, both with regard to European and non-European societies.

One of the traditional means anthropologists have used to overcome the problems this causes has been to take recourse to the concept of 'adoption'. This, however, often turns out to be an ethnocentric trap. It salvages the isomorphic notion of social reproduction by pushing the onus of the fiction from an etic to an emic level (from *us* to *them*). Thus, it is postulated that the new links of filiation resulting from 'adoption' are *like* the earlier (isomorphically social and biological) links of filiation, but that the responsibility for this fiction lies not with the ethnographer but with the people themselves. Adoption is a useful term for hasty comparativists precisely because European legal traditions treat it as a legal fiction. As we will see, such a confusion is at the very basis of the topic of the monetary purchase of persons in Macao.

The transfers of social relations commonly described by ethnographers by means of the notion of adoption may be very diverse. This diversity, it must be understood, lies not only in the level of complexity of the rights and duties to which it gives rise, but also depends on the nature of the conception of the person in that particular society. This is something that is often overlooked. The transfer of relations over a person assumes different aspects depending on what a person is in a particular society.

THE COURT CASE

The discussion in this chapter centres on a court case that took place in Macao in 1903. At the time that this case was taken to court, Camilo Pessanha was substituting the principal judge who was absent on leave. The Public Prosecutor was not satisfied with the verdict and appealed to the Court of Appeal in Goa (*Tribunal da Relação de Goa*). The report was accompanied by an interesting declaration from the principal judge, who had returned to Macao in the meantime, upholding Pessanha's decision. The Court of Appeal decided in favour of the original verdict. This case, therefore, came to constitute an important judicial precedent in Macao.

The first judge, Camilo Pessanha, is a fascinating character who deserves some introduction. He is perhaps the most highly regarded Portuguese symbolist poet. Born in 1867, the illegitimate son of a law student and a servant, he too read Law at the University of Coimbra. He was a Freemason and a Republican. Largely as a result of his penury and his political attitudes, he was obliged to accept an appointment in Macao in 1894 to become a high-school teacher. He lived there until his death in 1926, working either as a teacher, a private lawyer or a substitute judge. Furthermore, he held a number of other occasional bureaucratic appointments. He was a quarrelsome and erratic individual and his later years were marked by an increasing eccentricity, associated with a debilitating addiction to opium. Nevertheless, he achieved well-deserved fame as a jurist. The volume of transcriptions of his legal texts which has recently been published (Veiga de Oliveira 1993) amply justifies his reputation as a learned observer of Chinese customs and culture, whose views, marked as they are by his period, are nevertheless clear, critical and informed.

Briefly, the court case in point deals with the kidnapping of a boy aged eleven whose mother was a servant at the Government Palace in Macao. The mother's job meant that she could only return home every fortnight. During the intervening time, the boy was cared for by his disabled father.

The night of the kidnapping, the boy had crept out of his home, unbeknown to his father, in order to watch the *Auto China* (Chinese opera) in the grounds of a nearby temple. He was one of the *attais* that were such an integral part of these performances. There is a vivid description of these in Carlos José Caldeira's travel account (cf. Caldeira 1997). He reports what he saw in the 1850s, but these things had not changed all that much by the turn of the century.

> If the spectator happens to raise his eyes towards the ceiling he will see a bevy of *attais* (Chinese boys or urchins) of all sizes, who are hanging, lounging and climbing on the bamboo [roof frame], as if they were little monkeys. When driven by need or by invention, they take to urinating over the respectable audience. (ibid.: 313–14)

On his way back home, a hunchback carpenter offered to give the boy some white rice and a new jacket. The boy became suspicious but was easily overpowered. He was then placed in a hideout[71] from where he was taken to Chiac-Ham, a nearby Cantonese town. He was sold to Long-a-cam for the sum of 35 *patacas*. According to her, she bought the boy in order to resell him to her brother-in-law who needed a son for adoption. She charged 75 *patacas* for him, thus making a considerable profit on the resale.

MACAO'S LEGAL SYSTEM

At this point, a brief explanation must be made of the situation in Macao concerning the Chinese population's subjection to the Portuguese legal system. Macao was governed for nearly three centuries by an ambiguous but, on the whole, efficient system under which the Chinese population (who lived in theory outside the bounds of the Christian citadel) was ruled by Chinese magistrates.

The problems of communication between the Chinese inhabitants and the Portuguese Administration were resolved by the *Procurador*.

Originally founded in 1583, during the first days of the *Leal Senado*, this office survived all the various changes in Macao's history. For a while, the *Procurador* was even endowed with an official rank by the Chinese Emperor, under the policy of letting the 'barbarians' govern themselves. In the early nineteenth century, he shifted his formal allegiance from the *Leal Senado* to the Governor. The *Procurador* dealt with all matters connected to the Chinese population of the city: as a judge, as a municipal administrator in charge of taxation and as the principal link with the Chinese authorities of Canton After the *tso-tang* (Cant. *joh2 tong4*) magistrate left the city in 1846 (cf. Chapter 3), the *Procurador* took over some of his functions, becoming more powerful.

In 1894, however, in line with the then dominant Liberal policies of separating justice from administration, his judicial functions were removed. Then, for the first time, normal Portuguese courts had to deal with cases presented by Chinese natives. Up until then, the *Procurador* had assumed judicial functions and he had used as his referent Cantonese customary law. Under the Liberal regime, however, this was thought to be incorrect. So his judicial functions were handed over to the normal courts. This, however, raised the problem of relevance. If they were to be seen to dispense justice, Portuguese judges could not simply use Portuguese laws. They had to adapt themselves to Chinese custom.

Contrary to the African and South American colonial situations, in Macao, as indeed in Goa, the Portuguese had always recognized the right of the local populations to carry on their own traditional way of life. This was particularly the case as far as family law was concerned, for it was correctly felt that to apply Portuguese family law to non-Christian Chinese persons would simply prevent these people from taking recourse to the courts. A Royal Decree of 1869 established that, in judging cases involving Chinese natives, the courts should apply the Chinese Ways and Customs (Veiga de Oliveira 1993: 347).

As a result, in 1909, the Portuguese king signed a legal decree regulating Chinese family law, entitled 'Rights and duties of the Chins of Macao in relation to some of their ways and customs' (*Usos e Costumes*).[72] From an anthropological point of view this code, based on earlier judicial practice at the *Procurador*'s office, is a most valuable historical reference for the prevailing family practices in the Canton region at the time.[73]

The first decades of the twentieth century saw the start of a fierce debate in Macao – both in the press and in official committees – concerning the philosophical options underlying the application of law in the city. Everyone was conscious of the need to adapt judicial practice in the courts of the Territory to the prevailing Chinese cultural context, so as to avoid irrelevant judicial decisions. However, new colonial policies that challenged the Liberal ideals were becoming dominant.

Old Liberals like Camilo Pessanha – the man who served as judge in our court case – were strong upholders of the principles of equality before the Law, sovereignty of the State and general applicability of the Law. They abhorred institutions such as the *Procuratura* for they considered that these established differences between citizens who should be equal before the law. In fact, in 1912, Pessanha headed a gubernatorial committee that attempted to block the official creation of a court of law for Chinese residents and at the same time proposed the final extinction of the *Procuratura* (cf. Araújo 2000: 190). Eventually, in 1919, his line of thinking lost out. That year, a *Tribunal Privativo dos Chinas de Macau* (Private Court of the Chinese of Macao) was established. Only then was the *Procuratura* extinguished.

A new colonialist school of thought appeared during the last decade of the nineteenth century, strongly influenced by prevalent English and French colonial attitudes. People like Lourenço Cayolla, in his *Science of Colonisation*, argued that 'Judicial uniformity is an error and goes against the very nature of law, which must above all reflect the particularities of the environment where it evolved' (1912, II: 120). A new nostalgia for the old style *Procuratura* system was making its appearance in the Territory under the argument that the great majority of the inhabitants of Macao 'are of Chinese race, essentially traditionalists, who do not have the stature to accept, comprehend and follow a legislation which is created for a more perfected and cultivated society'.

> It was a rather disastrous mistake of the Portuguese government not to preserve the special legislation that existed in each colony. The French Revolution ideal of legal equality for all may well be true in cultivated Europe, whose civilization is homogeneous, but when applied to heterogeneous peoples, in the most diverse states of moral and intellectual development, it has counterproductive and prejudicial results.[74]

In 1903, therefore, for people like Camilo Pessanha who opposed such views, it was important to show that the Chinese residents of Macao could bring their complaints to the normal courts and receive judgements that made sense to them. The dispute between the judge and the public prosecutor, therefore, was not about the fact that Chinese people should receive justice that applied to their cultural condition, but rather whether or not they should hold full civil rights whilst maintaining their cultural specificity. The statements of the judges in our case are a particularly good example of the sort of problems that would have to be overcome if the ideal of equality before the Law was to be upheld.

In practical terms a situation of 'jural pluralism' prevailed throughout Macao's remaining history (cf. Santos 1991: 451–3). This meant that the Chinese population was always more or less free to choose whether it would take recourse to the *Procurador* (or later to the Chinese Court) or to the various types of semi-informal Chinese authorities that existed in the city. An ambiguous interpenetration between Chinese and Portuguese institutions seems to have prevailed with different intensities and manifestations in different periods.

The mother of the kidnapped boy managed to discover the boy's whereabouts by means of the *Procurador*'s 'secret police'. We found references to these police in the newspapers of the period but it is not at all clear to what extent they were 'secret'. In 1903, this magistrate still kept his administrative and diplomatic functions (in serving as a contact with the Chinese authorities of Guangdong Province) but had lost most of his judicial functions.[75] In theory, these had been handed over to the Portuguese courts and that is the reason why the boy's kidnappers were judged by Portuguese judges under the Portuguese legal system.

The 'secret police' managed to imprison the accused in Chiac-Ham, a nearby town under Chinese jurisdiction, and took them to a Portuguese court in Macao. This again can only be explained if we take into account the highly ambiguous role of the *Procurador* and his men.[76] However, we must remember the Macanese courts were notorious for their lack of efficiency. There is evidence that most Chinese inhabitants did not even attempt to take recourse to them. They preferred to turn to the Chamber of Commerce to resolve their small commercial disputes (cf. Araújo 2000: 194) and lawyers often worked as conflict mediators. So there is good reason to presume that the fact that the boy's mother was a servant at the Government Palace was crucial in explaining how she managed to get the police to help her, to get the case into court and to bring the judgement to a satisfactory conclusion.

In this case, the judges had to decide whether the accused had committed slavery, a crime punishable by law. The actual terms of the Public Prosecutor's accusation, however, concerned piracy. This was because Portugal had signed a treaty with Great Britain sixty years earlier (July 1842), which stated that any person attempting to enslave another would be punished with the penalties applicable to piracy. It would seem that the reason for this was that it was thought to be a more efficient and forceful way of dealing with slave merchants at sea, allowing British naval officers to lay hands on slave ships sailing under the Portuguese flag to America.

As both judges to our case explain (Veiga de Oliveira 1993: 344–5 and 383), this decision was primarily aimed at stopping the southern Atlantic trade in African slaves and was hardly applicable to the conditions of Macao. Nevertheless, the point in dispute with the Public Prosecutor was not related to this. Rather, it was whether the people involved in the sale of minors in Macao could justly be accused of having committed slavery. As it turned out, Pessanha's verdict created a precedent, for it was the culmination of three and a half centuries of debate among the Portuguese of Macao and Goa as to whether the Chinese could or could not be subjected to slavery.

SLAVERY IN MACAO[77]

The debate started at the very beginning of Macao's foundation. Already in 1562, a Jesuit priest complained that: 'Over four hundred pricey female slaves have been sent by boat to India; and in the last ship to leave for Malacca, a further two hundred girls were sent' (quoted in Teixeira 1976: 11). These girls were considered very valuable and attractive. The renowned chronicler Diogo de Couto too, complains that merchants left Macao for Malacca and Goa 'carrying with them very beautiful and white skinned girls, with whom they cohabited for many years' (ibid.: 12).

It was debatable, however, whether one could enslave a formerly free person. Clerical opinion, on the whole, was in favour of considering that the Chinese were, 'by nature', a free people and that it was, therefore, unacceptable to enslave them. In 1569, the Dominican Friar Gaspar da Cruz claims that he went so far as to visit Canton expressly to confirm his opinion that Chinese society did not recognize the condition of slavehood: 'And let no one claim anything else, because in order to study this, I worked for a while in Canton, as a number of Portuguese people claimed the contrary' (quoted in Veiga de Oliveira 1993: 389).

From very early on, it was recognized that the purchase of Chinese persons (particularly female infants) caused no particular problems in Macao, but that the export of these people as slaves was contrary to the safeguarding of peaceable relations with the Chinese authorities. This point is clearly made by a Royal Decree of 1624, where the King states that

> I have given you specific orders concerning the fortification of the city of Macao, and of making sure that no Chinese captives are taken

from that port as it is an issue about which they get very upset. I am happy to see that things are being done in order to fortify that city and that steps have been taken to prevent Chinese captives from being taken from there. [. . .] And in particular concerning the Chinese: I want it to be declared that they cannot and should not be made captive.[78]

These good intentions were, however, difficult to uphold in the Territory where the monetary purchase of persons was easily accomplished and the supply very abundant, particularly of young females. Were these people slaves, or were they not? Certainly, for the Portuguese, anyone whose services and freedom of movement could be bought for money was a slave. Furthermore, it was argued that their own parents were responsible for selling the children and that, as most slaves were subsequently converted to Catholicism, it was altogether a good thing to buy them.

Such arguments can be heard in the words of Goa's city council, complaining to the King in 1605 about an attempt on the part of the Jesuits to free Japanese slaves – to whom very much the same situation applied:

> Your Majesty orders that henceforth we should buy none of them. But these people are accustomed to sell their own children, and to sell them to other infidels like themselves. And since they sell them to heathen, surely it is lawful for Christians to buy them, since all those who are bought become Christians and are now so. (Quoted in Boxer 1948: 233)

Does one detect here the whiff of hypocrisy? It appears to me that we are faced with a most interesting example of equivocal compatibility. People learn, so to speak, to ride the wave of intercultural misunderstanding to their own benefit. Over a century later, for instance, the Judge of Macao (*Ouvidor*) was led to write to the King complaining of the Bishop, then a Dominican friar, claiming that he had maltreated him 'in words and complaints, for having forbidden the sending as merchandise to Malacca of boys and girls stolen in Canton, arguing that, by preventing him from selling these people, I was hindering the Sacrament of Baptism' (quoted in Teixeira 1976: 13).

By the eighteenth century, the Jesuits too, already distant from their earlier spirit of intelligent missionizing, had learnt the ways of equivocal compatibility. The office of the Father of the Christians, normally attributed to a Jesuit, had been created in the late sixteenth century in order to have someone responsible for the safekeeping of the interests of the recently converted. However, it was as the result of a number of complaints by Crown officials against the Father of the Christians that the final decree establishing the immediate abolishment of any form of slavery and servitude of Chinese in Macao was written by the Enlightenment dictator, the Marquis of Pombal. In the words of the decree, the aim was to discourage the 'barbaric behaviour' of those who, under the pretext of protecting children whom their parents would otherwise reject,

> (. . .) are introducing them to a general state of slavery which lasts for forty years, as is customary, and is made with the agreement of the Father of the Christians, who has it declared in the register of Baptisms according to what is asked by the person interested. This must be seen as an abominable absurdity, that cannot fail to make the Christian Religion odious in these regions, seeing how the Sacrament of Baptism, by means of which Christ Our Lord saved us from the captivity of guilt, is turned into a door for entering slavery. (Quoted in Veiga de Oliveira 1993: 398).

The Minister, whose hatred of the Jesuits eventually led him to expel them from all Portuguese dominions, raves on, complaining of the fact that the very same register of Baptism, with which such people prove they are Christians, should be used as a title of slavery.

THE TRADE IN PERSONS IN MACAO

Is the Minister justified in his claims that: 'the Chins are by nature free, so they cannot and should not by any means be made slaves' (Veiga de Oliveira 1993: 397)?

The fact is that, as James Watson states in carefully guarded terms, until the Communist takeover in 1949, 'China had one of the largest and most comprehensive markets for the exchange of human beings in the world. In many parts of China, notably in the south, nearly every peasant household was directly or indirectly affected by the sale of people' (1980a: 223). Both Pessanha and the principal judge in the case studied here confirm this point, stating that if one were to persecute all the people engaged in the sale of minors in Macao, then perhaps not a single Chinese home in the city would have been untouched (Veiga de Oliveira 1993: 384).[79]

Establishing whether the persons thus exchanged can be considered slaves is far more than a terminological quibble. The problem of definition arises most clearly in the text confirming the verdict written by the principal judge. He comments that

> There is no doubt that the purchase and sale of minors for the effects of adoption and domestic service is permitted in China; unless we wish to refuse the terms used, as most of the time it is not a price that one gives, and without a price there is no purchase; it is a *li si*[80] – a larger or smaller reward[81] that occurs in all of the Chinese contracts and acts of life! Otherwise, then, marriage would be a purchase, as the presents are nothing but the symbol of the price by means of which the man receives the woman who is lost to her parents! But there is also no doubt that, in China, slavery is severely punished and there are many sections of the Code of Law that deal with such a matter! (Veiga de Oliveira 1993: 381)

Our two judges, therefore, conclude that one cannot consider what happened to the boy a crime of enslavement but rather a crime of kidnapping. They take recourse to the Portuguese medieval legal concept of *cárcere privado* (private gaol), the punishment of which was less harsh than that of piracy. The liberal-minded Pessanha claims

> To proceed in any other way would be to fail to respect in its most sacred part (that of family organisation) the ways and customs of the Chins [. . .] Adoption is a kind of sale, not of the person of the adopted, but of the rights of paternity over him: to refer to an adopted son, the Chinese say bought son, and the Portuguese in Macao have adopted this term. Marriage, and more specifically concubinage (. . .) are equally a purchase; the former, in the majority of cases, albeit not always, only symbolically; but the latter is perfectly real, the price varying according to the conditions of the market and the graces and other attributes of the concubine or second wife. The intimate connection between Chinese family institutions and the deliverance of certain rights over its members by means of a price [has been repeatedly accepted by the courts in Macao]. (Veiga de Oliveira 1993: 347–8)

Pessanha's solution to the problem, therefore, seems to be on the line of the opposition between rights *in personam* and rights *in rem* that Radcliffe-Brown made famous in social anthropology (1952). The Chinese, then, would be selling rights *in personam* over their children and concubines, whilst the Portuguese would be buying rights *in rem*: that would be the nature of the intercultural misunderstanding. The Chinese sold relations, whilst the Portuguese purchased chattels. This being the case, he concludes, the carpenter who stole the servant's boy in order to sell him, and the woman who bought him for profit, were not engaging in slavery, for they were not exchanging a chattel, they were exchanging social relations; they were dealing with the boy's aptitude for being a son.

Brilliant as this solution was, I am not satisfied that it resolves our problem more than partially. In the first place, how is it possible that one should believe that one could force someone out of a social relation that is grounded in deep affection, such as that of filiation, merely by stealing him? In other words, the boy was 11 years of age, he was in his right mind and the judges even report some of his declarations. Would he accept his new parents in that context? Contrary to what a European person would think, the people who stole and exchanged him were convinced that he would. Otherwise, what would be the purpose of stealing him?

We will deal with this issue later. Let us now consider a second quandary. Is it really true that there are no slaves in China? On this matter, the two judges seem to disagree. Pessanha denies their existence in Macao or in China, acknowledging nevertheless that the Chinese law contemplated such a condition as a penalty for certain exceptional crimes (Veiga de Oliveira 1993: 340). The principal judge, however, gives us further evidence:

> The Kou Kong are a common class in China [. . .] – they are servants who differ considerably from the Nou Pi, properly speaking slaves.[82] The Kou Kong are raised in association to a specific family by means of a stipulated contract, which states the price and the conditions of servitude. At the end of the contract, they are equal to their former bosses, as happens in Europe! (ibid.: 382)

James Watson too, in his study of Chinese slavery (1980a), claims that there were slaves who functioned almost like a pariah caste and who were treated as expensive status symbols as they were thought to consume more than they earned.[83]

It would seem, therefore, that the European category of slavery is now, as it was in the past, unsatisfactory to describe the numerous types of relations between persons, and rights over persons, that were and, on the whole, continue to be mediated by monetary exchange in southern China. Even without entering too profoundly into the issue, it is clear that there is an enormous variation in the number of situations that fall into this category: from the man who pays a sum to his future parents-in-law, with the certainty that they will hand it back to him via his bride's dowry; to the man who purchases from another the right to the marital services of a woman, who had been the latter's concubine or wife; to the man who redeems a prostitute from her pimp in order to make her his wife or concubine;[84] to the man who buys a son to continue his name; to the single or widowed woman (an example given by Pessanha himself) who buys a daughter to look after her during old age and her soul after death;[85] to the same woman who buys a daughter to raise her and resell her for prostitution; to a couple who buy a small girl to give her in marriage to their small son, when he grows up, but, in the meantime, put her to work for them in a factory;[86] to the prostitute who has signed a contract that binds her to the payment of a certain amount of money compounded with interest; to the bond servant whose freedom is curtailed for a determinate number of years or even decades; finally, to the slave families who are prohibited from leaving the village and whose patrilineal descendants remain bound to the village's ancestral domain.[87]

Slavery turns out to be a useless term to refer to all of these relations.[88] But then adoption is no better. Suffice it to consider the difference between an adopted son, such as the boy in our court case was meant to become, and a *mooi1 jai2* – a young girl who is purchased in order to work for her masters and whose future husband must pay a brideprice to the masters.[89] Such girls could be resold or used to obtain an income through forced labour or prostitution. It was mostly their export from Macao as slaves that fuelled the slavery debate in the city.

The fortune of an adopted son was very distinct: contrary to girls, young men were bought in order to continue a name line. Confucian morals demanded that a couple who did not have male children should take a son to become the heir. He was to be favoured even over a resident son-in-law. In fact, article 13 of the *Usos e Costumes* positively obliges such a couple to do so: 'In the absence of legitimate masculine descent, the Chinese must take on an adopted male'. Preferably they should take the son of a close patrilinear relative, but the latter were seldom willing to give up their sons, so the boy often had to be bought. Such was the demand for boys that, according to James Watson (1980a: 233), the kidnapping of young men was the primary activity of bandits.[90]

We may, therefore, conclude that the application of the same term – adoption – to men and to women, in southern China, is largely arbitrary. But it is not only the terms slavery and adoption that raise comparative problems. For the sake of brevity I will refrain from demonstrating that the European legal notion of the marriage contract also fails to describe the negotiations and subsequent monetary exchanges that occur at the time of a Chinese marriage. The principal difference lies doubtlessly in the fact that the Chinese favour a logic of patrimonial transfer. As a matter of fact, this was one of the recurrent points of friction in the cross-ethnic marriages between Chinese or Macanese and Portuguese in the 1990s (cf. Chapter 9).

Thus we return to the initial point that the meaning of the exchange cannot be perceived without judging the nature of the things exchanged. No sense can be made of the purchase of persons if we fail to take into account the notion of person involved.

THE CHINESE CONCEPT OF PERSON

Let us now return to the question we left open above. What is implied by the fact that all of the accused in our court case reasonably expected the kidnapped boy to become a worthy adopted son?

If this fact puzzles modern Europeans, it is because of what we presume to be the normal reactions of people in such contexts. To make sense of that situation, therefore, we must avail ourselves of what anthropologists tell us about the Chinese concept of person. It is important to understand that there are two sides to this issue. On the one hand, we are concerned with the way in which persons conceive of other persons; and, on the other hand, we are interested in the way persons conceive of themselves, that is, their notion of self. Both of these aspects are socially constructed and, as we know, they interrelate dialectically.[91]

In other words, the man expected the boy to become a filial son according to a set of parameters of what he understood a filial son to be; and the boy, in all likelihood,[92] would have turned out to be a filial son. Not only would he have shared the man's conception of what a filial son should be like, but his social self was constructed in such a way as he would be disposed to be a filial son.

It must be noted at this point that the concept of 'filial piety' as enshrined in the Confucian tradition (cf. Hsieh Yu-Wei 1967) has, buried within it, a directionality of endebtedness that is very distinct from the relationship of filiation as characteristic of the Judaeo-Christian tradition.[93] The Mariolatry that has come to dominate the Catholic world in particular places at its centre the redeeming force of the maternal love enshrined in the image of the *Pietà*. This is contrary to the Chinese emphasis. Here, the parent–child bond must not be seen as mutual and paternal love is not what is emphasized. Rather, it is the bondedness of the child – for that reason paternal love is a secondary phenomenon and filial piety the starting point. The bond of gratitude one has towards one's parents becomes the very basis of all moral behaviour (Hsieh 1967: 170). In the words of a Taiwanese philosopher, 'A parent's love of his child is strictly biological, whereas filial piety, love and respect for one's parents is not biological but is moral, being based upon a sense of obligation or a debt of gratitude, and is therefore spiritual' (T'ang Chün-I in Hsieh 1967: 186).

Three aspects seem to stand out from the by now considerable literature that has accrued on the topic of the differentiation between Western and Chinese notions of the person.[94] The first of these aspects, and perhaps the most important one, is well characterized in Francis Hsu's argument that Americans tend to be *individual-centred* whilst Chinese are prone to being *situation-centred* (1981: 12).[95] By this he means that the Chinese place an enormous emphasis on appropriateness of place and behaviour, whilst Americans would be more concerned with coherence of individual expression. This has a reflection on the person's own notion of self – 'an organic conception of the self in relation to one's social and natural environment' (Bary 1996: 34). As Ai-ling Chin argues: 'the Chinese self has had his centre of gravity more exclusively in social relations and less solidly in himself' (quoted in Hsu 1981: 44).

Here lies one of the clues to our puzzle. Once wrenched from his earlier social context and possessed of a new social belonging, the boy would feel compelled to situate himself appropriately within it. The situation-centredness of his formulation of self would tend to override his initial sense of strangeness resulting from being dislocated from his original belonging.

The second aspect of differentiation would seem to be what Hsu calls the prominence of emotion in the American way of life, which would be countered by a Chinese tendency to underplay matters of the heart. Once again, the difference lies both in the way one approaches the emotions of others and in the way one experiences one's own emotions. Barbara Ward's paper on temper tantrums among the children of fishing-folk near Hong Kong is one of the important points of reference for this discussion (1989 [1970]). By observing the way in which adults failed to respond to temper tantrums, noticing them but not considering it necessary to respond, Ward argues that there are specific attitudes towards the socialization of children that result in what she calls an 'emotional self-reliance'.

Taking up this line of argument, Sulamith H. Potter undertakes to study the cultural construction of emotion by reference to a farming village also in the Pearl River Delta where she and her husband carried out extensive fieldwork (1990 [1986]). She finds that the management of emotions is characterized by a specific attitude of denial, not of the emotions themselves, but of their social relevance. People 'believe that experienced emotion is irrelevant either to the creation or to the perpetuation of social institutions of any kind' (ibid.: 182–3).

Thus, she argues that emotions are not thought to have a reflection on social relationships, reproducing them or injuring them, as tends to be the case in Western cultures. This means that people do not feel the need to repress them or even to stage their existence in order to endow the social order with authenticity. This has an important reflection at the level of the construction of the self. In her words:

> A Chinese person is a person whose emotions are understood as irrelevant idiosyncrasies, of no intrinsic importance to the social order. Such a person is significantly different from a person whose emotions are culturally defined as a fundamental aspect of the self, giving meaning to social experience, and providing a necessary validation of the connections between the individual and society. (ibid.: 188)

Thus, when her subjects of study wished to symbolize the strength of a social relationship, they did not automatically resort to an idiom of emotion, rather 'the critical symbolic dimension for the affirmation of relationships is work, and the related and subordinate concept of suffering, which is thought of as an intrinsic aspect of work' (ibid.: 189).

My own ethnographic experience in the urban contexts of Macao and Hong Kong would lead me to extend this notion of work to include the providing of services, mediated by transfers of wealth. Here, the primary symbolic medium is money. Potter points in the same direction, when she comments on the surprising efforts that daughters make to earn money for their parents, even though they know that they will not benefit from these efforts once they are married (ibid.: 193). She argues that these efforts, and not the expression of emotions, are what is seen as confirming and legitimating the relationship, both between parents and children and between husband and wife.

This being the case, we can go a little further in understanding the social relations and expectations that were at play in the events that led to our court case. The future father of the boy, having paid a considerable sum for him, considered that he had established a solid basis for a social relation of filiation. The boy, in turn, was not expected to experience any particular emotional bond towards his future father. If, in time, he came to feel it, so much the better, so long as he continued to behave in the correct filial manner. Furthermore, whatever emotions the boy may have displayed, he would in all likelihood have received the same treatment as he did after the temper tantrums that Barbara Ward witnessed. He would simply have been ignored until such time as he adjusted to his social environment.

The third aspect of differentiation to be considered is perhaps the most fascinating of all. East Asian civilizations (cf. Bary 1988) do not postulate the notion of a unified, monolithic and indestructible concept of the soul as is characteristic of the Judeo-Christian tradition. Ironically, one may note that, when the Jesuits of Macao thought they were saving a soul by baptizing it, they were in fact creating this soul. This is another area where the use of Eurocentric concepts to describe Chinese culture has resulted in great confusion. From a perusal of the literature on the topic, it would seem that the terms often translated as 'deity', 'spirit/ power', 'soul' or 'ghost' (e.g. Sangren 1987: 255–60, Mand. *shen, ling* or *ling-hun, p'o* and *kuei*; Cant. *san4, ling4* or *ling4 wan4, paak3* and *gwai2*) are all more or less related to the sense of inner personal identity, which Christians describe by using the notion of soul.

Perhaps the best explanation for this – albeit one that continues to depend on the Eurocentric notion of soul – may be found in Alan Elliot's pioneering study of spirit–medium cults in Singapore. 'The soul of a living man,' he tells us, 'is conceived as having two components, the *hun* or positive component, which has three parts representing the three spiritual energies, and the *p'o* or negative component, which has seven parts representing the seven emotions' (1955: 28). In Cantonese, the coined expression used to refer to this plurality of the inner person is '*saam1 wan4, chat1 paak3*' (three *wan4*, seven *paak3)*. In fact, the Cantonese with whom I discussed this issue corroborated Elliot's findings in Singapore that

> there are no very clear ideas as to how many parts of the soul there are, but there is a vague notion that there is more than one since its presence can make itself felt in more than one place after death. (1955: 29)

This plurality, then, is perhaps best understood by reference to Mayfair Yang's concept of the permeability of the Chinese concept of the person (1989: 39). In his classic paper on ancestor worship (1979), Maurice Freedman argues that there must be at least three souls – again the Eurocentric notion – as one of them is thought to undergo Buddhist judgement and reincarnation, another to remain with the bones (affecting the descendants by means of Taoist geomantic processes) and the third to stay at the tablet placed in the Confucian ancestral shrine. The main point he makes, however, is that 'the morality of the individual life leads to the rapid extinction of the social personality' (1979: 297). If the social personality of the ancestor lives on, it is only to the extent that it functions as a link between the living and their forebears, not because of its individual moral value. Thus, in Hsieh Yu-Wei's words, 'As the continuous flow of one's life in his offspring, together with his trade or mental achievement, was looked upon by Confucians as the perpetuity of his own life, then the question concerning the continued existence of the soul (and where his soul will be) is unimportant' (1967: 181).

There is a relational aspect to this. Thus, as Freedman argues, the descendants of a dead man may refer to him by the term *san4*, which most often means something that we would categorize as 'spirit' or even 'deity' – that is a principle of order which is associated to the notion of yang (Cant. *yeung4*). But the same deceased, to non-descendants, will be classified as *gwai2* – a term often translated as 'ghost' or 'devil', associated to the yin cosmological force (Cant. *yam1*) (Freedman 1979: 297). This term denotes disorder and uncleanliness and is the principal component of the expression used to refer to European foreigners, *gwai2 lo2*. Sangren has argued that what is at play here is a notion of power 'as a function of the mediation of order and disorder' (1987: 143). Such a mediation, therefore, is perceived as occurring in the very composition of the person.

This conception may help us understand how a person can be thought to lose some of his or her inner essence whilst continuing to live and think, albeit in a feeble condition. Marjorie Topley's example of the popular interpretation of fright neurosis in children in Hong Kong is apposite here. Children who suffer from this condition are supposed to have an unstable *wan4* (that is, the yang component) that leaves them and needs to be called back in order for the child to find his or her vital force again (1970).

Another good example comes from Taiwan. According to Hou Ching-Lang,

> Taiwanese tradition, still upheld today, claims that each man is the home of twelve original spirits, *che-ul yuan-chen* [. . .]. If they are all there, the body and mind are healthy; their absence, even partial, leads to sickness and to mental confusion. Whilst awake the mind functions integrally and the twelve original spirits are present; dreaming is explained by their adventures outside the body during sleep. If they are stopped in their way by hellish kings, gods or demons, the owner loses his life. (1975: 145)

If then we avoid using the Eurocentric notion of soul, we end up with the perception that the way in which the Chinese formulate the inner experience of individuality[96] does not presume uniqueness, essentiality or indestructibility. Rather, this permeable conception of the person can be seen as related to the emphasis placed on correct positioning rather than inner experience; on the material rather than the emotional side of social relations.

CONCLUSION

We are now in a position to begin to understand the sense of strangeness that confronted the Portuguese in Macao; first, merchants and priests and, later, jurists and bureaucrats. Pessanha stated it with the frankness and clarity which is so characteristic of his writing:

> What truly surprised me, newly arrived from Europe, was that apathy, that irritating kind of indifference, even to their very own suffering, that all of these people demonstrated, and which is, of all the traits of the Chinese people, the more invincibly odious to us, Europeans. (quoted in Pires 1992: 136–7)

Ethnocentric though he always remained, in time he became a keen and informed observer of Chinese ways, as the text of the sentence he pronounced clearly shows. But he never managed to bridge the gulf of the inner experience of the person. To the end, Pessanha continued to think that, 'all Chinamen are alike in the paradoxical processes of their intelligence and in the disproportion between their aesthetic sensitivity and their moral affectivity' (ibid.: 130).

He lived for over twenty years in intimate domestic companionship with a Chinese woman, Kuoc Ngan Ieng,[97] to whom he seems to have been very attached.[98] In all probability, he too had to purchase the right to her companionship, as tradition in Macao claims that she was a *pei4 pa4 jai2* (a young musician being initiated to prostitution) and that he had to pay the price of her freedom.[99] His last legal text is his own will. Even though most of it is dedicated to protect her interests and her well-being after his death, he fails to make a single comment that overtly denotes any kind of emotion and he insists that he remains a bachelor. Perhaps that can be interpreted as yet another of the equivocal compatibilities that are the very stuff of Macao's survival over four and a half centuries.

CHAPTER 6

STONE SILENCES: ORGANIZED AMNESIA[100]

In this chapter I will again deal with a public monument – this time a non-existent one. The argument will focus on the way monuments may be used – even in their absence – as markers of social belonging within an ethnically divided city. I will explore the notions of traumatic silence and organized amnesia in relation to the constitution and reproduction of the master narratives that legitimate political power.

A NON-EXISTENT MONUMENT

The events that I want to discuss in the first part of this chapter date to the mid-1950s – when the Portuguese presence in the Territory reached its four-hundredth anniversary. I first became aware of these occurrences in the early 1990s, whilst recording the family history of a Macanese employee of the Maritime Museum. He told me the following story in hushed but anguished tones. He felt very strongly about what he was telling me and there was a vindictive intention in his words. What he most resented was that, as he put it, the Portuguese from Portugal had betrayed the Macanese; as, according to him, they were about to do again in 1999. This is a literal translation of his words at the time:

> When four hundred years of Macao's existence had passed a monument was built . . . do you know where D. Maria is? Do you know the water reservoir? There is, at that point, a curve where the road turns downwards. Well, there, they had built a huge monument, very beautiful, to celebrate the 400 years of Macao's existence, of the Portuguese here in Macao. The Chinese did not let out a single sound, they allowed it all to be done; then, they were only three days short of the inauguration – the feast day of the city – all was ready, the invitations had already been sent, etc. . . . they gave 48 hours for the

demolition of the monument! 48 hours! It had taken a long time to build, but they gave only 48 hours to demolish the monument. What did they do? There was no time to lose. They put dynamite under the monument and sent it all tumbling down. It was all over! The party was all over – 400 years were all over! That was that!

This piece of information took me by surprise. I took a cab and went to the spot, but nothing recognizable could be found there. Furthermore, no book referred to the event. As it turned out, even the question of the date raised a problem, for the generally accepted date for Macao's inauguration is 1557 and I could find no reference to an occurrence of this nature for that year. Most authors state that no celebrations occurred in 1957 due to pressure exerted by the PRC (Gonçalves Pereira 1995: 61). As it transpired, it was no wonder that I couldn't find any reference to it, as it had all happened two years earlier!

The event was traumatic and was 'silenced', for it was yet another of those events which the Macanese feel have made them 'lose face' before 'the Chinese' – their ethnic counterparts.

In short, I had stumbled not upon one but two silences. The first was the stillborn monument celebrating the 400 years of the Portuguese presence in Macao; the second was the story of how that monument had been made to disappear. The first was a traumatic gap; the second was organized amnesia.

SILENCES AND IDENTITIES

Let us step aside for a moment and consider the relationship between silence and identities.

Social identities are not once-and-for-all. All identities are based on complex and continuing processes of identification and legitimation. The combination of these two factors means that identity building is a paradoxical phenomenon, as it is a dialectical process of construction that is based both on self-identification and other-identification. Identity, thus, is not only open to challenge; it is largely produced by a process of challenge and confirmation.

This means that all statements of identity involve both *choice* and *power*. Choice because they all correspond to the presentation of certain features and to the repression of others – a constant game of veiling and unveiling. Power because they require negotiation and occur within fields of force always previously marked by domination – be it through the exercise of violent domination, through hegemonic forms of domination or, more to the point, through a combination of both.

Shared silences, therefore, are a corollary of the need for choice in the production of what some authors have called 'master narratives', that is formulations of identity that prop up power relations. This means that the maintenance of hegemonic relations within any community depends upon forms of 'organized amnesia', that is constructed silences (cf. Jun Jing 1996: 73–4).

However, if some of the links of identification upon which an identity is built are forcefully challenged, a symbolic wound is produced creating chaos in the lives of the people whose social position depends upon that identity in one form or another (cf. Sider and Smith 1997).

The policing of these traumatic silences is of central import. Much like Freud's discussion of repressed urges, things that are communally silenced do not simply vanish; they often persist through time in a penumbral, silenced condition (cf. Pina-Cabral 1999b). Their potential re-illumination threatens the symbolically constituted equilibria of power. Like repression in individuals, traumatic silences are a threat to the master narratives of a group and, in this way, become powerful. Ironically, then, these symbolic wounds acquire the capacity to move people to gestures of compensation and over-identification, which in turn are central motors for identity building.

To take inspiration from Jun Jing's marvellous study of the martyred Kung village, people are apt to turn memories of suffering into sources of cultural revitalization, even though the task is an arduous one (Jun 1996: 165). And that was, precisely, what the man from the Maritime Museum was doing with me. We were talking in the early 1990s, after the die had finally been cast – the general conditions for the handover had already been decided. The traditional nightmare of the Macanese – that their claims to sovereignty in Macao might be challenged by their ethnic opponents, 'the Chinese' – had been decided upon and confirmed.

The organized amnesia around the silenced stones of that monument was now a lesser concern. For the Macanese, it became more important to claim special attention from the Portuguese from Portugal – such as myself – by making the latter feel that their own Portugueseness would be threatened if they did not protect their fellow 'Portuguese of the Orient' – as the Macanese often called themselves (cf. Pina-Cabral 1999a). Therefore, you will notice that, when speaking to me, he made no claims for the Macanese, but for the Portuguese in general – his actual words were: 'a huge monument, very beautiful, to celebrate the 400 years of Macao's existence, of the Portuguese here in Macao'.

AMBIGUOUS BELONGINGS

What precisely did happen to the monument? At the time I interviewed this man I knew nothing more about this story. Since then, however, the actual events have become clearer (cf. Fernandes 2000b).

The first problem was that I was researching the wrong year. The events relating to the monument had not taken place in 1957 but in 1955 – which turns out to have been an extraordinary year not only for Macao, but also for the international relations of China and its ruling Communist elite.

The root of all this is to be found in 1952. That year, Jack Braga, a learned Hong Kong Eurasian of Portuguese extraction, was invited to visit Lisbon to deliver a speech at the *Sociedade de Geografia de Lisboa* – one of the principal bastions of Portuguese colonial policy. We must remember that, in those days, Portugal was ruled by a conservative dictator, Salazar, who had a narrow-minded and jingoistic view of colonial development. The official view at the time was that all the colonies were alike and Portugal held total rights of sovereignty over all of them. Macao's special conditions were hardly ever publicly acknowledged.

In fact, like it or not, the regime was being forced to accept the need to engineer major changes to its colonial policies due to the new international order after the Second World War. In the early 1950s, there was internal resistance to these changes in Portugal and they were finally implemented only at the end of the decade and in what turned out to be a tragically inadequate fashion.

Braga's inflamed speech was in fact published. The following passage should give the general tone of his message:

> Thus, over the centuries and far from its home in Portugal, Macao has managed to accomplish an impressive number of feats; even though they were, at times, surrounded by hostile peoples, the inhabitants of Macao raised the Portuguese flag and it must never be forgotten that they were Portuguese by birth, by education, in their religion and in the culture and traditions that they transmitted. All Portuguese must be proud that their ancestors, who travelled to the Far East in such small and fragile craft, managed to accomplish so much in that small parcel of Portugal that they raised and maintained miraculously throughout all sorts of vicissitudes. (Braga 1952: 91–2)

At the end of the speech, and amidst heated cries of '*Viva Portugal!*', he proposed that the 400 years of Macao's existence be celebrated in

1955 and not in 1957. According to him, that was the correct date because Fernão Mendes Pinto, the famous sixteenth-century writer and adventurer, refers to the name of the city in a letter written in 1555 and says it has just recently been discovered. Somehow or other, this idea gained strength among the more nationalistic sectors of Macanese society.

The speech is interesting from another point of view. Although Braga expresses proud colonialist views verging on Lusitanian millenarianism, a certain ambiguity of cultural referents makes its appearance. For example, he begins by claiming that Macanese people (and by that he means the Eurasians) 'loudly proclaim their descent from the Portuguese pioneers' and that 'in their hearts, there is always a constant longing [*saudade*] for news of distant Portugal, their hearts fill with pride when the name of the fatherland is mentioned. They never lose the hope that some day in the future they can return in spirit, if not in person, to the great community that the Portuguese have created and that survives in so many parts of the world' (ibid.: 80).

Following this, however, there are long passages where he explains that, when the Portuguese arrived in Macao, the Chinese civilization was far more advanced than their own. The lecture continues with further passages dedicated to explaining how the Portuguese were physically less clean than the Chinese and how the Chinese used more adequate and civilized forms of dressing.

The speaker's personal history is relevant in this context. He was born to a Eurasian family in Macao but, like so many of his more active contemporaries in the first part of the twentieth century, he made a living in Hong Kong. He became a subject of the British Crown and distinguished himself in the local colonial administration (where the Macanese always played a central role). He is reported to have been a secret agent for the British during the Japanese occupation of their colony. He ended his days in Australia, where he left his library and manuscripts to a local university.

As with so many Macanese of the period, his association with Portugal was not that of a citizen, as he was British and he did not wish to live in Portugal. Rather, his heated claims to Portugueseness must be seen as a way of vindicating the right to the status of being European – which opened up a series of doors within the British colonial administration.

In fact, this vindication was a disputed matter within the colony. The Hong Kong census, for example, is ambiguous about it, separating Europeans from Chinese, from Eurasians and from Portuguese – as if the two latter categories were distinct, leaving the matter of the Macanese integration within one of the other categories to be decided.

Unlike most British colonial settings, the common practice in the Portuguese colonies was for Portuguese men to give their names to their children by local women. These became Catholic and were accepted as full Portuguese citizens – even though, of course, they were then subjected to numerous more subtle forms of internal discrimination (cf. Chapter 8).

In Hong Kong, the *capital of Portugueseness* of these Macanese was an important resource. Until it was wrenched away from them in the late 1950s and early 1960s by a rising Chinese middle class, the Macanese had an ethnic monopoly in the city: they controlled the middle ranks of the civil and financial administration. For over a century, for example, the Hong Kong and Shanghai Banking Corporation was run by 'Portuguese' clerks, as they were then called (Pina-Cabral and Lourenço 1993a).

For that monopoly to be maintained they had to distinguish themselves from the Chinese. When the British or other Europeans failed to recognize their difference, they felt deeply hurt and were traditionally prone to punctiliousness on this matter. I was told vivid stories by older people in Macao of how the British were prone to treat Macanese 'as if they were Chinese' even though, by the 1990s, such an assertion was no longer considered offensive.

Their *capital of Portugueseness* was an important resource that was carefully managed. Like so many of his fellow Macanese, Jack Braga was beginning to feel the pressure resulting from the new attitudes that prevailed in the dissolving British Empire after the Second World War. Ultimately, again like so many others, he gave up and moved to Australia, where people like him were less likely to feel hemmed in by a young and active Chinese middle class. The overzealous Portuguese nationalism of British citizens such as himself was an attempt to maintain a master narrative of identity before new rising hegemonies.

ZHOU ENLAI'S RESPONSE

So, in early 1955, the Governor of Macao, Marques Esparteiro, felt obliged to name a committee to organize the celebration of the four-hundredth anniversary of Portuguese Macao. It has to be said that he did this against his better judgement. We are told by the then Governor of Hong Kong, Sir Alexander Grantham, in his memoirs, that the Portuguese Governor was opposed to the celebrations but that these were imposed on him by the Overseas Ministry, back in Portugal (quoted in Fernandes 2000b).

He was quite right to oppose the celebrations, as 1955 was about the worst time to celebrate colonial glories on the doorstep of China. The Chinese Communist Party had come into power in 1949, after a very long struggle leading to a bitter civil war. The Korean War had ended in 1953 with a stalemate, showing how powerful China had become. China's economic and social reorganization – after more than a century of upheaval – seemed to have found the right path: 1955 was the year when the first five-year plan was finally put into action. Only in 1956 was Party authority challenged for the first time – leading to the famous 'Let a Hundred Flowers Bloom' movement and its infamous repression. That was the first significant sign of popular dissatisfaction with the CCP – but that didn't happen until the following year.

Furthermore, in 1956, the Bandung Conference was convened and Zhou Enlai played a central role in it. To quote Immanuel Hsü: 'The Geneva and Bandung conferences, in effect, accorded China leadership in the Afro-Asian bloc. As the underdog who has found a viable formula to reverse its destiny and to achieve quick elevation of national status, Peking [became] an inspiration to some underdeveloped nations' (1990: 662).

In 1956 too, Jawaharlal Nehru began his attempts to reclaim Goa back from the Portuguese. The Portuguese government, led by Salazar, refused to take this claim seriously – going so far as to court-martial the military officers stationed there after the Indians forcefully took over in 1961, as if it had been their fault. Notwithstanding, some people in the regime had understood that the time had come to change the basis of colonial power. Among the younger members of the ruling elite, people like Adriano Moreira were already starting to respond to the challenge presented by the Bandung conference (cf. 1955 and 1986). Their idea was to respond to the claims to freedom of the colonized peoples with a notion of a multicontinental Portugal. Thus, that same year, Macao was granted the status of an 'overseas province'.

The events leading to the destruction of Macao's monument involved Sir Alexander Grantham, the Governor of Hong Kong at the time. The Chinese decision to put pressure on the Portuguese via the British was probably a response to the fact that, even although their intervention in Macao's life was far greater than in Hong Kong, they had no direct link with the Portuguese authorities of the time. Sir Alexander reports on what happened in his memoirs. He was invited for lunch in Peking by Zhou Enlai.

> The lunch was proceeding happily when suddenly Zhou Enlai turned to me, and asked if I had heard that the Portuguese in Macao were

shortly going to celebrate the four hundredth anniversary of the founding of the Colony. Thinking that my host was still in a lighthearted mood, I replied that I had, that so far as I was concerned it would be a nuisance, as I should have to attend, dressed up in my plumes and feathers. As a matter of fact what I had previously heard about the proposed celebrations had caused me some uneasiness. A minister was coming out from Lisbon, and he was almost sure to talk about the 'sacred soil of Portugal', which would anger Beijing. Zhou Enlai now adopted a stern mien and said that the Chinese government and the Chinese people did not like these celebrations, nor would the Chinese in Macao and Hong Kong. The last was a thinly veiled threat that the Communists would stir up trouble, and probably serious trouble, in the two colonies. I suggested that perhaps it would be all right if the celebrations were limited to one day. No, the whole thing must be called off. I persisted for a little, but saw I could get nowhere, so the subject was dropped, but gloom prevailed for the rest of the meal. After lunch the men added for further talks and I returned to the charge, being reluctant to leave matters in such an unsatisfactory state. This time Zhou Enlai was more conciliatory, and agreed that one day's innocuous celebrations would be unobjectionable.' (1965: 186)

The outcome was that the PRC authorities took recourse to the more habitual means of publishing their diktats in the Chinese-language newspapers of Macao, and made three points: that China wanted peaceful coexistence with Hong Kong and Macao; that China would regard any celebration as a provocation; that, if celebrations went ahead, China would join up with India in claiming back the territories occupied by Portugal.

As soon as Governor Grantham informed Governor Marques Esparteiro of the threat, the latter cancelled all proceedings and eventually demolished even the statue's grandiose platform. No celebrations occurred either in 1955 or in 1957.

A THIRD SILENCE

We may detect in this series of events yet another silence: the silence that Zhou Enlai aimed to preserve.

The PRC had no formal relations with Portugal at the time and Salazar refused to engage in direct negotiations with China. So Zhou was forced to send messages via a circuitous route – the Governor of Hong Kong.

It must be further taken into account that Macao is and always has been totally indefensible, both from a military and an economic point of view. Had the Chinese Communists wanted to occupy the Territory, they could have done so at any time. To oppose any form of colonial occupation of its territory was one of the central policies of the PRC. It assumed an attitude of confrontation towards the Western powers, in contrast to the attitude adopted by their predecessors, the Nationalists and the Qing, whom the Communists accused of excessive feebleness (cf. Hsü 1990: 661)

Zhou's silence was due to the fact that, although Macao was by all accounts part of China, he could not afford to reclaim it from the Portuguese. There is something paradoxical in his stance. How could he, the foremost international speaker for colonial liberation, tolerate a colonial presence in his own backyard? As it turns out, he could tolerate it all right; what he could not do was admit to it.

At this point, we must consider Macao's role in all of this – one which has only now begun to come to light. In those days, neither the PRC nor Portugal were prepared to openly admit to it. The decision to maintain the status quo in Macao was taken by the Communists in February 1949, even before they took power, and was grounded on solid economic and political reasons (cf. Fernandes 2000a: 58). In the 1950s, the economic blockade of China by the Western powers meant that, once again, China was faced with its age-old problem of isolation – which had been at the basis of Macao's very foundation four centuries earlier. Furthermore, its role in Asian political struggles meant that it badly needed to rearm itself. Hong Kong was economically very important, but the way it was run prevented it from functioning as an informal portal to the outside world. Macao became a passageway for enormous amounts of products that were indispensable for the survival of Mao's regime: petrol, metals, cars, chemical products, etc. These were purchased by the PRC's representative in the Territory, the Nam Kwong Consortium.

This trade happened so openly that it led to repeated complaints directed against Portugal within the China Committee of NATO. Portugal eventually decided to take a stand, which only served to irritate China. The half-hearted attempt to curb the clandestine trade was at the source of the 1952 border incidents with China which, in traditional Macao manner, were eventually silently solved after the controls were again stopped.[101]

One of the most important products in question was gold. Having been a neutral country during the Second World War, Portugal did not sign the 1946 Bretton Woods Agreements that banned the importation of gold for private use. Being outside the International Monetary Fund, unlike Hong Kong, Macao could function as a clearing house for the gold that China needed in order to purchase products on the international black market. A quick look at the Macao government's official statistics immediately suggests the enormity of what was at stake. Between 1949 and 1973, a little less than 934 tons of gold entered Macao legally. There is ample evidence that this gold was re-exported, but there are no official figures whatsoever concerning export fees. If all that gold had stayed in Macao, the city would now be paved in gold (Fernandes 2000b).

It is perhaps of no small relevance that Ho Yin – who, together with Y.C. Liang, controlled the gold trade in Macao – appeared in 1955 in an interestingly dual capacity. He was appointed to Macao's Governing Council on 25 August 1955, as 'representative of the Chinese community', and was also appointed a member of the Organizing Committee of the colonial celebrations that Zhou banned. The latter committee was presided over by Ho's mentor – a figure of dubious reputation who practically ruled Macao in the 1940s and 1950s – Pedro José Lobo. Jack Braga, the originator of the whole idea of the celebrations, was also part of the committee.[102]

But Ho Yin played in both camps simultaneously. At the meeting of the Chinese People's Political Consultative Conference that took place between 30 January and 7 February 1956 in Peking, he was appointed representative of Macao for the Guangdong riding, having been personally received by Zhou Enlai on 27 January (cf. Fernandes 2000b: 131, 138).

Ho Yin eventually came to represent the CCP's claims to nationalist leadership of 'overseas Chinese' (Mand. *hua qiao*) in Macao in the capacity of leading 'red capitalist' (Mand. *hongse zibenjia*). Twelve years later, again in his dual capacity, he was a central participant in yet another deeply traumatic event, the *123*. Then, in the midst of the turmoil of the Cultural Revolution, the Portuguese Governor was forced to submit to him a declaration of surrender that represented, for the Macanese, the greatest and final 'loss of face'.

In short, considering that the CCP all but ruled Macao, why should some paltry celebrations be a matter of such consequence? Here we have to understand that, for the Chinese Communist leadership, the very existence of Macao and Hong Kong and their inability to take decided gestures against it was a symbolic wound.

In Immanuel Hsü's words, 'Though deeply committed to international communism, Mao and his followers were national communists at heart, keenly aware of China's misfortunes of the past century' (1990: 660). Anti-imperialism and nationalism were major driving forces for these people, who had seen their country divided, ruled by foreigners and brutally occupied.

Zhou Enlai, particularly, felt it very strongly. In the 1930s he had lived in Shanghai as organizer of the CCP's intelligence and internal security unit. In 1932 he had been forced to escape from the city disguised as a priest after the Nationalist Government managed to break through the Party's security arrangements. People like him could not forget that the White Terror, which permanently annihilated the urban sectors of the CCP, was jointly organized by the French Police, the Shanghai Municipal Police in the hands of the British and Guomindang's Public Security Bureau (Wakeman 1995). He had lived through the Japanese occupation of China and played an active role in the resistance.

The Chinese Communist leadership was quite happy to allow the Portuguese to remain in Macao for a further forty-four years; it was even willing to accept that people such as Ho Yin should play on both sides – first adopting the Portuguese nationalist rhetoric of the celebration committee and then the Chinese nationalist rhetoric that demonized the Portuguese presence. But it had to prevent celebrations.

A CHRISTIAN CODA

This, however, was not to be the end of the story. There was still one last attempt to leave a marker of the celebration of the 400 years of European presence in China. It was wrongly thought by some that, if the symbolic emphasis were to shift from Portuguese nationalism to the Catholic religion, the celebration would become more palatable to the Chinese.

I got word of this in 1993, before I had fully pieced together the events of 1955. At the time, the Chinese press had again lashed out against the building of a huge monument called *Portas do Entendimento* (Gate of Understanding) – an oversized tower-like structure in black marble which was raised slightly offshore on the western tip of the peninsula to celebrate the 1987 Joint Declaration.

The Government's decision to build this new and rather expensive monument caused a minor polemic in the city. Typically the CCP spokespersons made a lot of noise in the newspapers about wasted money, complaining that the sculptor and the marble had come all the way from Portugal and Brazil, when it would have been perfectly possible to find both the talent and the stone locally in Guangdong. This time, however, it was mostly non-sequential political posturing – contrary to the real willingness to act of the 1950s. Forty years later, anti-colonial rhetoric had lost its international appeal and Macao was about to be transferred back to China. No one cared to spoil diplomatic relations. So the monument was built and it will remain a visible feature of Macao's shoreline for the foreseeable future.

Curiously, one of the 1950s interveners, Father Manuel Teixeira, was still alive and living in the Territory when I did my fieldwork. As a young boy in the teens of the twentieth century, he was brought out from rural northeast Portugal to study in Macao's seminar. During his lengthy and active life he was a keen commentator and observer of life in Macao. His voluminous works on Macao's history constitute a rich source of references for anyone who studies the city's past. In the 1950s, he lived outside the Territory for a few years, performing pastoral duties in Singapore.

In 1993, in an angry response to the CCP-inspired criticisms of the new statue, he wrote in the Church-oriented Portuguese periodical *Gazeta Macaense*:

> I suppose that there are still Portuguese people here who saw what happened to a similar monument which was to be built in 1955 in the plaza in front of D. Maria, facing the ocean. It was all part of the commemoration of the four centuries of Portuguese presence in Macao. A specialist was brought all the way out from Viana do Castelo (Portugal) with fireworks. I personally came from Singapore in order to deliver a lecture. But Mao Tsetung raised his finger and all went up in smoke. (23/07/93, p. 2)

In 1955, when it had become clear that the celebrations could not go ahead as planned, Father Teixeira tried to turn the whole event to the Church's credit. He seems to have managed to convince Governor Marques Esparteiro that, if his Catholic parishioners from Singapore were to offer a statue of *Cristo Rei* (Christ the King), it could be placed discreetly on the existing pedestal. The Governor appears to have entertained the notion that this would be a convenient solution to the whole imbroglio. On 12 January 1956, he wrote a secret telegram to the Overseas Minister in Lisbon, where he espoused this proposal in an attempt to save himself from possible future recriminations:

> [. . .] As I mentioned [. . .] Chinese communists demanded the demolition, to which I offered every resistance. Later their insistence increased and the information from various sources indicated that, if

I resisted further, they would destroy the monument with a bomb, which was very likely, in view of other such attacks perpetrated on earlier occasions. If that took place, it would be a complete outrage against our prestige and political and economic situation, already so damaged. So, I took a decision to prevent such a gesture. I only removed [the statue] from its column, leaving the base and pedestal, on which I intend to erect a monument to *Cristo Rei*, having received an offer of such a statue by the Superior of the Singapore Mission, Father Teixeira. [. . .] (cf. Fernandes 2000b: 628–9)

In the course of time, it must have become apparent to him that the PRC was as opposed to Christian zeal as it was to Portuguese nationalistic sentiment. The whole project never went ahead and the very pedestal was blown to bits by the authorities in order to prevent the Communists from taking the initiative of placing a bomb there.[105]

At this point, I should stress that this non-existent monument is only one of Macao's many vanished monuments. You may live in Macao for a long time and not know their whereabouts, particularly if you lack all knowledge concerning the city's history. But as soon as you become curious or somehow involved, the history of the Territory begins to reveal itself to you from beneath the layers of concrete that fill the gaps. There are many more gaps like the one I have just described.

Before they left, the Portuguese hastily built seven oversized monuments (cf. Cheng 1999: 12) – one of them was even dedicated to Kun Yam, the Taoist-Buddhist goddess! But that was after the Chinese had finally found a way of allowing them to do so without 'losing face', that is without feeling that their master narrative was being challenged. All this, however, only happened after Deng Xiaoping's brilliant formulation of the 'one country, two systems' model. Even then, one last reminder of the ethnic and political anger of the mid-century still had to go: Ferreira do Amaral's statue.

CHAPTER 7

NAMES: PERSONAL IDENTITY AND ETHNIC AMBIGUITY[104]

> *'The embarrassment of limits is a general feature of social organisation'*
> Erving Goffman (1963: 148)

In this chapter I will explore the relation between personal identity and ethnic identity from a perspective that sees culture, to use Sangren's words, 'as a dialectically unified process of self and collective production' (1991: 80). I will be focusing on naming practices in Macao in such a way as to show that the negotiation of name conferral and use functions not only as a means of situating the person and of achieving personal strategic aims but also of constantly defining the sociocultural system or systems involved (cf. Herzfeld 1982: 288). I believe that the Macanese are a particularly good test case for this study, as they have lived for a long time in a marginal condition and thus they provide us with a clearer perception of what the practical limits of these sociocultural systems may be (cf. Terradas 1992).

ETHNICITY AND THE PERSON

In the last decades of the nineteenth century, due to greatly improved transport technology and to the new colonial world order, Portuguese people from Portugal started arriving in the Territory in greater numbers. In order to stand up to the colonialist prejudice of the European Portuguese in Macao and the British in Hong Kong, the Macanese found that they had to rely increasingly on the *capital of Portugueseness* with which they were endowed by their narrative of origins. As we have seen, this meant that, by the time the final confrontation with the Chinese middle class occurred, in the late 1960s, the Macanese had lost their Creole culture. Therefore, after the changes that took place in the Territory's ethnic alignment in the late 1970s (*the caesura of the 70s*), the Macanese found themselves in an intercultural condition, living between two cultural worlds to which they had relatively easy access. On the one hand, they could function reasonably easily within either cultural world. On the other hand, however, they constantly gave signs of incomplete integration to the people whose allegiance to each cultural world was more univocal. The potential for discomfort in such a condition is associated to a sense of betrayal that each of the camps feels in relation to the persons that navigate the frontier.

Linguistic proficiency is a major marker of identity in this context. Today, for the Macanese of the city, this is a far more significant factor of ethnic identification than phenotypic evidence of Eurasian ancestry. Since the late 1970s, most Macanese people are Cantonese speakers but their levels of proficiency (and their *boon2 dei6* accent) vary. In contra-distinction, the younger generations are much less proficient in Portuguese than they used to be.

After the Portuguese armed forces left the city in December 1975, a change occurred in Macanese ethnic positioning that resulted in the fact that, by the late 1980s, Cantonese slowly became the home language of most Macanese homes. A major contributing factor to this was the growth and strength of the Cantonese-speaking television of Hong Kong.

Thus, in the 1990s, even though the medium of instruction at school continued to be predominantly Portuguese, the Macanese were situated in a world where two cultural traditions overlapped. They shared a deeply felt sense of common origin and common destiny; they had a political and administrative elite which represented them; they held an ethnic monopoly over the middle ranks of the Administration (cf. Pina-Cabral 2000a) – thus it can be said that they are an ethnic group. Nevertheless, they did not have a culture of their own in the fuller sense of the term. Their cultural dispositions were constructed out of references to both the Cantonese world and the Portuguese world – and it has to be noted that these were often irreconcilable.

One of the major references of their ethnic identity was Catholicism and this, to a certain extent, provided a fixed point of reference. However, ever since they started converging with the Chinese middle class, they have also veered away from the staunch Catholicism of the former decades. Finally, they have maintained some of their distinctiveness in matters such as forms of speaking Portuguese and Cantonese and in food habits. These, however, are relatively small differences.

Concerted and repeated attempts have been made by Portuguese and French colleagues (e.g. Amaro 1992 and Scheid 1987) to find some form of phenotypic characterization of the Macanese. From what I have said earlier on, however, it must be quite clear by now that any such attempt is bound to fail, as precisely what characterizes the Macanese is their phenotypic variability (cf. Teixeira 1965). Now, one becomes a

Macanese because one is socialized in that way and we have no evidence that it was ever any different from that in the past. There are numbers of Chinese men and women who, having been brought up as Macanese, for one reason or another adopt full Macanese identity. There are people of African Creole origin who, having lived for generations in Macao, are treated as full members of the community. There are all sorts of combinations with Japanese, Malay, Timorese, Goese, Indian and European ancestries.

In spite of this, it must be admitted that, having lived in Macao for any length of time, a person learns to identify a Macanese. There are corporal dispositions and attitudes; there are forms of speaking, gesticulating and presenting oneself, that mark one's belonging to the group. These, however, are very fugitive markers and it must be understood that the Macanese constantly and strategically manipulate these visible distinguishing signs. Their personal identity develops in a context of greater uncertainty and, at the same time, of greater freedom than that of the European Portuguese or of the Chinese.

In this sense I find it useful to refer to Erving Goffman's notion of *stigma* to describe this process of ethnic identity management. He defines stigma as 'the situation of the individual who is disqualified from full social acceptance' (1963: 9). This may appear a contorted and negative fashion of formulating ethnic group belonging. Nevertheless, it becomes more significant when we consider that, again using the same author's words, 'stigma involves not so much a set of concrete individuals who can be separated into two piles, the stigmatised and the normal, as a pervasive two-role social process in which every individual participates in both roles, at least in some connections and in some phases of life. The normal and the stigmatised are not persons but rather perspectives' (1963: 164–5).

This formulation appears to me to be relevant if we are going to try to describe the emotional and experiential context of ethnic identity management in multi-ethnic social contexts. Indeed, ethnic identity functions as a stigma in all contexts in which one is forced to interact actively with people of another ethnic group. This is particularly the case in situations such as this one in which cultural diversity is so marked and in which prejudice flows in both directions with equal strength. Even though Chinese prejudice against 'foreigners' (whom they normally identify as *gwai2*, ghosts) expresses itself differently from European prejudice, there is no denying that it is at least as prevalent.[105]

The Macanese person, by relation both to a Chinese and a European, possesses a considerable number of the attributes that would qualify him or her as a full member of either ethnic group. This is the case in cultural terms – for they speak the language, they have a name in that language, they know and appreciate the food habits that normally accompany social intercourse, etc. – and even in phenotypic terms – for it may be rather difficult to tell whether or not a certain person of mixed ancestry is Chinese or Macanese, as the case may be. However, at the same time, this person carries a stigma, a sign of difference, which means that the person is either cast outside our ethnic universe or – even more preoccupying – kept to the margins of such a universe.[106]

Being Portuguese is as stigmatizing in a social situation dominated by Chinese ethnic belonging, as being Chinese in a corresponding Portuguese situation. However, the Macanese find themselves constantly in a potential situation of 'passing', that is, of changing their identity reference. In particular, in situations where his or her parents are fully Chinese but the person opts for a Macanese formulation of his or her social self, the personal uncertainty that thus results is characteristic of passing. Taking into account the existence of ethnic prejudice, the Macanese constantly encounter social situations where they are uncertain of acceptance or rejection.

Incidentally, this was one of the major problems that confronted me as a fieldworker. The solidity of my Portugueseness meant that I could potentially be a bearer of prejudice. My very presence in the field elicited this dynamic of personal uncertainty. 'Mixed social situations make for anxious unanchored interaction' (Goffman 1963: 29). People are anxious because they do not know what to expect.

Here, then, we can begin to approach the emotional infrastructure of the forms of relating interethnically. Anthropology does not provide us with a ready language to deal with the emotional aspects of social relations. If, however, we presume that society and culture are not given but have to be constantly recreated via the very process of personal interaction, we are then forced to take into account the emotional frameworks of such a process. One of the first characteristics of Macanese behaviour that confronts a person who arrives in Macao is that which I call the 'dynamic of despise' – a process through which a person, feeling that he or she is the object of prejudice, attempts to shift the burden of that prejudice onto some other person.

Goffman insists that the forming of a stigmatized individual is characterized by three processes. First, the interiorization of the culture's general value system; second, the realization that he or she does not fit into that system; third, the learning of a series of methods of overcoming the impediments caused by his or her stigma. If we then look at ethnic identity as a stigma, we can perceive that this process does not always occur in quite this fashion. For example, a Chinese person who never interiorizes the values of Western society, develops a simple hostile reaction to the apparent denial of these values with which he or she is confronted in cross-ethnic interaction. The same applies to a European Portuguese person.

For the Macanese, however, as well as for the Orientalized Portuguese or for the Westernized Chinese, the situation of cross-ethnic interaction is more akin to that described by Goffman's model. Indeed, in the Macanese case, a process of personal ambivalence characteristically develops from the overlapping of cultural references. This means that mixed social situations lead to personal anxiety – the 'touchiness' of which the Macanese are often accused – and to the attempt to 'cover', that is, 'To restrict the display of those failings most centrally identified with the stigma' (Goffman 1963: 126).

This process, however, is dynamic. When the stigmatized person sees one of their kind behaving in a way that exposes their stigma, they feel repelled. But, as they identify themself with the actor, they experience shame. This shame, in turn, is transformed into something to be ashamed of. Finally, they respond either by attempting to, so to speak, 'purify' the behaviour of the other person or by distancing themself from the other person, by imposing prejudice. Thus, this process of self-alienation leads directly to what Goffman calls 'a self-betraying kind of stratification' (1963: 131).

This stratification and its collateral effects are characteristic of a type of snobbery that is so often encountered in Macanese circles. No one is completely excluded from it, for it functions along various axes and is based on the long memory so characteristic of small and relatively closed communities. However, those persons and families who detain the greater capital of Portugueseness – locally known as 'traditional families' – as well as those that are richer and/or more educated are prone to discriminate against poorer, less educated families and against people whose family origin is based on a recent intermarriage between a Chinese woman and a Portuguese man. A person who is discriminated against develops a sense of ambivalence concerning their personal identity. They find solace in the ensuing anxiety by attempting to 'cover' their sense of personal weakness through the exposure of others.

The nature of the Macanese as a group is the product of these procedures of inclusion and exclusion as they develop in time, by relation to the external conditions that motivate people's interests. Thus, at a time when the capital of Portugueseness was a major source in a struggle for security and survival, the negotiation of Portugueseness was radically central to Macanese everyday life. Discrimination operated strongly along those lines, to the point where, for example, a member of a traditional family preferred his daughter to remain single rather than marry another Macanese whose claims to Portugueseness were somewhat weaker. Socialization too was deeply marked by that preoccupation: parents spanked their children if they failed to speak Portuguese at home; children who managed to enter High School did not mix socially with children who, failing to achieve the necessary level of fluency in Portuguese, were forced to go to the Commercial School.

As the importance of this capital became less apparent, in the late 1970s and 1980s, it also became less of a tool of social identification. People began experimenting with new forms of identification with the Cantonese culture which surrounded them. As 1999 approached, the management of personal identity started to shift in other directions. For example, a Macanese man of considerable prestige once explained to me that he had changed his signature in the mid-1980s. He eagerly showed me that, after a rather florid version of his Portuguese name, there was now a simplified version of the Chinese character for his Chinese name.

Indeed, names and naming practices are one of the most important ways through which such processes of personal identification are effected. Before attempting to show how naming practices have changed for the Macanese, however, we will briefly characterize the Portuguese and the Chinese naming systems, particularly as these are interestingly divergent.

NAMING SYSTEMS

Whilst the Portuguese system allows a considerable margin of manipulation as far as surnames are concerned, the Chinese system is absolutely coercive in this matter. Contrarily, whilst the Chinese system permits an enormous amount of personal fancy and manipulation at the level of first names, the Portuguese system is surprisingly conservative and coercive.

Curiously, the above formulation does not correspond to the vision that most Portuguese people have of their naming practices. If asked, most Portuguese persons will answer that parents are free to choose the first name of a child but that they are not free to choose the surname. It is said that a person must receive, after a first name, his/her mother's paternal surname followed by his/her father's paternal surname. It was, therefore, with some surprise that, upon starting to study bourgeois family practices in the city of Oporto, I discovered that many people did not name themselves and their children in this way (Pina-Cabral 1991a).

It became apparent to me that: (a) the stress on agnatic links implicit in this ideal system went against the predominant tendency of favouring uxorilateral ties; (b) people favoured prestigious surnames and tended to forget less prestigious ones, whether they were the mother's or the father's; and (c) people attached emotional significance to surnames, manipulating their use according to whether or not they 'liked' the relatives described by that surname. For example, I once met someone who signed her papers as Ana X. A few years later a certain person, Ana Y, sent me a letter. Upon meeting her personally, I was surprised to discover that it was the same person. I thought that she might have got married, but I was told that what had happened was that she had had a serious disagreement with her mother over her parents' divorce. In a spirit of vengeance, from then on, she stopped using her mother's rather more prestigious surname, adopting instead one of her father's.

Furthermore, as most people in Portugal have rather long names (usually consisting of three to four surnames), it is common practice to use an abbreviated form in everyday life. This may simply be a choice of one of the first names and one or two of the surnames, but this too can be manipulated. Later on, when choosing what names to give their children, people tend to opt for the names by which they are known. For example, a famous doctor at the turn of the century was known by a combination of his mother's surname and father's surname, Manuel XY. He married a wealthy woman and their children received the mother's father's surname, being called ZY. His daughter's son, in turn, received the mother's and the father's surnames, being called YW. This did not satisfy him, however, as he wanted a share in his grandfather's fame. Thus, he chose to be known as XY. As this is a 'good name', bringing with it prestige, this is the name that he passed on to his children.

It is also common to find that people use different combinations of names for different professions. For example, a doctor or a lawyer who is also an artist may opt for a pseudonym. But this is not the most common option. Rather, he may be known in one profession by one particular combination of his surnames and, in the other profession, by a different combination. So he is known as Dr Luís X but he signs his paintings as Luís X dos Y.

It is rather interesting that, contrary to what most people believe, Portuguese law allows for this broad margin for manoeuvre in the attribution and use of surnames.[107] Indeed, if we take into account the family system of the Portuguese middle classes, we may clearly understand the relevance of such a system. Family links are most important but there is no principle of descent. People have the freedom to choose the kinship links they want to activate and those they want to leave dormant. As family name is one of the major ways of identifying families, there has to be a way of manipulating it. However, there is a contradiction in this process. Whilst, on the one hand, paternal filiation is given greater symbolical precedence (cf. Pina-Cabral 1997), the widely prevalent uxorilateral preference in extra-domestic family ties means that one of the mother's surnames often represents the person in a way he or she deems to fit better with his or her personal identity.[108] This contradiction is experienced by people as jeopardizing their personal worth but only in a minor way. Thus, it is impolite to enquire from a person what right they have to their name, although it is equally common to talk about it behind their back.

All this, of course, is complete anathema to the Cantonese, whose view of the family is deeply marked by patrilineality. The predominance of agnatic ties remains unchallenged though, as a result of urbanization and of new attitudes to female participation in the labour market, we may now be witnessing a tendency for a softening of the exclusion of married daughters from family life (cf. Chapter 9). This means that Cantonese people are given only their father's surname. Moreover, although Chinese people are so numerous, there are very few Chinese surnames. Most people are called one of the old hundred family surnames (*baak3 ga1 seng3*). Thus, to them, there is something ridiculous and inappropriate about Portuguese surnames, both in the liberality of attribution and in the inventiveness of the names. For example, the last four governors of Macao were called: Chicken Axe; Watermelon; Myrtle Turnip and Rock Scallop.

Considering this, it is interesting that one of the commonplaces of Portuguese ethnocentrism in Macao should be a lack of understanding of the Chinese system of first names. For the Portuguese, it is considered bad taste and personally challenging for a person to receive a name that is not traditional. Preferably, the name should not mean anything and should be attributed in honour of an ascendant lineal kinsperson. Most parents opt for one or two of a very reduced list of traditional first names: Manuel, António, José, João, Pedro, etc.[109]

Contrary to the case of surnames, Portuguese law is very strict in matters of first names. In the name of the 'defence of purity and of the linguistic and onomastic patrimony' and in accordance with a so-called 'art of naming' at which the Portuguese are supposed to excel (Vilhena de Carvalho 1989: 60, 83), the law and its practitioners impose considerable constraints on what a citizen may call his or her children. There are limits to the number of names (ibid.: 71), to their spelling (ibid.: 76–7), to their relation to the gender of the person named (ibid.: 78–9), to political references (ibid.: 80) and to what is thought as 'excessive' imagination or eccentricity (ibid.: 60, 83). Furthermore, people cannot be called after animals, things or qualities, they cannot have inventive names (*denominações de fantasia*) and they cannot have the same name as their siblings (ibid.: 84).

There is a list of possible first names (all others being prohibited except in special circumstances). The bureaucratic process of decision of these cases where parents insist on giving the child a name which is not in the list are notoriously protracted. During these years, the child is considered to be bureaucratically non-existent, which means that parents lose all rights to child allowance and the child cannot cross borders.

Chinese first names, on the contrary, are entirely personal. Considerations such as the astrological moment of a person's birth, or personal life options are an integral part of a person's choice of name. In fact, contrary to the Portuguese, the name should mean something and its meaning carries semantic implications for the bearer. For example, these are names of acquaintances of mine in Macao: Crystalline Purity; Born in Macao; Grandiose Light; Spring Palace; Pure Unity; Beautiful Lotus; Red (the reference here may either be to Mao or to the auspiciousness of the colour red – depending on the intentions of the person's parents).

People will readily change their first names if they are not happy with them. Moreover, until the systematic use of public registers became obligatory, most men were known by at least three first names: the one they had received in childhood, the one that the father gave the son at the time of his marriage; and the name that he chose to be known by among his friends. For example, at a moment of crisis in his life, an aged friend of mine decided to change his name. As he was a man with modern views but was not a Communist, he called himself Healthy Criticism.

The Portuguese are very suspicious of people who use more than one first name and for a Portuguese person to decide to change their first name this usually means that they want to change their public identity in some very radical way. People whose name has gone out of fashion or has acquired new potentially comical implications usually prefer to be known by abbreviations and diminutives rather than change the name.

Thus, while the fact that a person may use different surnames in different contexts does not appear ridiculous or suspicious to a Portuguese person, the fact that most of the young Chinese people in Macao are known by an English or Portuguese first name of their own choice, strikes them as comical. For a Chinese person, on the contrary, the readiness with which a Portuguese person will discard his father's surname in favour of his mother's or of some personal recombination of surnames is seen as an indignity and a lack of filial piety.

INTERETHNIC NAMING

The two systems being so different, it is not surprising that there should be dual systems of naming in Macao. That is, it is common for Portuguese people to have a Chinese name and for Chinese people to have a Portuguese or English first name. The two processes, however, are not symmetrical, as one may expect from the difference in the naming systems.

The Chinese usually adopt a European alias and an alphabetical transliteration of their Chinese surname. Thus, they will present themselves as *John Tam* or *Philip Tse* or *Mário Lam*. Their full Chinese name remains the official designation, but they identify themselves completely with these forms of address, often preferring them even when used by other Chinese. Contrariwise, the Portuguese (Macanese or otherwise) who adopts a Chinese name, seldom uses it on formal occasions. This name is for Chinese-speaking persons as a gesture of politeness towards them. A Macanese man emphatically stressed: 'Our name properly speaking is the Portuguese name, the Chinese name is only a convenience'. This same person explained to me why he was not capable of telling me the Chinese names of his friends and family. He did not know them as he had no use for them. 'If I were to refer to them by that name', he said, 'they would be furious. They would immediately retort, "Have we arrived at 1999 already, that you should be calling me in such a way?"'

During the colonial period, European and Macanese people were usually known to the Chinese by a Chinese name. Many had nicknames. Where these were prestigious, the descendants still remember them. Beards being a prestigious and rare manly attribute among the Chinese, a number of Macanese told me that their grandparents were called 'Big white beard', 'Black beard' or 'Old man with a beard', etc. Most often, however, people were known by a Chinese transcription of their first name – Ian Lei Gei (Henrique), Eh Moon Do (Edmundo), Ah Baak Do

(Alberto), etc. – or, less often, of their surname – Ka Baak Lo (Cabral), Ma Dei La (Madeira), etc.

I have been told by descendants of some of the oldest Macanese families that, in pre-colonial times, their families had Chinese surnames. It is interesting, however, that they no longer know what these were. The Chinese surnames that Macanese people are using today are all rather recent. In some cases they date to the post-war period, but on the whole they were acquired in the 1970s and 1980s. These days, when a Portuguese or a Macanese person has a child in Macao, it is common for the child to adopt a Chinese name in which the first syllable of the Chinese transcription of the father's name is used as a patronym. As the integration with the Chinese middle class develops, Macanese people rely increasingly on their Chinese names. These are now assuming the aspect of full names, instead of being purely personal identifications mostly used by others in substitution of the European names that are considered difficult to pronounce and memorize. Moreover, people do not exercise the freedom of choice of the use of surnames that the Portuguese tradition allows. On the contrary, the new Chinese names are all patrilinear.

This trend was already apparent in the way the Macanese gave Portuguese names to their children during the colonial period. Macanese families are known by patronyms that pass patrilineally.[110] One speaks of the Manhões, the Rodrigues da Silva, de Sennas Fernandes, the Pancrácios, etc. An older informant claimed that 'In Portugal it is customary to give the mother's surname to the child. Not here. In my family this is the way we do it and I think this is the case also with the other families, with few exceptions.' These exceptions are precisely those cases in which the mother was a European Portuguese (this was considered a prestigious match in colonial days as it increased the capital of Portugueseness). In other cases, daughters were given the father's surname as well as the mother's, whilst sons were given only the father's surname. Another variant of this was for there to be two separate male full names in the family, which were passed agnatically. In one instance, the great grandfather was called António Ferreira Batalha, the grandfather José Marcos Batalha, the father António Ferreira Batalha and ego José Marcos Batalha. He claims that, if he had had a legitimate son, he would have named him António Ferreira Batalha. As we have seen, such a strict unilaterality in naming is absolutely contrary to Portuguese practice.

Whilst the adoption of Portuguese or English first names by Chinese is not problematic, the adoption of European family names is a different matter. This practice is perhaps the greatest area of embarrassment for it is characteristically associated to 'passing', that is the adoption by the individual of a different ethnic identity and therefore of a different social persona. In theory, it could function in much the same way as the Portuguese use of Chinese names. In practice, it causes feelings of unease on the part of the Chinese and it is usually interpreted as disqualifying the person on two accounts. They are a renegade, having left their people, but they are also guilty of not having filial piety. It is presumed that a person who does not use the father's name will also fail to keep the ceremonies of ancestral reverence.

The adoption of a Portuguese name, however, can take on two different forms with distinct implications. First, there are Portuguese surnames that correspond directly to a Chinese name, e.g. Leong = Leão, Kok = Costa, Vong = Fão. These people may revert, in Chinese circles, to their Chinese name without any risk of personal embarrassment. The adoption of a Portuguese form, however, indicates that they are integrated into the Portuguese-speaking society. They can be said to have abandoned the group but they cannot be said to have betrayed their ancestors. I am familiar with persons who, having lived their whole life within the Macanese camp, so to speak, slowly reverted to a Chinese identity as 1999 approached.

Second, however, there are those who suppressed their Chineseness completely, adopting a Portuguese surname once and for all. This could be the surname of their godparents, the surname of their wife, the nickname of their father or the name of a saint (Xavier) or an advocation of the Virgin (Rosário, Conceição).

This problem of surname changing is deeply rooted in Macanese history. Until 1841, the Qing Dynasty government prohibited all Chinese subjects from converting to Catholicism. That meant that, until then, all the Chinese converts had to abdicate their Chinese ethnic identity: they cut the hairpiece (thus symbolizing the end of their allegiance to the Qing), they dressed in Western clothes, they adopted a Portuguese name and they were taken in by the Portuguese community – whatever subsequent discrimination they suffered on the part of this community depended on the role they played in the life of the city.[111] This option, however, incurred a deep stigma. In the eyes of Chinese Confucian morality, this person had committed the gravest of sins against filial piety.

In 1846, during the establishment of the colonial era, the 'personal parish' of Saint Lazarus was founded in Macao to respond to the needs of the new converts who, under the new political regime, could now be Catholic and remain ethnically Chinese. In that parish, registers were kept in a mixture of Chinese and Latin and, contrary to the earlier practice, people could now preserve their Chinese surnames, even though they normally received a Catholic name (as converts still do today), which was usually in Portuguese or in Latin.

Prejudice against Catholics, however, remained quite strong among the general Chinese community. The following quote taken from an interview with a Chinese Christian refers to his youth in the 1930s – incidentally he retained his Chinese patronym:

> When I was a child, we used to bear a cross on a chain on our chest. Immediately the other boys would attack me. They attacked me in the sense that they insulted me singing: [here follows a kind of sing-song possibly in Cantonese but that I have failed to be able to identify]. It was just like all children everywhere. No hatred properly speaking. How do you say it: 'You have no fathers, you are men that . . .' Yes, because in those days the Chinese government of the Qing Dynasty forbade Chinese converts. They forbade the Chinese from converting to the Catholic religion. In that sense the Chinese who entered the citadel of Macao were baptized and adopted a European surname: de Assis, Jesus, António, etc. In that sense they committed a grave sin before the other Chinese, it is as if they ignored the existence of their ancestors.

The historical process is rather compressed here and the speaker does not refer to the fact that the problem was not limited to the use of surnames. In those days, the Catholic Church prevented converts from practising the rites of ancestral reverence. This, of course, has changed since the II Vatican Council but the sense of shame has also withered now that so many urbanized Chinese tend to forego most of those ritual practices. The fact is that the best option for these converts until the end of the colonial period was still to shift ethnic labels, to 'pass', and become Macanese. The result, however, is that they had a fragile sense of identity. They were *discreditable*, in Goffman's terms; that is, in their daily lives, they had to assume that their stigma was not known or immediately perceived by those around them (1963: 14). Nonetheless they had a skeleton in the cupboard and they knew that the other Macanese families often talked about them behind their backs. What was described as their lack of 'European blood' or 'European origin' was used as a tool within the process of 'self-betraying stratification' which we identified above.

Interestingly this process of passing does not seem to have stopped after the caesura of the 1970s. I have met people who were 30 to 40 years of age in the early 1990s who adopted a Macanese identity, having abandoned their Chinese name. This was usually a response to their schooling. If they were sent by their parents to a Portuguese school, they soon found out that they were left outside Chinese youth circles. In order to integrate into Macanese circles, they opted for a European identity.

Often the situation was compounded by the existence of complex conjugal situations. Macanese men in a prestigious position have always adopted the practice of keeping other women apart from their official wives. This is a practice that, in Macao, is largely associated with the Chinese cultural environment. Illegitimacy could be a stigma but it did not have the implications it had in Europe of fatherlessness.[112] Illegitimate children were usually recognized by their fathers and felt associated to them, although they were at times kept away from the father's main family. Cases of prolonged bigamy are very common. For example, a house was sold when I was in Macao whose proceeds were divided among twelve people. They were all legally registered children of a Macanese man, formally a bachelor, from four different Chinese mothers.

Cases such as this can lead to rather complex familial situations, where the reference to a patronym may appear in more than one form. For example, a Chinese convert who becomes an important man may well have a Macanese wife. Her children will inherit the father's prestige and fortune. If indeed the man is very important and the wife belongs to a good Macanese family, the children are quite secure in their ethnic position, they are not discreditable. However, this man is likely to have had a child with a servant or concubine. If the latter was Chinese, this child is likely to retain a Chinese identity. He may be named with the father's Chinese name. So, if the Portuguese name of the Eurasian father was Costa or Cabral, he will be called Kwok or Ga in Cantonese, respectively. They are left out for purposes of inheritance but the link with the father does not simply vanish. The father is likely to help them in their education, lending them some of his prestige, even if in a clandestine way, for the fact is that everyone knows whose child they are. This man's source of discreditableness is also the main source of his social position. If he marries a Macanese or a European Portuguese woman, he is likely to adopt her family name and their children are likely to be known by the woman's family name.

For a Portuguese researcher, who does not speak Cantonese fluently, it is easier to identify situations of change of ethnic reference in the direction Chinese→Portuguese (Macanese) than in the opposite direction. Some of the most influential people in the latter part of the colonial period were in this position. However, situations of passing from the

Macanese/Portuguese camp into the Chinese camp are less easy to identify. Nonetheless such transits do occur, I am told.

The study of the Catholic marriage records makes one very aware of the complexity of the naming situations in which these people found themselves. In truth, for some people, it is not easy to make a simple identification of ethnic reference. Some of these people 'passed' during their adult lives. Others started their lives in a process of Macanization but ended their lives in a process of re-Sinification. For example, a certain Mariano Vong da Conceição (where does he get his Portuguese surname?) is the son of a Chinese man (Fernando Vong) and a woman with a Portuguese name (Mariana da Costa). Although one of his marriage sponsors was Portuguese, he married a Chinese woman, so that the family now considers itself Chinese and is treated as such.

I will cite the examples of three men to show that some people are confronted with an ethnic option and that the motives for their decisions are imbedded in their personal histories, being largely imponderable. These are the sons of Chinese men who emigrated at the turn of the century to Latin America. Sometime before the Second World War, they brought their Latin American or Eurasian wives and children back to south China. Because of their mothers' race, these children had phenotypic characteristics that identified them as not wholly Chinese, so various options were open to them to resolve the ethnic identification question. These three men are all approximately the same age and they started their adult life in Macao as civil servants, although they later moved across to the private sector of the economy – they made this move at different points in their lives.

The first man (A) married various Chinese women and used an Anglicized version of his father's name throughout his life. In spite of having always worked in sectors connected with the Portuguese administration (he often functioned as intermediary in cross-ethnic business deals), he is considered to be Chinese by most of those who know him in Macao. The second man (B) is one of three brothers who, during their childhood, used their Chinese father's name and played in the Chinese football team. The one whose story I know better, however, married a Macanese woman. From then on, he adopted as his own name the ambiguously Hispano-Portuguese nickname by which his father was known in Latin America. He handed this name on to his Lusophone children as a patronym. These children systematically attempt to 'cover' their father's passing. The third man (C) never used his father's Chinese name. The father died when he was a child and his South American mother brought him up in Macao as a Macanese, giving him her Spanish family name as a surname. He presents himself as full Macanese and, to me at least, he spoke with derision of 'the Chinamen'.

CONCLUSION

To conclude, I would like to emphasize that Macao is a place where sociocultural change is readily observable. It is a border town which is dependent for its survival on an equilibrium between political forces that are largely unpredictable and have undergone profound changes over the past few decades. During long periods of its life Macao was a dormant and irrelevant outpost of the Portuguese empire, but then the winds changed and it became a place for fast money and hard and dangerous living.

Since the early 1980s there has been an unprecedented economic and demographic growth, so that the privileged rights of citizenship that the Macanese enjoyed were a highly valuable asset in personal terms. However the conditions were there for a yet deeper change. The capital of Portugueseness, which yesterday was a matter of life or death for the Macanese, lost most of its relevance during the period of transition. People who have spent their lives covering up the stigma of 'passing' are now confronted with new uncertainties, for the future of the city since 1999 is Chinese. At the same time, during the 1980s and 1990s, the illegitimate children of Portuguese and Macanese fathers who had entered the Chinese ethnic camp as a means of overcoming the prejudice from their more legitimate relatives were attempting to claim their paternity in the Portuguese courts in order to obtain Portuguese passports with which they would be able to escape if Chinese rule after 1999 proved too trying (cf. Santos 1991).

It is not only the Macanese who are changing. As the Chinese middle class becomes integrated into global culture – via modern education, consumerism and the mass media – cross-ethnic relations become less fraught with incomprehension. Furthermore, the perceived threat of 1999 was quite as strongly felt by the Macanese as by the Chinese middle class. Slowly, the political life of the city witnessed a greater participation by the Chinese population.[113] It was not in the area of power created by the shadow government of the PRC that the Chinese middle class looked for a means to express its fears and press its claims. Rather, they looked up to the area of formal government, until then controlled by the Macanese and Portuguese and largely ignored by the Chinese. On the one hand, this encouraged ethnic friction, as it threatened the individual position of Macanese politicians but, on the other hand, it favoured the creation of an objective convergence between the interests of the Macanese and the Chinese electorate, thus diffusing this friction.

A Macanese politician whom I asked to recount his family history kindly agreed to spend long hours discussing it with me, but omitted to tell me that his grandparents were converts who adopted a Portuguese name. I was soon informed of this by other families, who have other skeletons in their cupboards. However, contexts change and what today is a stigmatizing piece of information may become a trump card tomorrow. Two years later, this person delivered a speech in the local Assembly in which he justified his allegiance to the Chinese electorate on the basis of the fact that he himself 'only has Chinese blood in his veins'.

In conclusion, the Macanese person is constantly confronted with 'the embarrassment of limits' to which Goffman referred (1963: 148). I hope I have succeeded in showing that this affects not only the nature of the integration of the Macanese ethnic community, but also the nature of ethnic relations in Macao as a whole. As political, economic and cultural conditions change, so does each person's positioning towards ethnic belonging, both in terms of socialization and in terms of subsequent strategic aims. To the inhabitants of Macao, 1999 represented a major upheaval of the political, economic and cultural conditions of their lives. It is not only personal dispositions towards cross-ethnic relations that will alter as a result, it is also the very framework of ethnic differentiation that, as the generations pass, will slowly assume a new form.

CHAPTER 8

CORRELATE ASYMMETRIES: GENDER, CLASS AND ETHNICITY

Social differences marked by gender, by ethnicity and by socio-economic class are profoundly interrelated and mutually interdependent phenomena. These three factors of differentiation interrelate at each moment in history and evolve in correlation. All three of them involve asymmetries of power (in the broad sense of the term) and, as such, constitute fields of dynamic tension.

The relation between these fields often compounds the asymmetries, giving rise to discordant identitary pulls on the part of social subjects. Thus, people are prone to feel torn between their different belongings. This may well lead to internal crises so profound as to hinder the person's participation in normal daily living. Such situations can be deeply traumatic, initiating dynamic processes of repression and resolution both at a personal and at a group level.

In this chapter I will focus on relations of parenthood and cohabitation (matrimonial contexts) that cross over the boundaries between the principal ethnic groups in Macao – the Chinese, the Macanese and the Portuguese. The expression 'matrimonial context' is intended to cover situations of cohabitation of sufficient duration to permit the raising of children.[114] It includes wedded couples, common law marriages (*uniões de facto*, in Portuguese), long-term situations of concubinage and situations of cohabitation and co-parenthood that may involve little more than a master–servant bond. The argument will concern itself with the identitary problems facing the Macanese Eurasian community during the colonial period (1846–1967). Finally, I will outline the changes in marriage patterns which occurred in the post-colonial period (1967–87) and which prepared the way for the transition period (1987–99). It will be shown that the changes that took place involved correlations between the asymmetries in gender, ethnicity and class.

THE MATRIMONIAL CONTEXT OF PRODUCTION

During the colonial period, when ethnic relations were marked by greater mutual exclusiveness than today and were traced over class boundaries, the children of people with different ethnic belongings were obliged to make identitary options that often involved traumatic experiences. Such traumas marked the person's and the group's identity so deeply that they did not simply disappear once the conflict itself was resolved. Rather, they acted as a dynamic springboard for corrective identitary action – 'feelings' that functioned as 'driving forces'. This is particularly the case since these traumatic wounds were often transmitted to the children in the form of continued identities.[115]

In order to give the reader a sense of the personal dimension of such traumatic experiences, I have decided to transcribe a short work of fiction. Its Macanese author, Deolinda da Conceição, died prematurely in 1957, one year after her book *Cheong-Sam (A Cabaia)* was published in Lisbon (1987a [1956]). The book is a collection of short stories that she had published in a Portuguese-language newspaper of Macao (*Notícias de Macau*) for which she worked throughout the 1950s. In spite of the relative naïveté of her style, the work deserves a reading by anyone interested in the position of women in wartime China. It is fair to assume that she consciously wrote these texts in such a way as to cover the gamut of tragic possibilities that confronted the women of her times. Having returned to her native Macao as a war-time refugee from Japanese-occupied Shanghai and from a broken marriage, with children born of two different men – at a period of deep moral conservatism in Portugal – she was no stranger to tragedy in spite of her personal strength and beauty (cf. Conceição 1987b).

Alms-giving

The crowd was thick on the small pier. People were restless and impatient, longing to put an end to a duty that etiquette imposed, but that was so disagreeable, as one was only there because it did not look proper to be absent.

The hour of departure approached and the young man began to say goodbye. He was a student who was leaving his birthplace in order to continue his studies in a distant land, where he would meet his father's family.

His eyes scanned a crowd that seemed larger than it was due to the small size of the pontoon to which the boat was moored. He saw his colleagues, some of his teachers and the few friends his father managed to collect. His face dropped at the sight of people whom he knew to be there for interest's sake and not as a mark of true friendship. He felt vilified by this slighting of his dignity as a man. He had felt wounded ever since, as a child, he noticed that there was a difference between himself and his companions. This feeling had been the driving force behind his capacity to spend so many long hours tethered to his books. He had abdicated from what was due to him as a child, in order to make real the dream that he held so dear of managing to free himself from his humiliating circumstances.

His soul was wounded by the injustice of destiny. Why did he have to be born under such circumstances? Why did Nature endow him with such uncommon intelligence, only to make him all the more conscious of his sad fate? So many times he had asked himself whether he would be able to escape the environment that depressed him! Would he manage to flee from under the shadow that oppressed him, the shameful shadow of bastardy? In fact . . . he felt it was not his own fault. So he suffered with such anger that it shook his inner self.

His father, he knew only too well, had left distant old Europe disillusioned with life. Embittered and desperate, the father came to this corner of China in order to bury his pain or even worse, who knows, his humiliation. His mother was a poor Chinese woman, ignorant and barefooted, without the merest hint of education, whom his father had brought home one evening. She remained there to that day in a kind of uncertain condition. No one knew very well whether she was a servant or a kind of wife unprotected by matrimony. Yet he knew she was his mother – the mother he loved in his heart but of whom he felt so ashamed in society; a mother with whom he should not be seen in public. She did not understand him at all but it was her that raised him, breastfed him, hit him in moments of unrepressed anger. Her boorishness had freed her to vent out her annoyance with his childish misdeeds at the top of her voice.

Father hardly talked to her as he barely understood her language. The student, however, had been obliged to learn to speak both languages fluently in order to talk to both of them. Never had they gone out together, never had they shared a stroll. They had never been seen exchanging opinions concerning their life together. Ever since he could remember, he had been a witness to father giving orders and mother obligingly complying. At table, she ate with chopsticks from her bowl, whilst he and his father ate with fork and knife. Christmas or other such like festivities simply made no sense at home. When he got sick, father took him to a European doctor. Mother, in turn, carried him out to the healer. Of course, this was always followed by a string of recriminations and a scene. All he could do was try to calm down father's anger at her, whilst explaining to her why father thought that a doctor was the thing. He would grumpily hear out their mutual complaints, which left him in intimate despair.

Why had he been born this way? Why him? Why?

The hugs of his friends left his eyes dry. He thanked them for their good wishes but, whilst holding their hands, he knew they had not gone there out of genuine friendship. He felt dizzy but controlled himself. Soon enough he would be free of this entire repugnant atmosphere.

His father opened out his arms and he allowed himself to be shaken by a hug that he was not able to reciprocate. He hated himself then, but how could he be to blame for what took place in his heart? This man was indeed his father – the father who, in spite of his vulgarity, had always heaped him with affection. The father who, in his equivocal language, had always showered on him so much love – as if to compensate for the sadness of his fate.

He would have liked to feel proud of a man that had always unswervingly endeavoured to remove any hindrance from his path. But all he felt was compassion. After all, it was this man who should be held responsible for his hateful life, his ignoble condition.

His soul was burning with hunger for affection. He hungered to be able to embrace his father and mother. Only, as it happened, these two creatures would never have been the parents he would have chosen for himself. They just could not satisfy the desire that burned within him from the day when, as a child, he had asked himself why his parents were so different from those of the other children. Now, he knew he would soon free himself from all that. He would be able to walk past his new friends and companions without having to withstand the inquisitive gaze of those that searched his face for evidence of the stigma of his origins.

He worked hard at his studies; he closed off his ears to the cruel words, so that he might now conquer for himself the good name that he had not inherited. He would achieve that aura of dignity, which had always been denied to him, and he would touch shoulders with others, feeling newly cleansed.

He had asked his mother not to come to the pier. He had said goodbye with a broken heart, as he knew he would never see her again. But, at the same time, he had agonised over her ample gestures, all that crying and snorting – all those theatrics of emotion that were so characteristic of her position. He watched her as she cleaned her eyes with her *cheong-sam*.[116] Once again he observed how grotesque and ungainly her posture was. Half grieving, half relieved – he just ran away.

Distractedly he carried out the task of shaking everyone's hand, as he heard a colleague commenting that it was time to get into the boat. Suddenly, he was stopped short as if he had received a blow. Crying aloud, a Chinese woman was trying to get to him through the crowd. Her dishevelled clothing and her loud laments were an undeniable mark of her lowly class. This was obviously a working woman, or at least one who had once been, as the ageing in her face clearly indicated that she was past hard labour.

The face of the young student suddenly became pale and severe. He searched for his father with his eyes, only to discover that he had quickly turned away, incapable of dealing with such a situation.

When the woman finally reached him, before she fully expressed her lamentations, he put his fingers into his waistcoat pocket, took out a coin and placed it into the hands that reached out to him, as if in prayer before his eyes. Then, trembling nervously, he turned round and mounted the gangway with feverish steps.

On the pier, with her eyes wide open with craziness, the woman repeated amidst her convulsive crying: 'He gave me alms, he gave me alms in exchange for the life I gave him!' (Conceição 1987a: 51–9)

The story of the Macanese student who rejects his own mother out of despair about his Eurasian condition makes little sense to the Macanese students of today (cf. Pina-Cabral and Lourenço 1993a: 104–13). By the time I arrived in the city in the early 1990s, there was little to be gained from claiming that one was Portuguese or denying that one was Chinese. But this was not the case fifty years earlier.

Marriage patterns have changed drastically; ethnic relations have lost their aggressive edge; class discrimination has become less blatant; utter poverty less prevalent. When this story was written, ethnic, gender and class prejudices were more violent. Things changed in such a way that, by the 1990s, the feelings and actions of the story's characters had come to seem puzzling.

The student in the story saw himself obliged to ignore his mother in public. This is an act that, even then, would have seemed hideous to anyone. The detail of the coin, of course, might be considered fictional exaggeration. Nevertheless, I insist, the plot is grounded on verisimilitude, as was confirmed by the older informants with whom I discussed it. They all argued that such a situation could well have occurred at mid-century. I was personally told of people that, to this day, continue to hide the fact that their mothers had been lower-class Chinese women – often even *tanka* (fishing folk) women who had relations with Portuguese sailors and soldiers.

Henrique de Senna Fernandes, another Macanese author, wrote a short story about a *tanka* girl who has an affair with a Portuguese sailor. In the end, the man returns to his native country and takes their little girl with him, leaving the mother abandoned and broken-hearted. As her sailorman picks up the child, A-Chan's words are: '*Cuidadinho . . . cuidadinho*' ('Careful . . . careful'). She resigns herself to her fate, much as she may never have recovered from the blow (1978).

Now, it may be claimed that such an ending is a product of the male-orientation of the author. My conviction, however, based on interviews with him and with older Macanese people who lived during this period, is that there is verisimilitude in this story too. They claim that the mother would have believed that her child would have a life of incomparably greater ease as a European in Portugal than as a lower-class Chinese woman in Macao.

When dealing with a community such as that of the Macanese – the result of centuries of interaction between two deeply differentiated worlds[117] – we have to be clear about the processes that allow for the reproduction of the group's identity across generations. The tragedy of being a Eurasian during the heyday of colonialism should not be forgotten (cf. Spitzer 1989), even today, when it has become possible to trace a Eurasian ancestry as a claim to prestige (cf. Hall 1992).

A community such as that of the Macanese had two distinct points of entry. On the one hand, there were *matrimonial contexts of reproduction*. These occurred when two members of the community married each other and produced children that were born within the community. During the colonial period, the close identification with Portugueseness meant that marrying a Portuguese person in Macao was a way of reproducing community belonging and should be seen as a type of matrimonial context of reproduction.

On the other hand, there were *matrimonial contexts of production*. These were situations where a Macanese or a Portuguese person married an Asian person. In the vast majority of cases, their children were brought up as Macanese – that is, Catholics and Portuguese citizens, bearing a

Portuguese name. Such people were fully entitled to be considered Macanese *and* Portuguese. They were, however, often subject to internal forms of discrimination – they were members of the group, but laboured under a kind of diminished condition.

Let us return to a comment that Deolinda puts in the mouth of her character. At one point, he asks himself whether he would 'manage to flee from under [. . .] the shameful shadow of bastardy'. Technically speaking, however, he is not a 'bastard'. His father and his mother fully recognize him and do so publicly, to his grief. What the sentence implies is that *he* does not recognize *them* – that is, he feels his historical insertion into a legitimate continued identity has been severed. In denying his mother's heritage, he makes himself a bastard, even though he was not born one. But he did so because of the pressures upon him and against his own better judgement. He did so because he had no alternative in a world where there was no identitary middle ground between being Chinese and being European (although being a 'Portuguese half-caste' was a diminished condition of Europeanness in colonial Hong Kong, where so many Macanese eventually found a livelihood).

THE ASYMMETRY IN INTERETHNIC SEXUAL RELATIONS

Deolinda's short stories are an outlet for her revolt against the condition of women in wartime China. Furthermore, a number of them demonstrate how, in situations of interethnic misunderstanding, the main victim was always the Chinese woman. She uses her fiction to reveal in an almost pedagogic fashion that, at that time, interethnic sexual relations were essentially asymmetric.

In fact, in those days, the *matrimonial context of production* was usually constituted by Chinese women of low socio-economic status who were married to or concubines of Portuguese or Macanese men. Very rarely did Chinese women of higher status agree to marry a Westerner. As Deolinda argues in one of her short stories,[118] should they have wanted to do so out of romantic infatuation, they would not be allowed to. In the family histories I compiled, I did not come across one single case that broke this rule. It was only in the 1980s that Macanese or Portuguese women began to marry men who defined themselves ethnically as Chinese.

In fact, even ambiguous cases reveal, on closer inspection, this general tendency. For example, a prestigious Macanese family, one of whose daughters is married to one of the principal figures of the Territory, originates in an interesting series of events. In this case, at the turn of the twentieth century, a Portuguese lawyer helped a wealthy Chinese man to solve a legal wrangle. As payment for his services, the wealthy man gave the lawyer an exceptionally beautiful adopted daughter as a concubine. The lawyer was so taken up with the concubine that his Portuguese wife felt she should separate from him and return to Portugal. The lawyer remained in Macao and he and the concubine had a large number of children, who played an important role in the Territory in mid-century. The relevant fact here is that we are not dealing with a full daughter of the wealthy man, but with an 'adopted daughter' – in all probability a *mooi1 jai2* (cf. Chapter 5), the status of whom was very much inferior to that of an adopted son.

Interethnic sexual relations were indeed unidirectional and they often reveal Erving Goffman's dictum that 'mixed social situations make for anxious unanchored interaction' (1963: 29). A man of Chinese origin could only marry a Macanese or Portuguese woman if he had previously abandoned his Chinese ethnic identity. But this left him with 'a skeleton in the cupboard'. Such passings normally occurred very early on in life. The men who made them had usually been brought up as Portuguese, either as a result of adoption or because their lower-class parents had sent them at an early age to the seminary or to a Portuguese school – both of these being fully state-subsidized. However it is important to emphasize that, although such situations did occur, they were never abundant.

These men had converted to Catholicism early on in life, used a Portuguese name (often with no sign of their Chinese heritage) and spoke Portuguese as their mother tongue. Cases such as Pedro José Lobo – the main negotiator with the Japanese at the time of the Pacific War – fell into this category. These men, however, had to contend with the phenotypic evidence of their Asian ancestry and with the competitive envy of their neighbours who were only too keen to put them down by referring to their Chinese low-class background. These forms of 'self-destructive discrimination', to use another Goffmanian notion (1963), were very characteristic of life in Macao. If, as in the case of Lobo, the man became politically and economically powerful, he rose above such preoccupations. Even then, the 'traditional Macanese families' with greater prestige might hesitate to encourage one of their daughters to marry such a man.

The female version of this process was numerically far more significant. Many abandoned female children were raised as 'orphans' by the Italian order of Cannossian Sisters in their Holy Infancy Asylum. They were known as *bambinos*, in reference to the asylum's Italian name. Often, Portuguese soldiers or sailors who decided to remain in the Territory, or Macanese men of low economic status, would opt to marry one of these girls. When they left the orphanage at adolescence, they were put out to work as servants in Macanese families and, from there, they usually got married or found some form of employment. The number of such women is rather startling, but we must not forget that there has always been a large contingent of abandoned or transacted young females in Macao. From 1876 to 1926, the Cannossian Sisters raised 32 960 girls and 1446 boys.[119] The disproportion is of itself plain evidence of the sexist preferences of Cantonese parents.

Taking into consideration the process of reproduction of the Macanese as an ethnic community, I have classified as *matrimonial context of production* the situations where a Macanese or a Portuguese man constituted a family with a Chinese woman. The two situations just outlined above – of people who transferred their allegiance to the Macanese camp at an early stage in life – were marginal situations between that and the *matrimonial context of reproduction*. Here, the couple was constituted by two Macanese persons or by a Portuguese and a Macanese. It must be noted, however, that all of these situations had something in common: the children who were born to these couples had no active kinship relations among the Chinese population of Macao. The conjugation of gender difference with ethnic difference gave rise to an asymmetry that functioned almost perfectly to block relatedness (cf. Stafford 2000).

When I tried to establish among my older informants how they demarcated their kinship horizons, I was surprised to discover that Chinese women did not function as links in a chain of relatedness (and even less so 'orphan' girls or men who abandoned their Chinese ethnic identity). The children who were raised as Macanese did not know the Chinese people who might have been their relatives.

This ignorance was partly responsible for explaining something that was initially very surprising to me. I was puzzled to hear persons who displayed clear phenotypic evidence of an Asian ancestry declare that they had no Chinese relatives. Once I started systematically drawing up family histories with my older informants, the reason for this became quite clear. On the one hand, the names by which their descendents knew them were the Portuguese names they assumed upon conversion. On the other hand, as the links of relatedness with Chinese ascendants were severed, the links with collaterals lacked any social significance.

Taking the first family histories I carried out in Macao as a sample,[120] it is easy to conclude that some sort of blocking process was occurring.

The nine informants gave information about 670 people to whom they claimed to be related. Of these, there were only sixty-one persons (forty-eight women, thirteen men) whom the informants declared to be Chinese.[121] They only knew the name of twenty-nine of these sixty-one persons. In fourteen instances they knew the full name, in fifteen instances they knew only a nickname or a Portuguese or English alias. In only two instances did they manage to provide a full name for a Chinese relative whose relationship was more distant than the mother, the mother's mother or the mother's brother. In both instances, we were dealing with Chinese men of considerable reputation in the city.

This draws our attention to the fact that gender and ethnic asymmetries are deeply intertwined with socio-economic class. The Chinese women that entered into Macanese kinship networks were normally lower-class women. Their relatives, had they been around, would not be considered as valuable allies. In any case, as they were poor and often dislocated women, their relationship with their relatives would always have been tenuous.

We can detect here another type of equivocal compatibility (cf. Chapter 5). It is not only a case of the Macanese of that generation being overly keen to safeguard their *capital of Portugueseness*. Cantonese society also contributed towards the blockage in relatedness. As has been argued (R. Watson 1986), Cantonese women are generally 'nameless', to the extent that they do not function as transmitters of identity and are usually referred to by means of technonyms.

Finally, one thing must be stressed: this ignorance of names was not due to any kind of linguistic blockage. My Macanese informants (and those of their relatives whose relatives would have been Chinese) were all fluent speakers of Cantonese and had no difficulty in recognizing, pronouncing or memorizing Chinese names.

THE MATRIMONIAL CONTEXT OF REPRODUCTION

To return once again to Deolinda's words, identitary traumas function as 'driving forces', but their power does not exhaust itself in the first generation – it can be passed on in the form of continued identity to the descendants. The matrimonial contexts of reproduction, thus, were not immune to the sort of conjunction between the asymmetries of gender, ethnicity and class that have been traced above.

The following story was told to me by a woman who reached her adulthood in the early 1930s and concerns the conditions under which she had her first two children. She was a member of a prestigious family of Macanese Eurasians. Her grandfather had acquired an aristocratic title at the end of the nineteenth century. She fell in love with a Macanese schoolmate who was unacceptable to her parents as a marriage partner because his own parents had been raised in matrimonial contexts of production.

Being a close friend of Pedro José Lobo – who was a Timorese-Chinese convert raised in a seminary – her lover managed to obtain employment in the firm owned by Lobo in Timor. Later, he entered the colonial administration. Once established, he sent word to his sweetheart to join him. One afternoon, she eloped in the company of the old *aia* who had raised her from childhood. With the aid of Lobo's men, she was taken to Timor where they got married. Their happiness, however, was short-lived, as the Japanese invaded Timor and interned the couple in one of their infamous concentration camps. Their first two children were born there. In each instance, when delivery approached, the Japanese officers in charge allowed the couple to isolate themselves in a place near the sea where there were some large, flat rocks. There, the man delivered his own children.

When the Japanese left Timor, the family returned to Macao but did not feel at home there and went on to live in Africa. It was only much later, after her family had lost its fortune and got dispersed throughout the world, that the wife's links with her family were re-established.

The 1950s saw a great change in racist attitudes worldwide. Previously, Portuguese Eurasians throughout the world – and there were communities similar to the Macanese in most places where the Portuguese expansion has left its mark – were constrained by the racist attitudes which were dominant among the principal European colonial nations (cf. Spitzer 1989). Every one of these people felt the sting of prejudice and its correlative socio-economic disadvantages. Being in an ambiguous position in relation to the European/Other divide, they often felt the need to soften the blow by pushing the onus onto someone else. Thus, self-destructive discrimination was always waiting round the corner.

The bitterness and sense of personal humiliation that accompanied such processes took a long while to disappear. Normally, it accompanied the subjects who had been wounded by it early on in life to the end of their days. Often, it even affected their children.

A Macanese woman, whose parents were affected by racist legislation in the early 1940s, still protested about it in the 1990s when I interviewed her. Her father had come to Macao with the army in the late 1920s. He married one of the *bambinos*, the convent-raised orphans. As she put it,

'The convent raised orphans, so he went to fetch her there'. By 1941, when her parents already had two children, new racist legislation was enforced as part of Salazar's early colonial policies. This meant that her father would never again be promoted. He eventually decided to leave the army, stay on in Macao and work in commerce. His daughter never forgot this heavy blow to his prestige and that of his family.

Note the tone of self-destructive discrimination that pervades the way in which she first told me about it:

> Those who went there as part of the [policies of] colonisation before Salazar, stayed on. Salazar was the one that spoiled it all. He even made laws for blacks, forbidding marriages. He forgot that, in Macao, people were not black, isn't it? The law Salazar created for the army prevented officers from marrying with black women, so as not to produce little blacks, and forbade marriages. So, as the law was applicable to our case, the daughters of a Portuguese man could not marry an officer!

Very few people today in Portugal remember this legislation which, in fact, goes against the lusotropicalist and anti-racist declarations that became the official ideology of the Portuguese colonial state after the onset of the African wars of liberation in the early 1960s.[122]

> Art. 4 – Army officers who ask for a marriage permit must prove that their future spouse is of Portuguese origin (*portuguesa originária*), never having lost that nationality, daughter of European parents, not divorced, and that both of them possess means of subsistence sufficient by relation to the degree which they will occupy in the military hierarchy.
>
> Art. 5 – In considering the concession of the permit, the wife's social situation will be considered, as well as her past and her family's past, the difference in ages, the possible existence of infant children or of single daughters of either partner. (. . .)
>
> Art. 10 – Any army personnel who marries without licence will be demoted if he is an officer, struck off the army if he is a sergeant and punished (. . .) if he is a soldier (. . .).[123]

Clearly the legislation was applied leniently. A daughter of one of Macao's most distinguished aristocratic Eurasian families told me of her sister's marriage: 'In order to marry lieutenant T, my sister X had to prove that she was not black or yellow back to the fourth generation'. This, however, is a simplification of what actually happened, as I learned during a later interview. The officer terminated his career as a distinguished general, but when he lived in Macao in the late 1940s he was only a lieutenant from a middle-class family. His bride, however, was considered a good prospect as she descended from a prestigious aristocratic family, in spite of being Eurasian and there being very little left of the original family fortune made in a ship chandler's business at the time of the coolie trade.

The solution they found, it turns out, was reasonably well tested in those days. They went over to Hong Kong for a weekend and discreetly arranged for a religious wedding, after which they started living as husband and wife. Clearly, therefore, they had the compliance of his superior officers – in spite of the rigours of the law. Later, when he went to Portugal on leave, they obtained the document that 'proved' that she 'was not black or yellow back to the fourth generation'. In Portugal, there was no one who knew of her family background to report against her. By the time they returned to Macao, they were fully and officially married.

Such a solution worked in their case because hers was an old Eurasian family who had been Portuguese citizens with registered Portuguese names for a number of generations. For the man whose wife was raised as an orphan in the convent, such a solution was not available. His military career was irremediably severed, and all those years later, his daughter continued to protest bitterly about it.

THE CAESURA OF THE 1970s: MARRIAGE PATTERNS

Eventually this system of relations between gender, class and ethnicity that compounded different forms of subalternity came to an end. Things slowly began to change shortly after the end of the Pacific War, when a modern Chinese middle class first made its appearance in Macao.

This is how a woman who was born in the late 1920s described the change to me:

> The Chinese community lived apart. It was not as if we established a separation. We did not discriminate against them. Only, they did not join us socially. For example, if I met a Chinese acquaintance on the street, I would speak with him or her: this and that. But we did not mix in social matters. They did not enter our clubs. They did not go to the Tennis. There was no conviviality up until the end of the Second World War. Perhaps the Chinese were not interested – that is, those with sufficient social status (*nível*). To play tennis, to frequent the clubs – they had no interest in our style of life.

When the Communists took over China, a number of merchants and industrialists started to flee to the south. They would send their families ahead to set up home. And, as houses in Macao were more affordable than in Hong Kong, there was a great infiltration of Chinese families into Macao. These families had another type of status (*nível*), they started joining Catholic schools. That was when the Chinese and the Macanese began to meet socially.

Earlier on, the Macanese had encountered two very different types of Chinese across the ethnic divide: either an impoverished lower class or a very restricted group of traditionalist capitalists to whom many Macanese owed personal allegiance – people such as Kou Ho-Neng or Fu Tak-Iam, the holders of the gambling contract previous to the present retainer.

At the time the gambling contract changed hands (1961), a generational change occurred in the city's elite. Pedro José Lobo's role as political negotiator with the Mainland was handed over to his successor, Ho Yin, who saw himself not as a Macanese but as a modern Chinese. This was also the more extremist Maoist period and the period during which the Portuguese colonial empire and Salazar's dictatorship were slowly collapsing. Indeed, from the mid-1960s to the mid-1970s, Macao lived through a period of heightened ethnic conflict – which I have called the *caesura of the 1970s*. After the new democratic system had been implemented in Portugal (1974–6) and the Deng Xiaoping regime was put into place in China (1978), a new era of ethnic relations emerged.

In order to assess the change in marriage practices of the Macanese, I carried out a study of the marriages that involved at least one Macanese or Portuguese partner in two of the older Catholic parishes of the city.[124] The first period selected was 1961 to 1964, because by 1965 the atmosphere of open ethnic conflict that was going to explode violently in December 1966 (the events known as *123*) was already noticeable.

It is interesting to note that, contrary to what older informants stated, in those days there was a considerable percentage of Macanese people marrying Chinese partners (33.7 per cent). Nevertheless, the number of Macanese endogamous marriages was significant (32.7 per cent) as was the number of Macanese who married Portuguese persons (17.9 per cent). If we compare marriages leading to *matrimonial contexts of production*[125] (49.4 per cent of all marriages) with those leading to *matrimonial contexts of reproduction*[126] (50.6 per cent) we conclude that the latter were marginally more significant.

Now, it must be noted that, at the time, the female partner was Chinese in roughly 80 per cent of the cases of matrimonial contexts of production.

We may, thus, conclude that there was a situation where the ethnic boundary between the Macanese and the Chinese camps was reproduced and reinforced across generations.

The second period (1965–74) corresponds to the caesura of the 1970s. These were times of deep uncertainty for the Macanese. It was clear to anyone that the Portuguese colonial empire was coming to an end. The Chinese authorities had not wanted to take over the city in 1966/7, but their shadow government was fully operational. Should they ever wish to, all they had to do was cross the border. Macao would one day be Chinese, anyone could see that.

Across the *Portas do Cerco*, however, Maoist China did not seem a viable option. The information the Macanese had about this – via the thousands of refugees that escaped across the shallow waters – revealed a particularly frightening picture. Unfortunately, metropolitan Portugal bore no appeal as an alternative. It was underdeveloped and culturally isolated and its population was emigrating throughout the world in search of better living conditions.

The Macanese responded by increasing the marriages among themselves (44.3 per cent) and decreasing marriages with Portuguese partners (10.2 per cent). The remaining 42 per cent married Chinese partners. What this meant was that marriages leading to matrimonial contexts of reproduction increased to 54.5 per cent of all marriages.

In December 1975, having granted independence to its other colonies, the new Portuguese regime terminated its military presence in the Territory. Law and order were maintained by the police force, which was mostly staffed by Chinese residents of the city. That same year, Mao died and shortly after Deng Xiaoping took over. Almost immediately, there was more prosperity in China and Macao's economy took off. The atmosphere of gloom lifted. In the wake of new gambling contracts that granted the government increased revenue, the city's infrastructures as well as its administrative apparatus began to grow rapidly. A new type of Portuguese person started to arrive in the Territory – bureaucrats and technocrats who stayed for short periods and brought their families with them. Marriages between Macanese and Portuguese decreased almost overnight.

The interesting aspect is that the percentage of Macanese endogamous marriages also fell rapidly (1975/81 – 34.4 per cent). As the Territory's economy boomed and the process of transition to Chinese rule was increasingly consolidated, this tendency increased (1982/6 – 33.7 per cent; 1987/90 – 19.8 per cent).

In 1970–4 the majority of Catholic marriages still led to matrimonial contexts of reproduction (56.3 per cent). However this was radically inverted after 1975. By 1987–90, only 24.7 per cent of the marriages led to matrimonial contexts of reproduction. Furthermore, the gender balance also changed. By the 1990s, marriages between Macanese and Chinese partners evened out in terms of gender, as Macanese women began marrying into Chinese middle-class families.[127]

Interethnic marriages are far less marked by asymmetry. A Macanese man with whom I was discussing what happens to a Macanese woman who marries a Chinese man told me:

> This depends on the role that woman plays within her family. For example, my sister-in-law [wife's sister] is married to a Chinese. The son cannot speak a word of Portuguese. He goes to a Chinese school and doesn't even have a Portuguese name. The other sister-in-law [also wife's sister] is also married to a Chinese. But all of their children have Portuguese names [aside from their Chinese names, of course]. Well, all right, they do go to a Chinese school. And why? Because she also has a say there. It all depends on a person's education.

THE CAESURA OF THE 1970s: DOMESTIC ENVIRONMENT

The cultural atmosphere of the Macanese homes also changed. During the colonial period, Portuguese had become the first language of the Macanese. By the time of the Japanese invasion, *patuá* had disappeared as a domestic language. A Macanese person's first language had always been some sort of non-elite version of Cantonese – this was the language used by the *aias* who raised them. Macanese parents, however, were deeply preoccupied with teaching their children to speak, read and write a European language (Portuguese in Macao, English in Hong Kong). An informant born in the early 1930s, for example, explained to me that every time he said a word in Cantonese in front of his parents he was slapped. This was their technique for obliging him to become a fluent Portuguese speaker.

After the caesura of the 1970s, however, all this changed due to two independent processes that concurred, making Cantonese the domestic language of the Macanese. On the one hand, the Macanese were no longer so concerned that their children should learn Portuguese, as Cantonese had become a perfectly acceptable middle-class language and they could well see that, in the future, Macao would become part of China. On the other hand, profound linguistic changes had occurred in the city's Chinese ethnic camp.

The Cantonese spoken in the streets of Macao had changed. After 1949, the Communist government had intensified the process of linguistic standardization that the Nationalists had begun, which meant that, by the 1970s, the Cantonese spoken in Macao was no longer the rural Sekkei dialect but was Standard Cantonese as spoken in Canton. This was what the city's Chinese schools taught the children of the new middle class that took over the city's economy.

Furthermore, the enormous development of the Hong Kong mass media – and particularly the Cantonese-language television channels – had a strong impact on the city. After the caesura of the 1970s, young people – Macanese and Chinese alike – no longer looked up to European culture as their point of reference. They looked towards Hong Kong and Taiwan and, beyond that, to Japan and the United States.

Gradually the style of dressing came from Hong Kong, the songs that are endlessly repeated in front of the *karaoke* screens were in Cantonese, the film stars who shape the imagination of young boys and girls were Hongkongese and Taiwanese, the comic books were either Japanese translations or produced in Hong Kong, written in a version of Chinese that aimed to portray spoken Cantonese.[128]

In short, by the 1990s, only the Macanese 'traditional families' with special political associations to the Administration insisted on teaching their children to speak fluent Portuguese. However, even these people, used Cantonese as their everyday home language. This did not mean that the Macanese had lost interest in the Portuguese language; the large majority of them managed to speak it reasonably well. Furthermore, only late in the 1980s did the Macanese start worrying about learning written Chinese.

In fact, when one comes across a Macanese family in a restaurant carrying out one of the regular family meetings that are so important for the constitution of their sense of community (cf. Pina-Cabral 2000), one is surprised by the linguistic medley that characterizes their speech. There is a constant fluctuation between Portuguese, Cantonese and English that makes up for a rather fascinating style of communication. They mix the cultural references to the three linguistically specific mass media that meet in Macao (television, radio and press in Portuguese, English and Cantonese).

CONCLUSION: CORRELATE ASYMMETRIES

Between the late colonial period (1946–67) and the transition period (1987–99) a major change occurred in Macanese life styles that I associate with the *caesura of the 1970s*. This change involved a reconfiguration of the way in which gender differences, ethnic differences and class differences related to each other in producing subalternity.

In class terms, the colonial period was characterized by the existence of a profound differentiation within Chinese society: on the one hand, a traditional upper class and, on the other, an impoverished proletariat. The second half of the century saw the appearance of a Chinese modern middle class. In Hong Kong, they took over the middle ranks of the financial and colonial administrations in the early 1960s, expelling the Macanese from an area that had been virtually their own for over a century.

In Macao, the Macanese managed to prevent this, for two main reasons. First, contrary to the more forward-looking policies of Hong Kong colonial government, the Salazarist regime resisted the entry of Chinese into the Administration. Second, the alliance between the traditionalist elite and the Communist regime (personified in the figure of Ho Yin) meant that the Chinese modern middle class had a lesser margin for growth in Macao.

When the economy took off in the 1980s, therefore, the Macanese managed to retain their control over the middle ranks of the Administration. Nevertheless, the Chinese middle class became increasingly important in the private sector of the economy. After the subsiding of the open ethnic conflict that characterized the late 1960s and early 1970s, the two sectors of the middle class in the Territory started to converge.

The changes in marriage patterns and in domestic language identified above reflect this approximation. They also reflect the changes in the way in which gender asymmetries structured ethnic relations. Increasingly, interethnic marriages became more common and Macanese women started marrying Chinese men.

During the colonial period, Macanese marriage strategies reflected the desire to increase the capital of Portugueseness. After the caesura of the 1970s, however, Deolinda's story of the student who rejected his mother no longer made any sense. The European heritage of the Macanese was no longer a door to privilege. In order to lay claim to a special position in the Territory, the Macanese found it necessary to emphasize that which they previously had to hide: their Eurasian condition. It was precisely that condition that endowed them with the means to mediate between the European and the Asian worlds. Their capacity to bridge between the two worlds became a positive source of privilege – a *capital of intercultural communication*.

During the first half of the twentieth entury, colonialism was globally dominant. Since the 1980s the world has become increasingly globalized, the capacity to connect different cultures is seen as a positive asset. In the early 1990s, for example, Deolinda's son, an artist and clothes designer, created a collection called 'The Silk Route' with which he achieved some international acclaim. His idea was to emphasize the way in which Macao can be a 'meeting point of cultures' – the phrase which served as the motto for the Administration's cultural policy during the 1990s.

CHAPTER 9

HABITS OF THE HEART: MODERN WOMEN AND FILIAL PIETY[129]

This chapter is dedicated to exploring one aspect of the relationship between tradition and modernity in East Asia: the apparent incongruity between the symbolic subalternity and the practical empowerment of southern Chinese middle-class women. Whoever has come to know one of Macao's or Hong Kong's (or, for that matter, Canton's) female entrepreneurs — be she a high-level professional, a business woman or a market-stall seller — knows immediately that this is not a subaltern person. On the contrary, one is confronted, surely, with some of the most self-sustaining, enterprising, hard-working people that one may chance to meet anywhere. And yet such modern women are immersed in a lifeworld where deep traditional strains are readily perceived. These traditional strains point towards a logic of gender relations that, in other contexts, have implied serious female subalternity.

This insight necessarily leads us to approach the supposed schism that separates modernity from tradition in a less Manichaean fashion. We are obliged to consider 'the continuing role of tradition in providing the rich texture of an evolving modernity' (Tu 1996: 6). Such tradition both constitutes a durable background to practical decisions and provides the social actors with the major symbolic lines of integration of their existence, thus structuring their emotional responses.[130]

I was captivated by the double meaning implicit in the expression 'habits of the heart' that Tu Wei-Ming uses to refer to the Confucian heritage in present-day capitalist East Asia. He argues that, although the PRC has lived through repeated and systematic opposition to Confucianism, 'this by no means implies that the habits of the heart in Mainland China have ceased to be Confucian' (1996: 259). Here, he develops de Bary's argument that, just as Europe exists today in a post-Christian condition, so East Asia is living in a post-Confucian era (1988: 109).

'Habits of the heart' point to two preoccupations that have accompanied me throughout this book. First, the way in which persons both create and are created by culture and, second, the way in which various forms of social differentiation (e.g. ethnicity, gender and class) generate and are generated by people's emotions.

For the hasty comparativist, the familial arrangements of the middle-class Chinese of Macao may simply appear 'modern' like anyone else's. For example, (a) they are not members of anything that might be called a lineage (cf. Chun 1996);[131] (b) their daughters are all as well educated or almost as well educated as their sons (Ng 1989); (c) most of the women are engaged in extra-domestic paid employment; (d) most households are neolocal; (e) married women often contribute financially towards the upkeep of their parents; (f) there is a consensus that it is totally wrong to exclude daughters from inheriting; (g) there are no arranged marriages properly speaking; (h) there are no polygamous households; (i) divorce proceedings are often instituted by the wife; (j) it is thought to be wrong to grant all of one's estate to only one son; etc.

And yet, when asked, they state clearly that, above all, they are Chinese and that to be Chinese is a quality that emanates directly from a kind of familism (cf. King 1996). This connection between social identity and a deep attachment to the family is not unique to China. The Portuguese peasants and urban professionals that I studied in my earlier fieldwork experiences also characterized themselves as deeply familistic. But it was not the same familism. This became all too apparent to me when I analysed what happened to the Macanese Eurasians in the 1980s and 1990s. As they slowly approached the life style of the city's Chinese middle class, they had to shed some of their earlier emphatic 'Portugueseness'. What did this process involve in terms of family practices?

A Macanese man in his sixties, whom I befriended, kindly invited me to the wedding of his son who was marrying the daughter of a Chinese restaurateur. Being a stranger to local habits, I was obliged to ask him what to expect. So he apologetically explained to me that things no longer were as they had been. When his parents had got married in the 1930s, they had organized a fully Portuguese wedding to which they had invited one or two of their more distinguished Chinese patrons. When he married a Macanese woman in the 1960s, they had been obliged to organize two receptions because their families wanted a Portuguese *copo de água* (reception), but their Chinese friends would have been offended if they had not put on a full Chinese banquet. So they arranged for a Portuguese lunch and a Chinese dinner, to which different people were invited. Now that his son was getting married, it made no sense to invite anyone to a Portuguese meal, he complained, as people simply did not like that anymore.

I went to the church wedding, which took place in the late morning. It was celebrated in Portuguese but by a Chinese priest and according to the Taiwan-style liturgy. The bride was dressed in white and the congregation was almost entirely constituted of the two families. After the wedding, whilst the couple were having photographs taken, I went home. In the evening I went to the first sitting of the reception at a Chinese restaurant. The bride changed dresses several times, one of them being the traditional Chinese embroidered red wedding dress. Many hundreds of people came, writing their names with black felt pens on the red wedding cloths and handing in their red *lei6 si6* envelopes containing different amounts of money which were meant to reflect the nature of their relatedness to the couple.

MARRIAGE PROPERTY TRANSFERS

I found it very easy to speak with people about the theatrics of wedding receptions. In fact, in characteristic Cantonese style, this was a favoured theme of discussion – where it had taken place, what dishes were served, how much money should this or that kind of person put in their *lei6 si6* envelope, how good the restaurant was, etc. When I tried to delve into the more private aspects of the wedding negotiations, however, I was made far less welcome. My Macanese informants confirmed that, if one married a Chinese woman, one had to follow Chinese custom. But they put an end to my queries by declaring that they knew that the negotiations involved financial matters, but they did not know how that was done.

The issue was a touchy one, not primarily because of the privacy of the financial deal but specially because of the presumed responses of Portuguese people. I later had an experience which made me aware of the depth of emotional response that this could cause. My informants were protecting themselves from what they reasonably presumed would be my likely response.

I had been asked to give some classes to law students of the University of Macao, where I discussed kinship theory. In one of these classes I dealt with the issue of bridewealth. After the class, a Portuguese student approached me to ask whether I could give him some private advice. He was very disturbed. Having arrived in Macao a few years earlier, he had begun to date a Macanese woman and they had eventually decided to get married. To his enormous surprise, when they announced their intentions to her parents, instead of immediately declaring their joy, they stated that it was not possible to make a final decision before reaching an agreement concerning payments.

Now, in Portugal, it is the bride's parents that pay for the wedding reception and very often it is they who contribute most actively towards the settling of the new couple in their new home. The notion of having to pay in order to be able to marry a woman whom he had been dating with her family's open consent for a number of years seemed totally outrageous to this student, particularly as the girl's family were fluent speakers of Portuguese and were Portuguese citizens. To him, the notion that he should compensate her family for taking her away was strange, as he was not, in fact, taking her away and, in any case, how could one compensate for the transfer of a person with money? That would be to buy a person and to buy a person is denying that person's personhood, a revolting crime.

I advised him not to worry and to do as he was told. On the one hand, the interpretation he was making of the payment was ethnocentric and blatantly incorrect and, on the other hand, his bride would probably bring with her property of a greater value than the sum which was now being asked of him. Eventually, exactly that happened and, through him, I managed to obtain considerable information concerning the wedding practices of the family of his bride and their Macanese in-laws.

He offered to do some research among his new in-laws and the families that were related to them by marriage. Since the 1970s roughly two-thirds of all marriages in those families had involved bridewealth payments – and increasingly this was happening even in instances of marriages such as his that did not involve a Chinese partner. The negotiations were carried out at a lunch meeting in a restaurant (*yam2 cha4*). Again, in roughly two-thirds of the cases, the two entire families had been involved in the negotiation. In slightly less than a third of the cases, the bride and bridegroom had taken all the decisions on their own. Cases did exist, however, where the parental couples had shouldered the responsibility of the negotiations without anyone else's intervention, as used to be the custom, but these were very rare instances.

Again according to his in-laws, the amounts given by Macanese bridegrooms were almost ten times smaller than those given by Chinese bridegrooms of similar social standing. He told me that the amount agreed was supposed to cover the costs of the banquet (which were, in any case, offset by the *lei6 si6* payments of the guests) and the bride's dowry. In short, as my own Chinese friends had led me to believe, it was considered a matter of prestige for the bride's father to hand back in dowry most of what he had received, or even more in some cases.

Curiously, it would seem that the negotiations were carried out in terms of the price per year of age of the bride – as if what was at stake was to compensate the parents for the costs involved in raising her. This, however, is a purely symbolic form today. If one takes into account the fact that most middle-class Macanese brides in the 1980s and 1990s underwent normal secondary schooling, the amounts of between MOP $10 000 to $20 000 that the bridegrooms paid would not even cover the costs of school uniforms!

It is important to distinguish between three distinct types of property. First, there is what I have called bridewealth – *lai5 gam1*, lit. courtesy or ceremony gold. Then there is the dowry – *ga3 jong1*, lit. marriage property – which the bride takes with her to her new home. Finally, there is the property that the bride takes with her, or that she comes to acquire within marriage, but which does not belong to the new household which she is about to enter, remaining attached to her own self – *tai2 gei2*, lit. (for) own body or *si1 gei2*, lit. (for) private self.

At this point, it is probably worth noting that, as was the case with adoption, the act of getting married is not classified by a single word for men and for women. The comparative implications of this are considerable (cf. Chun 1996: 439). Thus, what the bridegroom does is *chui2* – a character that is composed of the characters 'get, obtain' and 'girl, woman'. What the bride does is *ga3* – a character composed of the characters 'girl, woman' and 'family, house'. The implications being that, whilst the bridegroom obtains a woman, the bride goes to a different household.

The ritual of serving the tea to the bride's parents-in-law is considered the central point of the marriage ceremony and it continues to be practised. Even though many of the middle-class brides go to live in neolocal residential arrangements (apartments in high-rise buildings) after their wedding, the ritual of virilocality continues to make sense to all of the people involved.

This asymmetry, implicit in the terms and in the rituals, involves a directionality that is important in order to understand the relation between these three different types of property. The bridewealth goes to the bride's parents to compensate for her absence, the dowry is what she contributes to her new household, but the *tai2 gei2* is what she has as her very own. In Qing and Republican China, the bride's status in her new household depended on the nature of these payments. As Ruby Watson has stressed, 'the possession of a dowry was an important economic expression of the differences that set her apart from concubines and maids' (1991: 250).

It is interesting to note that the code of family law (*Direitos e Obrigações dos Chins de Macau com relação a alguns dos seus Usos e Costumes*) that the Portuguese Crown proclaimed for use with Chinese residents of the city in 1909[132] should begin precisely by contemplating the different nature of such payments, thus implying their centrality to the system. After two clauses setting the context, it states:

> Art. 3 – The husband may, without the wife's consent, dispose of his property and go to court, except if there is an antenuptial agreement stating the contrary.
>
> § 1 – The real estate part of the dowry is the couple's joint property; the husband may only dispose of this with the wife's consent.
>
> § 2 – The property entitled *T'ai-Ki*,[133] that is the jewels and clothes given by her father at the time of marriage, belongs to the wife alone, and she may dispose of it freely.
>
> § 3 – All other property is considered to be the husband's.
>
> § 4 – *T'ai-Ki* are all the items of property that the wife takes into the household, whether given by the father or acquired by her previous to marriage, to which there is no reference in the antenuptial agreement.
>
> Art. 4 – The husband is in charge of administering all the property belonging to the couple.
>
> § – The exception to this is the *T'ai-Ki* property, the administration of which belongs to the wife.
>
> Art. 5 – The couple may, by means of an antenuptial agreement, stipulate that the property that the wife takes into the household, as well as that which she may come to acquire in the course of the marriage, is administered by her.

In Portuguese law, the only legal term that exists for marriage transactions is 'dowry' (*dote*). Thus, the legislator's option was to omit bridewealth (as it has no effect after the marriage has taken place) and to treat *tai2 gei2* initially as if it were a part of the dowry (Art. 3, § 4), but then to differentiate it clearly (Art. 4, §). Ultimately, in practical terms, the difference between the three types of property emerges clearly. The bridewealth is a payment that compensates for the woman's transfer, so it has no implications during matrimony. The dowry (*ga3 jong1*) is a kind of devolution and corresponds to items that may have a productive value (such as real estate). It is the common property of the new couple. But the *tai2 gei2* is the wife's personal property that in a sense shields her, even if only partly, from the insecurity of her new situation.

Such a concept is totally strange to Portuguese law. Therefore, it comes as no surprise that the *Procurador* Pedro Nolasco da Silva and his friend, the gambling magnet, Lou Lim-Ioc – who were the principal members of the committee that drafted this code around the time when Camilo Pessanha judged the boy's kidnapping (cf. Chapter 5) – should have decided to leave this term in Chinese.

MATRIMONIAL INSECURITY

The conception of marriage underlying these practices is one which sees it as 'the acquisition of a woman who crosses over to live in her husband's family' (Chun 1996: 439). The major difference with Western Europe, thus, does not lie in the practice of virilocality: on the one hand, virilocality has been prevalent historically in parts of Western Europe and, on the other hand, neolocality has become a prestige option for middle-class couples today in East Asia. It would seem that the major difference lies in the founding role attributed to the couple in Western Europe. The image of the couple as the central reproductive nucleus of family life does not have the same appeal in China. Thus, the reproductive continuity of the family is seen to be based on men and not on women.[134]

Western legal codes presume that which we may call *stabilitas* following the Canon Law concept, as suggested by Philippe Ariès. According to this historian, 'the most important fact of the history of Western sexuality is the persistence throughout the centuries and up to the present day of a compulsive model of marriage – monogamous indissoluble marriage' (1983: 138). This model of marriage made its appearance in Western Europe between the ninth and the twelfth centuries. Until then, canonical prohibitions were mostly associated to incest (defined in very broad terms). *Stabilitas* (the word used by Canon Law for the indissolubility of marriage) was declared as universally applicable in the Fourth Council of Latran (1215) at the same time as the reduction in the incest prohibition from the seventh to the fourth degree (Ariès 1983: 145). The reinforcement of conjugality produced by *stabilitas* seems to have been contemporaneous with a weakening of the principle of descent and of the rules of exogamy that are associated with it.

It should come as no surprise, therefore, that whilst the codes of family law that were being written at the end of the nineteenth century by Portuguese legislators for use in Portugal were deeply inspired by the *stabilitas* tradition (cf. Pina-Cabral 1993), the *Usos e Costumes* freely contemplates both divorce and concubinage, reflecting the importance that such practices have in the Chinese system.

Art. 6 – The dissolution of the marriage can only be judicially declared at the husband's initiative in cases where the wife has committed adultery.

Art. 7 – The separation of residence and property [*separação de pessoas e bens*] may be judicially declared at the husband's initiative for any of the following reasons:

1st – Sterility of the woman, after thirty-five years of marriage;

2nd – Serious cruelty or insult;

3rd – Leprosy;

4th – Being a gossipy woman, prone to theft or to jealousy.

§ – Should the husband be a leper, the wife is also permitted to ask for judicial separation.

Art. 8 – In both the cases of dissolution and of separation, the children remain in the husband's care.

§ – In the case referred in § of Clause 7, the children remain with the wife.

Art. 9 – If dissolution or separation are declared, the wife only has the right to withdraw from the household her personal property.

Art. 10 – The husband may, both in the constancy of the matrimony and after its dissolution, take concubines.

Art. 11 – The children that the husband has of this concubine are in all ways equivalent to those of the legitimate wife.

Art. 12 – The concubine can only be repudiated under the same terms in which the husband can ask for dissolution of marriage or separation of residence and property. [cf. Art. 6 and 7]

Upon reading such a set of rules, one begins to look differently upon the way brides are decorated, with their forearms covered in gold bracelets. What at first seemed just another manifestation of *nouveau riche* brashness suddenly acquires a deeper meaning. Even when the heavy bracelets of soft yellow 24-carat gold are borrowed for the wedding – as apparently has been known to happen – they still represent the bride's father's desire to provide her with security in the face of divorce and abandonment.

There are no more concubines in South China. Macao's households are often neolocal and never polygynic. The women we met would never agree to their husbands bringing a rival into their homes. Furthermore, divorce can be declared both at the husband's and the wife's initiative and, at least in the case of educated middle-class women, it does not imply that women will be stigmatized or incapable of remarriage.

When I asked modern women about their *tai2 gei2* property, they usually smiled. Yes, they would show us the jewels that they had brought with them into the marriage, but these are not very significant today in financial terms. They are all working women whose monthly salaries over the course of time will amount to much more than any amount of gold bracelets in the bank safe.

And yet, when one starts to unravel the implications of the way in which these women formulated their personal interests, one suddenly becomes aware that, much as the 'habits of the heart' have changed in the intervening century since the *Usos e Costumes*, strong logics of continuity do exist.

> As with couples everywhere, matters of finance are a central topic of debate between our friends X and Y. They usually agree, but . . . Y is an educated professional. These days her salary is even marginally higher than X's income as a civil servant. He has less formal education, but he has been quite successful in getting qualified professionally in his line of work. Now, is it fair, he asks, that all the expenses of the house should come out of his earnings, whilst she pockets hers, contributing very little to the household? She counterargues smilingly: what sort of husband would he be, if he could not even provide for his own household? After all, whose household is it? Whose child is hers? In any case, she is not going anywhere with the money and it can only be good for her to save it, as it is extra security for her and their child. And he should not complain, because they eat most days at her parents' house, which represents a considerable saving. Later, he tells me on the side, that he knows she hands over money to her parents. She should not really do it, but as they can afford it, he chooses to ignore it.

We soon became aware that the matter of concubinage continues to be a very heated topic in the city. Our entrepreneur friends who have opened up businesses in Zhuhai, across the *Portas do Cerco*, told us that all their employees who earn above a certain amount are expected, as a matter of prestige, to acquire a second younger wife and to provide for her in separate domestic arrangements. Many of the 'astronauts' – who sent their wives and children to Canada, to the States or to Australia, as a form of security during the transition period – ended up having a secondary wife. Wealthy businessmen in Hong Kong and Macao whom we met confessed to having domestic set-ups in more than one city.

Thus, although co-residential polygamy has completely terminated and although, today as in the past, the legitimate wife usually manages to preserve primacy, a form of polygamy has continued to be prevalent. This form of polygamy implies new dangers for the wife. In the past, the children of the concubines also owed allegiance to the legitimate wife. Today they do not, so the husband's enthralment with a younger woman and her children may jeopardize the financial security of his legal household.

In Macao and Hong Kong, as well as in the nearby Special Economic Regions of Zhuhai and Shenzhen, there is a surfeit of young women looking for a *boon2 dei6* partner who can provide them with residence permits as well as with greater prosperity than is available to them in their rural areas of origin. He may even decide to divorce his wife – then she will be in a difficult situation, particularly if she is past her prime. We came across many cases of marriages which were kept together by the age-old threat of revenge suicide.

Women in mid-life are often quite bitter about this, being prone to portraying conjugal relations in an agonistic tone that, with the passing of the years, often tends to soften.

> W. is a secondary school history teacher – a handsome forty-year-old with two school-going children. She told my wife that she does not contribute any of her money into the house. She claims that it is her husband's responsibility to provide for his family – he is the man of the house. So she saves all her earnings and only uses some of it for extra expenses for her and her children when, for some reason, he cannot be persuaded to pay up. She keeps it in an account to which he has no access. She explains that husbands cannot be relied upon and that 'These days, whenever a man walks out of the house, you can't be sure that he will return.' All those younger women out there looking for a sugar daddy are a real temptation for middle-aged men like her own. She claims that she has not had any problems so far, but who knows what may happen? In principle, even if he found

another woman, this would still be his home, but will he be able to provide equally for both families? And, in the end, who lands up having the upper hand? The younger woman with whom he is infatuated will do everything she can to harm his first household.[135]

A Portuguese woman, who married a Macanese man in the 1960s, told me in a critical tone:

> When I arrived in 1963 I used to say with horror, 'Every time I go out, I learn of yet another man who has a second woman.' Yes, indeed, they had various, but they always carried out all of their duties. So, it was not noticeable, as he never let his children down. He might let the wife down, but never the children. The woman, in turn, due to her sense of shame, because of the way she had been educated, stayed at home, sad but submissive. All she ever did was frequent tea parties with the ladies. So, when I arrived here, there was a lady's society and a gentleman's society. [. . .] There was no shortage of family spirit at home. The men did what they could. New Year they stayed until midnight in one place and then they went to the other. I don't know how they managed, but they succeeded in being everywhere at once. As a matter of fact, there was an outward respect that, whilst being purely formal, nevertheless never harmed the children.

Beneath the kind of reckoning of interests discussed so far, there is a concept of the family that differs in significant ways from the Western European *stabilitas* model. Today as a century ago, 'The children that a man may have from [a concubine] are, in all matters, equivalent to those he has from the legitimate wife' (Art. 11). The implications of this are less of a legal nature than of a moral nature. Recent Portuguese legislation, for example, grants children out of wedlock that are duly declared (*perfilhados*) the same rights of inheritance as children of both spouses in wedlock. The concept of 'illegitimate child' has been legally prohibited. But, in fact, the concept continues to be implicit in the jurisprudence on the matter. It continues to provide an emotional structure to the family system. A father out of wedlock has less rights of paternity and his paternity is less clearly protected by the law than a father whose child was born in wedlock (cf. Pina-Cabral 1993).

In practical terms, this means that a Chinese wife cannot claim any special privilege for her children by comparison with the children her husband had out of wedlock. The latter are as much entitled to his favours and to the property of his household as her own children – even if there may be a differentiation in matters of prestige. The implications of such a difference from the Western European *stabilitas* tradition are hard to pinpoint if we try to generalize and describe them analytically but they are nevertheless easily perceived anecdotally in situations where they can be shown to provide the framework for emotional responses.

For example, a certain Macanese professional was married to an educated European woman. They were childless, so they adopted a niece of the wife. I had interviewed this man extensively concerning his family history and, out of respect for his primary wife, he had never told me about his secondary wife and their children. The European wife died of a tragic disease, which shook him very deeply. At the funeral, he was accompanied by his two sons, who took on the role of mourners, granting a secondary role to the niece. His second wife was also present and she too put on mourning attire. In Portugal, such a practice would have been considered deeply offensive – in Macao, even in a Portuguese-speaking Eurasian family, it was correctly understood as a sign of respect.

Thus, today as in the past, the essential prototypes that structure people's spontaneous understanding of family relations in Macao do not focus on the Western European (supposedly 'modern' and 'biological') image of the conjugal couple and child (Christ's Nativity Scene as the prototype of some sort of 'natural family' – but more on that later in this chapter). This has profound implications for people's sentiments of justice.

For example, a case was reported in the city's newspapers in the mid-1990s of a woman whose mutilated corpse was found floating in the sea. Ultimately no one was indicted for her death, but the newspapers clearly associated the murder with an inheritance dispute. Her father had died unexpectedly leaving a valuable piece of industrial real estate that was the family's principal source of revenue. She was the only daughter, so she declared herself sole heir. At this stage two young men appeared who claimed they were his sons from a secondary household. The mother and daughter responded in an emotional way, refusing to admit any rights of inheritance to these men of whose existence they were supposedly ignorant. The people with whom I debated the issue suggested that her death might somehow be associated to her half-brothers' feelings that she was denying them their legitimate rights.

WORKING WOMEN

These anecdotal instances clearly show the importance that extra-domestic paid employment has had in changing the condition of middle-class Macanese and Chinese women in the Territory. This was a widespread phenomenon in East Asia. Already in the mid-1980s, Barbara Ward claimed that 'Eastern girls are beginning to marry later and go to work earlier' (1985: 223). In fact, part of the approximation between the two ethnic groups that has occurred in the city since the caesura of the 1970s is tied up to the way in which the biographical profiles of marriageable women of both groups have tended to approximate to each other.

This tendency towards marrying later is associated with a more active female participation in the educational system. Since the 1950s, Chinese and Macanese parents have been led by economic and prestige considerations to further their daughters' schooling (cf. for Hong Kong, Ward 1985: 215). In the Macanese case this might have happened even earlier, as we found women of the declining generation (born in the 1920s and 1930s) that underwent university education.

Although we do not have figures to establish clearly the evolution of the female student population in the second half of the twentieth century, interviews with school teachers indicated that the situation is very similar to that of Hong Kong. Among the twenty-two Chinese families studied by Ng Chun-Hung in Hong Kong, there was no evidence of any difference in treatment between sons and daughters concerning education. Parents denied any kind of tendency to favour male education (1989: 13).

The study I carried out of Catholic marriages (cf. Chapter 8) indicated that age at marriage did indeed increase throughout the 1970s and 1980s for both Chinese and Macanese. As for extra-domestic employment, a major change seems to have taken place. Whilst the middle-class women of the declining generation[136] (born in the 1920s and 1930s) did not have a professional career, many of the women of the controlling generation (born in the 1940s and 1950s) had professional lives, and the majority of those of the emerging generation (born in the 1960s and 1970s) took it for granted that they would continue to engage in extra-domestic paid employment after getting married. The Territory's economic boom in the 1980s and early 1990s and the insecurity owing to the processes of transition to direct PRC rule encouraged this tendency, as people urgently felt the need to earn money as a source of security.

These tendencies are integrally associated with the reduction in the number of children per couple. It is common to associate this reduction with the birth policies of the PRC, but there is reason to believe that it would have occurred in any case. In fact, the Macanese family histories I carried out exemplify a similarly dramatic decrease in the number of children per couple at mid-century and the Macanese have never been subjected to PRC birth policies.

These changes occur concurrently and cannot be seen as independent factors. In fact, they are also related to class factors as Barbara Ward wisely noted:

> Where the women of the poorest classes work from necessity, those of the next higher income groups tend to stay at home, partly because domestic work demands their presence, partly because social prestige for their families may depend upon their being different in this respect from the poor. The upper strata that can afford to give their girls both education and freedom from domestic tasks can also afford to ignore this particular badge of social prestige. (1985: 222–3)

FILIAL DAUGHTERS

Looked at from our comparative perspective, two aspects of the narratives we have transcribed deserve to be singled out: these working women (a) use their salaries as a means of improving their condition (b) within contexts that are still ideologically framed in such a way as to presume women's subalternity. This emerges clearly even in cases where women have achieved a certain contentment and self-sufficiency.

> An older non-specialized worker at one of the government services in Macao once told us that she was almost certain that her husband suspected that she earned more than she declared to him, because people knew more or less the salary levels of civil servants. But he probably did not mind. In fact, all those years ago, when they were young and she received her first salary, she told him that she was going to receive less than she really did. Her mother was alive then and she felt she needed to help her. So, she put aside every month a small amount for her mother which he did not know about, as he probably would have thought that it was unfair to his family for her to hand over money to her parents. Since then, even although the mother has died, she kept up this lie. Now, even her children are grown up, but she feels that the money that she accumulated gives her greater independence. He works in the boats that cross between Hong Kong and Macao, so in all likelihood he has another younger wife in Hong Kong. But he never failed to bring his salary home and he treats her well and with respect, so she decided that she preferred not to know. She has become a very devout Buddhist, which keeps

her busy out of working hours – and even during work, she is often found reading devotional texts that she openly admits are a little beyond her understanding. But her master told her that, if she kept reading, she would eventually reach understanding.

When women talk of their practice of keeping money aside, they often frame the argument in terms of protecting their uterine families from male abandonment. But the truth is that the danger of men failing to protect their children is considerably less than that of failing to protect the abandoned wife. So it might be more profitable to see these practices rather as strategies of empowerment on the part of these women. They aim to counter the structural subalternity that they find at home in situations that, even though apparently neolocal, are conceived as being virilocal.

The matter of the relationship between the woman and her parents deserves particular attention here. Charles Stafford has provided us with the useful concept of the '*yang* cycle' to argue that what is at stake in Chinese family systems is the existence of 'cycles of mutual obligation between parents and children which centrally entail the transfer of money and the sharing of food' (2000: 42). Such is the situation in Macao. These women feel deeply the need to provide for their parents in some way.

On the one hand, this need is a sign that they want to affirm their personal value. By continuing to contribute towards their parents' well-being, they are performing the essential duties of 'filial piety' – those which, according to the Confucian *Analects,* are the very basis of human morality: 'in the complicated relations among men, filial piety forms the primary and most fundamental unit of mutual connection between two or more persons' (Hsieh 1967: 171). By managing to hand over money to their parents these women are affirming themselves as worthy according to their culture's primal standard of worthiness and, as such, are partially cancelling out their inborn impairment as women.[137]

K. is one of five sisters and one brother. She is thirty-eight years old. Both she and her older sisters have handed over their full salary to their parents ever since they started working. She said that she started out that way and that now she cannot do otherwise. So, whenever she needs money for herself she has to ask them for it. She admits that, as she grows older, the system is becoming increasingly inconvenient. The younger sister has started to work recently and they all advised her not to hand the full salary to the parents.

Nowadays, the parents do not need the money as much as they did when the eldest sister started working. In fact, K. has been doing two jobs for quite a few years. She claims that the parents do not know that the reason she leaves every night after dinner is that she goes to this other job. The money she earns there and that which she makes out of the classes she gives during weekends, she keeps for herself.

This narrative suggests that, should these women feel that they were being exploited by the parents, they would have the means of putting an end to this exploitation. Nevertheless, they go to considerable efforts in order to continue to provide for their parental household, even though they know that when they get married this money will not be returned to them and, in any case, eventually the brother will be the main heir. Their reward, however, is the worthiness they feel.

In comparison with Portuguese society, the most surprising aspect of these money transfers is the way in which parents boast of them publicly. When a son or daughter gives money to his or her father, the father publicizes the worthiness of his child. In Portugal, a son or daughter may well assist his or her parent financially, but this somehow diminishes the parents in their parental role as providers. It is something that must be done, but with circumspection, as it has two implications – filial love and parental failure. In fact, it would seem that the practice of contributing regularly towards the parents' household is far more prevalent among the Chinese than the Portuguese. In Hong Kong, for example, it is claimed that 65 per cent of the sons and 44 per cent of the daughters do so regularly (cf. King 1996: 268).

This is not the place to consider the momentous issue of the divergent attitudes towards money in post-Christian and post-Confucian societies. Rather, I would like to stress the fact that, much as nurture of children is paid back with nurture of old people in the *yang* cycle (Stafford 2000), the mutual obligations that are thus created are essentially asymmetrical. To return again to Sahlins' formulation, it is a redistributive and not a balanced reciprocity. In the words of John Haley, 'Those below owed filial piety and loyalty to those in authority who, in turn, owed benevolence as a reciprocal but not conditional social duty' (quoted in R. Smith 1996: 159).

Thus, we come to the second aspect of these women's narratives which deserves attention: the fact that, whilst wanting to affirm themselves publicly as filial children by making regular monetary contributions to their parents, they feel that they must hide this fact from their husbands. Often, as we have seen, it is an open secret that the husbands smilingly ignore. But other husbands have been known to protest. What must not be forgotten is that husbands also hand over money to their parents. More husbands do so than wives and they do it more regularly and in higher amounts.

Barbara Ward has claimed that modernity leads to a weakening of patrilineality and more balanced gender relations (1985: 255–60). Although in practical terms this seems to be true, the essential prototypes of familial association – the habits of the heart – have survived. Although middle-class working women have started to hand over money to their parents, and modern urban living allows for greater rates of neolocality (thus allowing for a reduction of tension between mother-in-law and daughter-in-law), the Chinese people of Macao remain attached to a notion of marriage as essentially virilocal. Working women have found one means of affirming themselves as worthy social subjects in the light of their society's major values, but the centrality of the image of agnatic filial piety as the most basic form of relatedness has not simply vanished.

DIVERGING DEVOLUTION

The various attempts I made at clarifying the issue of whether daughters do inherit or whether fathers are morally entitled to leave everything to one son were met with uncertain responses. People were eager to claim that they did not follow the old ways, but in many ways I could see that familial relations were marked by clear traditional characteristics. How come when two brothers were working in their father's factory, one was always clearly the boss and the other was his trusted employee? How come that money was so freely lent to a son to start a business, but the daughters had to work at night in order to pay for their university studies?

I have to confess that this situation surprised me less than it might have done had I not remembered what happened when I carried out fieldwork among rural folk in northern Portugal in the late 1970s. Then, when I asked about inheritance, I received very emphatic egalitarian responses. Later, however, when I managed to obtain detailed information about specific cases of property division, I realized that something else was happening, something that people were not capable of formulating in clear terms. In short, if some children had not been systematically favoured over others, the ideology of the 'house' (*casa*) would not be practically realized. The property of the house (which defined it symbolically and spatially) would have to be divided at each generation and each couple would land up forming a definitionally new 'house'. This, however, was not happening: 'houses' survived across generations as recognizable entities. A 'house' is not simply a building. It has a social presence that involves a name, prestige, a territory, cattle, etc. Eventually I worked out how this contradiction was resolved practically without people needing to go against their egalitarian principles. Parents felt that the child who stayed in the house and looked after them in their old age (usually a daughter and often a younger daughter) should be recompensed for her extra efforts on their behalf. Thus, she was usually granted that part of the parental patrimony that was symbolically and spatially more definitional of the house. In this way, the identity and basic sustainability of the main house was not jeopardized in the generational change (cf. Pina-Cabral 1986).

As far as the Macanese are concerned, I came to suspect that their responses to my questions were aimed more at 'representing themselves as modern subjects' than at 'representing their actual practices when confronted with inheritance situations'. When I asked if sons were favoured over daughters, the response was emphatically negative. However, the few cases of disputed inheritances that were reported to me suggested that, not only were sons favoured, but there was usually one son who was installed as the father's successor and who accrued greater benefits from the family's property base (whatever nature it might have had). Usually, but by no means always, this was the eldest son.

There was even a curious terminological pointer to this. In Portugal the words *mano* and *mana* (respectively male and female) are used reciprocally as qualifiers of any sibling, usually with the implication of emotional closeness. In Macao, however, reflecting Cantonese custom (*daai6 goh1*, lit. big brother), the term *mano* has a very specific local usage. It is not a reciprocal term and it applies, as a sort of title, only to the male firstborn of the siblings. When used by third parties it is qualified not by the person's first name, but by the family name: e.g. *o Mano Siqueira* or *o Mano Rodrigues*.

Among the Macanese, the term is particularly associated with men whose fathers died young leaving a large number of children and who functioned *in loco parentis* to their younger siblings. When it is an older sister who assumes this role, she might also be known as *Mana*.

Curiously, the conversations that we had with our Chinese friends were equally inconclusive. People did not seem to be clear about the issue of inheritance. Although the Chinese were more willing to admit that sons were favoured over daughters than were the Macanese, the fact is that they too denied that one might simply exclude daughters or younger sons.

This ambiguity is somewhat clarified by reading the *Usos e Costumes*. There the legislators are quite specific as to how inheritance should function among the Cantonese (interestingly, the code's application was restricted to the Chinese of the Two Kwangs, as it was believed that other provinces followed different customs, Art. 31).

First of all, 'Should there be no legitimate male descendants the Chinese must take on an adopted male' (Art. 13). Furthermore, bereaved parents must adopt a grandson to succeed a son who dies without descendants and similarly widows whose husbands had no sons must adopt a son (Art. 19). Then,

> Art. 22 – Succession by death of the parents only applies to male descendants.
>
> § 1 – The legitimate quota of the firstborn or of his representatives will be double of that of any of the other sons.
>
> § 2 – Single daughters do not inherit, but they do have the right of receiving a dowry, for their marriage trousseau, of a value equivalent to one fourth of the portion attributed to second-born sons.
>
> Art. 23 – The widow keeps the right to alimony until such time as she marries again.

In short, we may conclude that this was a system of diverging devolution (where males and females inherited) but one that favoured some children over others (cf. Goody 1990: 21–136). What this means is that when one asks people in Macao if one can leave everything to the eldest son or whether daughters may be excluded from inheritance, the response will be necessarily ambiguous. For, whilst both second-born sons and daughters are less favoured than first-born sons, neither are fully excluded. The old anthropological distinction between inheriting and succeeding can help us here: all children are heirs, but only some are successors.

I managed to obtain information from other sources that allows me to complement the interview material. The first source is a questionnaire applied by the Territory's Department of Census and Statistics to a 'representative sample' of the Chinese population of Macao in 1999[138] concerning the attitudes of the Chinese towards the judicial and police apparatuses. This was part of the effort systematically carried out in the last two decades of Portuguese administration to implement a system of justice based on the Portuguese legal tradition. In considering the results of this questionnaire, one must bear in mind, first, the distinction referred to above between representing oneself and representing one's likely actions when faced with a real situation; and, second, because of the ethnic complexity and judicial pluralism that characterizes the city, that the responses cannot always be interpreted as having the same meaning.

For example, when asked from whom they would seek help if they needed to resolve a conflict over division of an inheritance, 67 per cent of the respondents claimed that they would go to a lawyer. This seems a simple enough response, leading us to believe that people would eventually resolve their problems by having recourse to the courts and, thus, to the applicable legal codes. Does this imply that the Chinese of Macao are measuring the legitimacy of their family practices in accordance with the Portuguese Civil Code?

There is no simple answer to such a question. The role that a lawyer might play in such a situation is not at all straightforward and it seldom has to do with official judicial practice. In his study of the Territory's judicial system, Boaventura Sousa Santos states:

> The sociological characterization of the lawyers' practices of Macao is a complex task . . . [since their] activity bears a contradictory relation with the currently valid legal system, as it frequently occurs outside or only partially in connection to the latter. It must be stressed that the issue is not that illegality or paralegality are desired as such. Rather, an apparent or fictional legality is pragmatically created which, in Macao's sociological conditions, almost always functions as real legality.
>
> These two characteristics converge in the creation of something that may be termed 'lawyer's law' (*direito advocatício*) – a sort of parallel and unofficial legal system that constitutes one of the important dimensions of Macao's judicial pluralism. As it is a concurrent legal system, it 'runs' in parallel to the official legal system – at times nearer to it, at times more distant. Often, however, the two cross and combine giving rise to 'mixed formations', which are at times so complex that it becomes difficult to establish where the official system ends and the concurrent system starts. (1998: 362–3)

No wonder then that informants and respondents should be somewhat unclear as to the legal question of inheritance. In the questionnaire distributed by the Department of Census and Statistics, when asked whether a father is allowed 'to leave all of his patrimony to the eldest son', the responses were curiously divided: 42 per cent claimed that he is allowed, 57 per cent claimed that he is not. But when asked whether it is fair for a father to do so, the percentage of those who responded nega-tively (60 per cent) increased slightly.

When we cross the nature of these answers with the data characterizing the respondents, we discover that people with higher education are more prone to claiming that the father is legally allowed to leave all of his patrimony to one child. We have to presume that these are the ones that are better informed concerning the actual operation of Macao's judicial pluralism – as there is also a significant correlation with income level.

Curiously the differences between the answers to the two questions are more marked when we divide the respondents by gender. Whilst women are as prone as men to believing that society allows the father to leave all of his property to one son, there is a higher percentage of them that is opposed to it. In short, while only 55 per cent of the men oppose the system, roughly two-thirds of the women (64 per cent) do. I interpret this to mean that women feel more victimized by the system.

However, I managed to obtain information that allows us to lift the veil of Macao's paralegality somewhat and to judge the nature of the inheritance system as it really functions in Chinese homes.[139] The Portuguese legal system is strictly egalitarian and leaves very little leeway for parents who might want to manipulate it by means of a will. Now that the *Usos e Costumes* are no longer applied, Chinese residents should have been legally subject to such a system. In spite of the paralegality described above, the need to register property legally obliges the Chinese residents who own real estate or valuable commercial permits, to perform legal acts of inheritance. As the Administration began to operate in more modern and efficient ways in the 1980s, Portuguese courts became aware that either they resolved the issue expeditiously or they would be totally incapable of organizing modern registers of property.

The solution was interestingly contrary to the spirit of the law, which is to ensure 'fairness' in the distribution of the parental property. Portuguese Law contemplates the possibility of the division of property due to inheritance being carried out by means of a court inventory, both when there are minors among the heirs and when the division is litigious. Finally, it opens up the possibility of an Optional Inventory (*Inventário Facultativo*) should the heirs ask for one. Since procedures of this type are normally very expensive and may well take years if not decades to conclude, the option makes very little sense. Therefore, people almost never ask for it.

In Macao, however, the majority of legally registered acts of division of property due to inheritance are carried out by means of such a procedure. The system has been simplified and expedited to such an extent that the court delivers a decision in less than a month. The property values indicated in such cases are always purely symbolical and often the property remains undivided at the end of the process. In almost all of the cases, the heirs are jointly represented by only one lawyer who works for the family seniors (*gal jeung2*).[140] Normally the female heirs simply sign a blank slip of paper that is appended to the case and that supposedly proves that they have already received their share in cash. Such a system would be perfectly compatible with the *Usos e Costumes*, as women were supposed to receive their (much smaller) portion as dowry (Art. 22, § 2).

Eighty-five such optional inventories relative to the years 1990 to 1992 were studied. In practically all of the fifty-five cases where there were heirs of both sexes, there was clear evidence that female co-heirs had been excluded. Except in the cases where the mother was co-heir (and, upon her death, a similar procedure would have to be carried out), female heirs declared that they had already received their portion in cash. Interestingly, in the few cases where female co-heirs refused to sign the declaration and claimed their full share, they were found to be educated women who had lived abroad.

A cursory study was undertaken of a number of cases where the inventory was demanded by the judge as the result of declared conflict. These cases were the direct result either of the existence of a concubine of the deceased whom the children of the principal wife were trying to exclude or of a mother who tried to retain the control of the business against the successor's will.

CONCLUSION

In this chapter, I have discussed extensively two of the central links that constitute familial relations, the links of filiation and of conjugality, but nothing has been said of fraternal relations. Now, one central differentiating aspect of Chinese family in contrast with the Western European tradition is that, in China, these are not conceived in relation to an egalitarian ideal. On the contrary, a couple's offspring are markedly different from one another and the way families operate is based on that difference. Thus, daughters are different from sons; elder or dominant brothers are different from younger brothers; children of the first wife are different from those of the concubine; adopted sons have different rights from other sons.

A model of authority is deeply embedded in fraternal relations, having its clearest manifestation in the Confucian concept of 'fraternal submission' (cf. Hsieh 1967: 177ff.). I am not claiming, of course, that today's sisters or younger brothers in Macao are all necessarily submissive. What I am saying is that there is no presupposition of the desirability of equality between siblings as there is in Western Europe. This must be understood if we are to make sense of the processes of generational devolution that may be observed in many family firms. Time and again I encountered situations in Macao, Canton or Hong Kong of one brother succeeding the father as boss and the other brother (usually, but not always, the younger) operating as his trusted employee.

But the concept of fraternal submission is far more significant than this, since it functions as a major structuring metaphor of modern daily living, performing a central role in the attribution of meaning to the interpersonal relations of subjection and mutual support that are the very stuff of young male association – both in entrepreneurship and in youth gangs. The genetic link between familial feelings and political allegiance, which was drawn out by the neo-Confucians, has not simply vanished. The term for elder (dominant) brother (*daai6 goh1*) has an equally widespread usage to mean boss, chief or leader. The respective term for younger brother (*sai3 lo2*, lit. small fellow) again stresses the element of protection and submission. The brotherhood bond (of submission and mutual loyalty) is thus a major structuring element in the symbolic construction of the relations of male cooperation that are omnipresent in Cantonese daily living and economic relations.[141]

Such formulations of the essential links between human beings are not independent of the human beings in question. I mean that notions of the person and the processes of emotional constitution of the person, as were discussed in Chapter 5, are basically interdependent with the way in which the fundamental human links are formulated.

Modern as they indeed are, the Chinese of Macao structure their lives and experience their sentiments in relation to major prototypes of familial relations grounded on their cultural tradition. By dealing with representations of the past, people confirm and reconstruct prototypes of human relations that, whilst explicitly not referring to their present world, are still somehow seen as genetically related to it. The role played by historical fiction in this regard must not be understated. The importance of martial arts fiction in modern China is a clear example of this. The works of Louis Cha (Jin Yong), for instance, are clearly illustrative of such a process.

In turn, the appeal that certain images have to a particular public tells us much about the prototypes in reference to which they structure their experience. I would like to terminate this chapter by citing an example of this that I believe illustrates many of the issues so far discussed.

Macao has always been a commercial entrepot. Particularly during the 1990s, it functioned as an exit point for much of China's huge clandestine antique market. As such, walking the streets, you were bound to come across large numbers of all types of paintings, statuettes, engravings, ceramics, etc. My mother is an avid collector of Nativity Scenes (*Presépios*). She has collected hundreds of pieces from practically all over the world. When I go to foreign places, it is taken for granted that I will be on the look out for one for her. So, I went through numberless shops, workshops and storehouses trying to find an image that could, even if by approximation, approach the traditional Nativity triad of father, mother and child. It soon became clear to me that this particular image did not constitute a meaningful metaphor for the Chinese residents of the city. Nowhere was there one to be found.

There were images of Kun Yam[142] with a child – which, incidentally, forward-thinking nuns were using as substitutes for Our Lady in their missionary shrines in the poor quarters of the city. There were numerous representations of older men with male children and even with female children. And, of course, there was the lovers' theme that ranged from prudish manifestations to an inexhaustible variety of erotica. The only Nativity Scene that we managed to buy for my mother had been imported from the Philippines.

I am not claiming, of course, that no Chinese artist ever thought of painting a scene of a couple with their young child. All I am saying is that such an image appears not to have any special appeal to Chinese imaginations, so that even the many Chinese Catholics of the city do not seem to feel the need to represent their world by reference to such a pivotal image.

In the post-Christian world, representations of the 'nuclear family' in the form of the Christian Nativity triad are pervasive and have an appeal that is by no means limited to those who consider themselves to be actual believers in the Christian message. Our supermarkets at Christmas time are obvious proof of that.

I have often warned my students that one of the central teachings of the anthropology of kinship is the need to distance ourselves from the obviousness of the Nativity metaphor – that 'graphic proof' that nature and god jointly reveal that the father–mother–child unit is the essential element of human life.

As the years passed, I became increasingly certain that my difficulty in finding a Nativity Scene – which placed me in an unfilial situation every time my mother reminded me that, now that I was going to Macao again, I should remember to bring her a Chinese *Presépio* – was indeed something significant. It pointed to the fact that, for the post-Confucian imagination, conjugality is not the essential reproductive nucleus of the primary social unit. Rather, the father–child, and in a smaller way, the mother–child links – the links of filial piety – are the essential founding links.[143]

CHAPTER 10

TRIAD WARS AND THE END OF PORTUGUESE ADMINISTRATION

In 1987, Macao started preparing itself for the transition to direct Chinese rule. The Territory was undergoing an economic boom and the new population that had arrived from the Mainland in the late 1970s and early 1980s was starting to adapt to the city's more cosmopolitan ways. The first half of the 1990s was a heady period of excitement and prosperity, with an unprecedented building boom that saw the land surface of the Territory more than double due to new landfills. Casino business prospered tremendously with visitors coming increasingly from the Mainland and leaving behind vast amounts of their recently acquired earnings. In the VIP rooms enormous sums of money moved nightly across the tables, apparently coming from nowhere and going nowhere. There were baccarat tables where the minimum bet was HK$ 20 000 and the maximum bet HK$ 900 000. Chips of HK$ 1 000 were moved about in large heaps.

As the business of preparing for the transition was going ahead smoothly, with relations between Portugal and China at an all-time high, there were increasing signs of instability in the city's underworld. Things came to a head at the time of Hong Kong's troubled transition (July 1997) with the Asian economic crisis as its backdrop. Suddenly, the city found itself to be the battlefield of a major war between its various underworld elements. Furthermore, a media campaign led by the Hong Kong press catapulted this information into the global arena. Previously, Macao had only made its way into the international press as an exotic outpost – with 'seedy' and 'sleepy' as the favoured adjectives. Now, a rhetoric of fear with cinematic overtones became the dominant mode and any homicide was reported in the following day by Reuters and Xinhua. One of Macao's underworld leaders (Wan Kuok-koi) was even interviewed at length by *Newsweek* and *Time*; CNN and BBC considered it worthwhile posting his face in their Internet news pages.

Local police and government repeatedly insisted that the population need have no fear, as the events were clearly delimited to a settlement of accounts between gangland figures and did not affect the normal daily life of the city. But the Hong Kong press met these comments with derision, even though they were perfectly correct. All sorts of secondary actors entered into the fray, trying to cash in on the atmosphere of gloom: PRC military officials claimed that, if they had been ruling, law and order would have prevailed; local pro-China politicians used the occasion to argue that the death penalty was definitely required; local pro-democracy politicians blamed it on Portuguese and Chinese corruption; the Portuguese press had a field day, blaming everyone all round; the United States and the Australians declared Macao out of bounds for their naval personnel!

Finally, as the tension mounted, a tone of discomfort entered into the diplomatic relations between Portuguese and Chinese authorities. Previously, it had been established that no Chinese troops would be stationed in Macao after December 1999. The Chinese authorities, however, used the events as an occasion to declare unilaterally that they would station troops in Macao and, indeed, a few hours after the handover ceremonies were finished, Chinese troops did enter the city. By then, however, the whole storm had quietened down.

Clearly, by the time the most newsworthy gangster was sentenced (Wan Kuok-koi, 23/11/99, a month before the handover), a new balance had been reached between the underworld and the new authorities. In fact, at the height of his power, in 1997, this man had told reporters that, one way or another, the crisis in the gangland would be finished by December 1999 (*South China Morning Post*, 31/07/97).

This was not the first time that South China gangsters resolved their conflicts through a murderous turf war and it is unlikely to be the last. Nor was it the first time that such an event occurred in Macao even though it was not specific to the Territory. Indeed, the main protagonists had as many ties with Hong Kong and the People's Republic of China as with Macao. Furthermore, there are clear indications that the same protagonists were linked to scandals concerning casinos that erupted in the Philippines, Taiwan, Peking and Mongolia.

In the light of the Territory's history, however, the events that took place between the Hong Kong and the Macao handovers (1997–9) were more than a regular trial of forces in the underworld: they were yet another *incidente* – the last one to occur within Portuguese administration. For that reason they constitute a fitting theme to close the present book. In the first chapter, I argued that these recurrent crises of legitimacy were structurally linked to the basic contradiction between *rights of sovereignty* and *rights of citizenship* that has characterized the political history of the Territory. Did this contradiction simply vanish after the handover? I believe that the following analysis of the events shows that, whilst the principal forces involved in this structural contradiction have undergone a realignment, the basic imbalance will remain during the next fifty years of life of the Special Administrative Region of Macao.

Writing about events of this nature involves problems that demand that I should make a disclaimer at this point. Carrying out ethnographic research of the 'Triad Wars' as they occurred was not possible for obvious reasons. Thus, the information I managed to gather was mostly obtained through press reports – much of it, however, was further confirmed by information I gathered in the city in the late 1990s and in 2001.

Ironically, I was helped by the unusual interest that the Hong Kong press demonstrated in publicizing Macao's troubles during this period. Associating it with the reports provided by Macao's Portuguese-language newspapers, I acquired a rich supply of information that, once cross-checked and compiled, turned out to be far more systematic than at first seemed possible.

Thus, it should be made clear that, whilst I was careful to rely only on information that seemed trustworthy in the light of my knowledge of the city, and confirmed in terms of other sources, I seldom had the means to establish the absolute veracity of the newspaper reports upon which I based my account. At times, this was not important as, for example, when the very existence of a persistent rumour was of itself a significant event. At other times, it would have been desirable. Whenever the information seemed open to doubt, I made an effort to declare it so.

Within these limits, I believe the following synopsis of events is adequate. The truth, in any case, is that the portion of what happened that can be solidly proven by legal means is extraordinarily limited. Not a single one of the many murders perpetrated in the city during this time was finally proven in court, in spite of the Public Prosecutor's genuine efforts. When Wan Kuok-koi was forced out of action by being sentenced in November 1999, little more could be proven than that he had participated in organized crime. In the end, his actions turned out to be less significant than the fact that it was him to be imprisoned and not another one of the principal protagonists.

OUTLAWS OF THE MARSH

On 30 March 1962, at the Overseas Ministry in Lisbon, Stanley Ho signed the first of a series of contracts for the exclusive right to run Macao's casinos. On 18 May of the same year, he ceded the contract to the newly founded *Sociedade de Turismo e Diversões de Macau* – STDM – whose principal partner was Henry Fok (Huo Ying-dong). This retiring man, whose association with the Communist regime has been steadfast since the time of the Korean War, was destined to become fabulously rich and to play a central role as a tutelary figure in the handovers of both Hong Kong and Macao.

With Stanley Ho as its figurehead, STDM preserved its monopoly to the post-transition period. In July 1997, the month of Hong Kong's handover, STDM signed the last of its contracts with the Portuguese government. By agreement with the Chinese authorities, this contract will be valid until December 2001, two years beyond Macao's handover. Will it be renewed, will it be granted to someone else, or will the monopoly system be broken up – opening the ground for new entrepreneurs? This was perhaps the central question that fuelled the conflict that erupted in the Territory in the second half of the 1990s.

The control of Macao's gambling establishment is no small local matter. Indirectly it affects most of the gambling and underworld interests of China and Southeast Asia. Furthermore, whoever controls it can tap one of the greatest sources of easy fortune in the region. For example, the *Far Eastern Economic Review* states that 'Bankers who were given a rare look at STDM's accounts in 1986, when the company considered floating some shares of a related entity on the Stock Exchange of Hongkong, say that after Macau government levies, capital spending and recurrent overhead costs, the company's net income margin is 35–40%' (06/09/90, p. 60).

Macao's casinos are monitored by a Gambling Inspectorate. The inspectors are present in all rooms at all times, so as to make sure that the laws regulating casino business are followed. Their role is central in keeping casinos safe and comfortable, even though legality often seems to be interpreted here in a slightly less strict manner than might be the case elsewhere. Furthermore, the Territory has three other police forces, the PSP (Public Security Police), the Customs and Naval Police and the Judicial Police.[144] The disagreements between these different corporations seem to be endemic and they were part of what had to be addressed by the Administration, when the whole crisis erupted.[145]

Casino business is of necessity an activity that will spawn a whole series of marginal interests that are not amenable to absolute control. The borders between legality and illegality are all too easily overstepped. Money lending easily becomes loansharking, money spending becomes money laundering, prostitution becomes slavery, easy money leads to smuggling, drug peddling, arms dealing, etc. These activities cannot be simply ruled out, merely controlled.

In the course of the twentieth century, a *modus vivendi* was reached between the different actors involved: the Administration, the casino management, the Gambling Inspectorate, the various police forces and the various underworld interests. Furthermore, in the case of Macao, the powerful Chinese State across the paper-thin border and the underworld interests that it spawns, also necessarily became important local actors.

Macao's marginality in terms of its relation to State power means that, over the centuries, underworld interests have managed to find a safe haven there. I have referred earlier on to the Qing 'anti-pirate' campaigns at the turn of the eighteenth century (cf. Murray 1987 and Guimarães 1996). But in the 1920s and 1930s, for example, the South China Sea pirates were still using Macau as a port of rest (cf. Lilius 1991). Moreover, the city has always been an important platform for the Chinese secret societies, also known as 'triads', as was already evident in the days when Sun Yat-sen used it as a trampoline for his overseas travels (cf. Guedes 1991). It has been noted that these secret brotherhoods have historically been strongest where the Confucian state has been weakest (Ownby 1993: 16).

The most common Cantonese word to refer to these loose confederations of associates is *hak7 se5 wooi2* (lit. black or dark social organization or gathering). The alternative term 'triad' is the literal translation of *saam1 hap6 wooi2* (lit. three cooperating organizations) and carries with it the cosmological implication that heaven, earth and man are conjoined into a mystical whole. *Tin1 dei6 wooi2* (Mand. *Tiandihui*, lit. heaven–earth gathering) is supposed to have been the name of the mythical first sect legendarily associated with the Monastery of the Fighting Monks of Shaolin (cf. Ter Haar 1993: 153).

In fact, in Macao, we are not dealing with any very formal kind of organization, but rather with loosely connected groups of male (and to a lesser extent female) age-mates which tend to link up through relations of what we might call vassalage between leaders. There is a processual aspect in the formation of these networks. A group of youngsters (often gathering around a dragon dance society or a martial arts centre) will form relations of fictive brotherhood and accept the leadership of an 'elder brother'. By linking up with the leader of an older group, they will function as 'soldiers' to the older men and, at the same time, will be given opportunities to improve their condition. Some of these agglomerates can become very large. The largest in Macao, the 14K, was supposed to have at its disposal a number of men considerably superior to the 4500 security agents of the Administration in 1997. It is doubtful, however, whether all of these people ever responded in any ordered way to a single, unified leadership.

As David Ownby has demonstrated, this kind of organization functions due to the conjunction of three constituting elements that are traditionally present in Chinese culture: collaboration for mutual aid; fictive kinship; and the blood oath. The latter is probably the only ritual element of today's triads in Macao. As in the early modern cases referred to by this author, 'the blood oath both bound these young men to one another in the face of potential risk and perhaps made them appear more fearsome to outside groups' (1993: 47). Of itself, however, this oath is not specific to secret societies. In fact, the *Usos e Costumes* provides us with an example of an oath of the kind, with the corresponding Chinese text, to be used as a model in the Territory's courts.[146]

Both the authorities and STDM have learnt to cohabit with these groupings over the years. In fact, the normal condition of the city implies a kind of regularly recreated pact of invisibility. The Administration (and now the SAR Executive) cohabits easily with this alternative source of power, so long as it does not challenge the State's legitimacy by declaring itself too openly. This pact is, at times, negotiated frontally, as when the police call on the leaders of the triads to meet (such a meeting is supposed to have happened in the offices of the Public Security Police in July 1997, for example). Usually, however, the pact of invisibility is maintained by the informal but eager mediation of a large number of people in the city. In order to achieve their own private goals, they all contribute to the pact, each in his or her own capacity, by providing bridges between the legal world and the underworld: be they policemen, inspectors, businessmen, solicitors, lawyers or simply housewives.

If one does not happen to be one of its victims (for example, a prostitute who becomes a debt servant, a gambling debtor, a drug addict or an overzealous officer), the relationship functions admirably well, which explains why Macao's streets are normally so safe. When the peace was shattered in the mid-1990s and violence suddenly erupted in the streets, the surprise was all the greater for the previous invisibility of the danger.

The equilibrium with the authorities was based, in characteristic fashion, on an ethnic polarization. Most Portuguese people in Macao being civil servants, they were forbidden by law from gambling in the casinos, except for a few days around Chinese New Year. European visitors also seldom felt at ease in the seedy environment of Macao's casinos. Thus, they were kept out of the potentially violent implications of an involvement in gambling-associated activities. It was in everyone's interests to keep them out of the fray. Portuguese women repeatedly tell me that they find it safer to circulate at night in Macao than in Lisbon. For the Macanese, the boundary has never been quite as invisible and many of them made a living out of exploiting it.

Every once in a while one was reminded of the existence of this underworld by, for example, a news item reporting that a mutilated corpse with some pawnshop tickets in its coat pocket had been dredged out of the waters of the Delta or by discovering that someone, with a rather menial job, drove an excessively expensive car. Otherwise, the truce was only broken sporadically when a change in allegiances demanded a test of force.

Indeed, this sort of mutual dependence between the State administration and the secret sects is by no means unique to the Territory. Here, as elsewhere, the immutability of the centre turns out to be as apparent as the perishability of the margins (cf. Pina-Cabral 1999b). They are mutually dependent, not only in Macao, but in China as a whole. By making reference to the legendary origins of the triads, a kind of legitimacy is attributed to them, which allows for a certain amount of collaboration. This myth of origins, therefore, functions as a structure of symbolic mediation that validates the attribution of agency to the triads, even if in an ideologically reduced manner.

As the new 'one country, two systems' formula began to be implemented, the PRC authorities felt obliged to broadcast the fact that the transfer of power over Hong Kong did not jeopardize the triads – aiming, in this way, to neutralize possible feelings of mistrust over the handover. The press repeatedly quoted Deng Xiaoping's comment that the secret societies in Hong Kong were also 'patriotic' (e.g. *Sunday Times*, 30/08/97). Moreover, Wong Man-fong, a former Chinese diplomat in Hong Kong, is reported as having declared in May 1997 that he met with triad leaders before the signing of the Sino-British Agreement of 1984, to tell them that, if they did not disturb the stability of Hong Kong, the government would not spoil their business. Finally, in April 1993, the head of the Public Security Bureau, Tao Siju, told the press that some 'patriotic' triads might constitute excellent allies, as long as they showed concern for the stability and prosperity of Hong Kong (*Associated Press*, 14/05/97).

In the 1980s, as the economy of the Pearl River Delta boomed and China opened itself to outside influence, the nature of the clientele of Macao's casinos changed imperceptibly. By 1990, anyone who visited a casino could see that the traditional Hong Kong clientele was increasingly being crowded over by Mainland customers, recently arrived from across the border with pockets full of fresh money. A pale notion of the sheer size of the sums could be judged from the regularity of the corruption scandals involving Chinese officers and managers of public enterprises. In Guangdong Province alone, between 1991 and 1994, twenty people were sentenced, involving a total of RMB 80 million of public money. On one day, in November 1994, eight such convicts were executed in various courts of Guangdong (*Ou Mun Yat Pou*, 01/11/94).

From the second half of the 1980s to the early 1990s, Macao underwent a building boom that made absolutely no sense in terms of the city's planning and internal needs. It seems to have been a response to the need to circulate money. As casino business prospered and became more complex due to the increased pressure for various forms of money laundering, STDM found it expeditious to clear itself of the task of organizing these activities. Thus, at the time of the 1986 renegotiation of the contract (that led to the formation of the Orient Foundation), it started operating VIP rooms. Legally, it was forbidden to sub-contract casino space. In fact, however, this is exactly what was done with the Administration's discrete agreement. VIP rooms were sub-contracted to 'tour-operators' for a percentage of the casino's gains.[147]

Outwardly, the system is supposed to function in the following way. Tour operators invite players from abroad, all expenses paid and with a whole set of attractive perks. The player pays for his chips in the place of origin. These chips cannot be cashed, but played only, so that the gamblers can only cash the chips they win over and above the original batch. In this way, they cannot stop playing before they lose all of the original chips. Junket chips are colour coded so that they can only be used in the VIP room sub-contracted to whoever sold them, thus ensuring the operator's earnings.

The system was particularly useful for people who, in this way, paid money in one country and received unimpeachable cash in another country. Recently, Xinhua reported a case that exemplifies the sort of uses to which this system can be put. A member of the municipal government of a northern Chinese city was seen to spend vast sums of money in Macao's casinos. Upon investigation it was discovered that the money did not originate in the public purse, as was at first thought, but corresponded to corruption payments made by underworld elements to a number of his city's top officers. These were being laundered and then re-invested in real estate before being pulled out of Macao (*Ponto Final*, 09/01/01).

As the amounts of money that crossed the tables were very large, the system could be a cover for all sorts of activities of this nature. For instance, in 1998, the *Camberra Times* complained that dirty money was brought to Macao from Hong Kong by courier. He changed it into chips and proceeded to lose some of it in a VIP room, after which he cashed it all and received a cheque that could be safely deposited anywhere in the world (quoted in *Ponto Final*, 25/09/98).

When, in late 1995 and early 1996, Macao's underworld became increasingly unstable, newspapers were keen to insist that this was a 'turf war'. Profits were reduced due to the Asian economic crisis[148] and to the ensuing collapse of the badly overbloated real estate market of Macao and so the thugs were battling with each other for profits. Another theory was that gangsters were escaping from Hong Kong, now that it was going to become a Special Autonomous Region, and were coming to Macao. In fact, as time passed, it became increasingly apparent that these were excessively partial explanations and that the implications of what was happening were far more wide ranging, involving a whole restructuring of the major equilibrium of forces at play in South China.

A SYNOPSIS OF THE TRIAD WARS

Ng 'Kai-si' Wai was one of the pioneers in running VIP rooms. He is known as 'Kai-si' (lit. market) Wai, because he started his life working the protection racket in Mongkok Market in Hong Kong. In the mid-1980s, when STDM made an agreement with the Marcos administration to develop casinos in the Philippines, he moved over there. He came back in 1987 in the company of a Chinese Mainland woman, Si Tou Iok Lin, who also played an important part in later events (*Ponto Final*, 10/05/98).

In order to control the VIP room business, 'Kai-si' Wai made a partnership with Wan Kuok-koi, better known as 'Bang Nga' (lit. broken tooth) Koi. The latter was a rising star in Macao's biggest triad, the 14K.[149] This man is an uncharacteristically boisterous figure, clearly possessing considerable personal charisma, which makes him capable of charming his opponents. One of the officers of the Judicial Police involved in capturing him in the 1970s, Arturo Chiang Calderon, later became his trusted advisor and strategist; and the Director of the Central Prison where he was held, José Redinha, later became his personal lawyer.

'Kai-si' Wai and 'Bang Nga' Koi joined forces in order to push out Mo Peng Deng, then leader of 14K. The last years of the 1980s were a heady period and 'Bang Nga' Koi's power as leader of the largest group of young armed men in the Territory was growing steadily. His tendency to indulge his showy side provoked a strong dislike for him on the part of the other more traditional leaders of the underworld and the casino business.

By 1990, however, there were signs that external elements were pressing in on the Macao turf. In 1993, a triad leader from Hong Kong was killed during the Grand Prix, indicating that the field of allegiances was moving. 'Kai-si' Wai became increasingly involved with Mainland interests associated with military circles. In fact, he made considerable investments in Peking and Si Tou Iok Lin went so far as to open a showy casino near the capital.[150] This distanced him from local triad interests and, as a result, in 1995, 'Kai-si' Wai is rumoured to have broken up relations with 'Bang Nga' Koi.

Newspapers reported that, sensing problems were looming ahead, Macao's Public Security Police organized a meeting between the four main triad leaders of the Territory in order to discuss with them the best way to combat the entry into Macao of organized crime from Mainland China and Taiwan (July 1995). Allegedly, a short-lived alliance called the 'Group of Four United' was then created. It would seem, however, that the different security forces were not cooperating. One month later, the Gambling Inspectorate gave signs of taking a biased view on the issue by banning 'Bang Nga' Koi from entering Macao's casinos.

The first public sign that a violent struggle was about to take place was the explosion of a bomb outside Grandview Hotel, Taipa, in January 1996. This hotel was owned by a certain *Anran (At Peace) Co.*, which newspapers associated with China's Ministry of Public Security (MSP). Furthermore, STDM was also changing its policy, as Stanley Ho's relations with Peking began to improve. Allegedly under the influence of one of its female partners – a former ballet dancer from Mainland China – STDM began encouraging 'tour operators' from outside Macao to bid for its VIP rooms (*ASIA, Inc.*, August 1997). One of STDM's Public Relations officers was murdered as he was returning to Macao from Zhuhai (the Special Economic Region, immediately to the north of Macao) in November 1996.

For the first time since anyone could remember, Portuguese members of the Administration were now openly involved in the fray. In April 1996, the Undersecretary for Security was publicly gravely humiliated as he was leaving a restaurant with his wife. In October of the same year, there was a bomb threat at the hotel where the wife of the President of the Republic of Portugal was staying. Finally, in November 1966, Manuel António Apolinário, a Vice-Director of the Gambling Inspectorate (earlier head of the Judicial Police) barely survived a murder attempt. Newspapers openly laid the blame on 'Bang Nga' Koi and the police suggested as much, arguing that it was vengeance for having improved casino security. In the years that followed, however, this thesis became less and less probable.

A struggle between 'Bang Nga' Koi's 14K men and the groups associated with the second most important triad – Sui Fong[151] – led to a number of very publicized murders. In December, 'Bang Nga' Koi was detained for questioning and later released. He received a three-year suspended sentence for having failed to respect the court order to keep out of casinos. At that time, he seemed to have outsmarted 'Kai-si' Wai in the control of the VIP rooms and the Sui Fong leader was on the run in Vancouver. He had clearly won the first round. Early in December he even gave an interview at Macao airport – a most unusual step.

At about this time, government and military elements of the People's Republic began putting pressure on the Administration of the Territory, making allegations that crime was out of control in Macao. Indeed, in 1996, there had been twenty-one triad-related murders, an enormously high figure compared with Macao's usual records. Stanley Ho reacted telling the press that things were so badly out of control that they could only improve with the introduction of the death penalty. This being one of the touchiest points of dispute between the Portuguese and the Chinese governments, a matter on which the earlier always stood firm, the meaning of this statement could hardly escape notice.

In the early months of 1997, as the countdown for Hong Kong's handover progressed, all hell broke loose in the streets of Macao. This was a war which took advantage of all the accoutrements of modern filmic chivalry: murders were executed by pillion riders on fast motorbikes or by hitmen covered with black helmets who calmly entered restaurants with pistols ablaze in both hands; shops were attacked by throwing burning motorcycles running at full speed through their front doors; youngsters at games arcades were attacked by helmeted figures carrying heavy chopping knives; cars were set on fire; people were shot as they stepped out of the lift; bombs exploded in the garden of the

Government Palace; police barricades were crashed into; dozens of parked motorcycles were set on fire simultaneously in various spots in the city. Most of the armament and ammunition used in these attacks was Chinese military issue and the hitmen reportedly came from across the border, did their worst and immediately returned to China.

Even though he was at the peak of his power, 'Bang Nga' Koi's visibility made him a particularly easy target for blame. Mainland police issued a warrant against him. Hong Kong police declared a ban on 'suspected gang members entering Hong Kong from Macao' and the courts of Macao also issued an arrest warrant against him. He was forced to leave the Territory, only to return at the end of July 1997, after a Portuguese judge dropped his arrest warrant under rather surprising circumstances.

In the meantime, during his absence, 'Kai-si' Wai attempted to oust his followers from the VIP rooms they controlled by bringing in Hong Kong gangsters faithful to himself. He is said to have made a deal with the Sui Fong triad which rekindled the fight with 'Bang Nga' Koi's 14K men. 'Kai-si' Wai's new casino, the New Century Hotel, was ready to be inaugurated. However, its launch ceremony in August 1997 was marred by fear of what 'Bang Nga' Koi's men might do. Newspapers reported that 'Kai-si' Wai's life was threatened and that the hotel was like a bunker, heavily guarded by ex-army types specially brought out from China.[152]

Two days after the bungled inauguration ceremony, newspapers reported that Peking's Public Security Bureau (PSB) had sent an order to hunt down 'Bang Nga' Koi. Ten days later a warrant was issued by the Guangdong branch of the PSB in Taishan. However, by September this warrant too had been dropped, as the judge that pronounced it was found to be involved in the 'corruption' scandal that surrounded the closing of Si Tou Iok Lin's casino in Peking.

'Bang Nga' Koi's public visibility was constantly on the increase even though there were signs that his control over his own men was slipping. *Newsweek* and *Time* magazines published lengthy articles on him and the film telling his life story that he had commissioned from a popular Hong Kong film crew was ready to be launched.

The fighting continued in the streets of Macao, involving the murder of three police officers between September 1997 and April 1998. This deeply disturbed the Administration and fuelled the claims on the part of Mainland authorities that 'stronger measures' were needed. From March to July 1998 a guarded media battle took place between the PRC and Macao's Administration concerning the responsibility for events.

The former accused the Territory's police and judiciary of being incapable of controlling events, whilst the latter responded that the greatest problems came from across the border. It soon became clear that what was at stake was a posturing concerning the role of the Chinese military in Macao after the handover.

On 1 May 1998 something happened that considerably altered the course of events. A bomb exploded under the car of the Director of the Judicial Police whilst he was out jogging, in conditions that were never clarified, remaining highly suspicious to this day. Blame was immediately placed on 'Bang Nga' Koi and was used as an excuse to arrest him. In fact, a few months later, police came to corroborate his statement that he had nothing to do with it.

That evening, the Judicial Police carried out a television-style raid, with the cameras of the international media clicking around them, as they arrested 'Bang Nga' Koi in a restaurant of Macao's main casino, where he had gone to watch an interview of himself on Hong Kong's TVB. The film of his life story had its première, five days later. This man's impact on the Territory was clearly tremendous. The Acting Director of the Prison resigned, so as not to be forced to impose special high-security regulations. A former head of the Public Security Police, who had remained behind in Macao as a consultant, decided to return to Portugal in order not to be forced to turn witness against him, according to newspaper reports.

After his capture, criminal activities increased again with enormous violence. Slowly, however, as events unfolded, suspicion started to mount that he and his followers were being used as scapegoats and were not necessarily responsible for all the havoc that was taking place.

At the end of May 1998, the leadership of the municipality of Zhuhai was changed in order to bring it closer to Chinese military circles. By July there were signs that the collaboration between the different defence forces of the Territory and China's Ministry of Public Security had improved. A number of 'liaison officers' and 'experts' were now working in the Territory. On 18 September, at the start of the 3rd Plenary Session of the Macao Special Administrative Region Organizing Committee, Vice-Premier Qian Qichen declared that a small garrison would be stationed in Macao after the handover as 'a symbol of China's sovereignty' and in order to help with 'security problems'. This ran counter to explicit earlier agreements between Portugal and China that had been publicly confirmed by Lu Ping in 1997. The Portuguese side manifested surprise but without great vehemence.

At the end of September, STDM invited the People's Liberation Army military band to Macao, thus signalling their agreement with the new *status quo*. By October there were signs that cooperation between the Chinese and Macao defence forces had been reinforced and the Ministry of Public Security launched a major 'land and sea anti-crime drill' involving over 1000 men in Zhuhai.

'Bang Nga' Koi's closest supporters were picked out one by one, killed by other gangs or captured by the police. In November 1998 his considerable financial assets were frozen by the court. By that time, newspapers reported that there were indications of an internecine struggle within 14K. In March 1999, there was an attempt to pass judgment on 'Bang Nga' Koi, but his case was adjourned and the judge returned to Portugal. Finally, four weeks before the handover (23 November 1999), he was sentenced to fifteen years' imprisonment, his huge assets were confiscated and his main supporters were also sentenced.

In 1999, police reported thirty-seven homicides. However, in the first ten months of 2000, there were only seven homicides in the city. It would seem that, with 'Bang Nga' Koi sentenced and the People's Liberation Army in occupation, the pre-1995 calm had returned to the city, as 'Bang Nga' Koi himself had predicted in 1997.

According to a White House report on criminality divulged by newspapers in January 2001 (cf. *Ponto Final*, 09/01/01), the Triad Wars resulted in a generational change in the gangland and in a scattering of allegiances. The effect of this was that Macao's underworld was split into a series of smaller groups and that it was penetrated by new interests coming across from the Mainland.

THE TRIAD WARS AS AN *INCIDENTE*

It might be argued that a crisis of this nature was inevitable. Two factors contributed to make it more violent. First, the Asian economic crisis and Zhu Rongzi's government's response to it of tightening the internal credit facilities to prevent a devaluation of currency and second, the fact that STDM's monopoly was put into question.

Throughout the 1980s, STDM had been a major driving force behind Macao's economy and its relationship with the main interest groups in the Territory had been on the whole pacific. After 1986/7, with the subcontracting of the VIP rooms and with gambling profits rising sky high, the system slowly began to change. Clearly, the monopoly situation was no longer, strictly speaking, being enforced and other groups were asking for a larger share of the profits. In July 1996, 'Bang Nga' Koi is said to have attempted to convene the 'Group of Four United' to do just this.

In July 1997 (twenty days after the Hong Kong handover), STDM signed another contract that carried its monopoly across the 1999 handover until December 2001. Nevertheless, by then, it was clear to everyone in the city that other interests were claiming a share of the profits of Macao's gambling. Stanley Ho's public attitude suggests that STDM had come to accept this. By the time the Triad War ended, the local interests most opposed to this arrangement – represented by 'Bang Nga' Koi – had been pushed aside.

Early in 2001, the government of the Special Administrative Region indicated that it had decided to renew STDM's contract in 2001 but without the exclusivity. New entrepreneurs, therefore, will be allowed into the terrain (*Diário de Notícias*, 07/02/01). According to local reports, however, the PRC leadership, in its drive against corruption and in order to preserve Macao's autonomy, is supposed to have given indications that, at least formally, these will have to be headed by local Macao capitalists.

This war was the last *incidente* in Portuguese-administered Macao. As with previous *incidentes*, it was a crisis in political legitimacy and its resolution demanded a local realignment of forces. In many ways, however, the main protagonists had changed. What was at stake here was no longer the traditional confrontation between Portuguese and Chinese interests, with the Macanese operating as a margin for negotiation. Even though the Portuguese Administration was being slandered by the press for being incapable of controlling the city's criminality, they only played a secondary role in this drama. The main protagonists were now, on the one hand, the local Chinese – the *boon2 dei6 yan4* – and, on the other, the people in control of the PRC.

Thus, it would seem that the opposition between *rights of sovereignty* and *rights of citizenship* that I proposed at the beginning of this book can still describe the operation of this conflict. Whilst the PRC and the people who are close to its centre have the ultimate capacity to control the city (and this is clearly stated by the presence of the military), the local people have the right to run the Territory and hold the privilege of benefiting from its exceptionality. In the 1950s, for example, Zhou Enlai had used Macao as a means of breaking the UN blockade and had prevented the Portuguese from celebrating their colonial presence as they wanted (cf. Chapter 6). In this *incidente* the Mainland determined that the profits from the exploitation of gambling must be distributed more widely. In both instances, however, as again in all the other major *incidentes* in Macao's history, the Chinese State stopped short of destroying Macao's 'special' status, giving clear signs that it considers the Territory's autonomy a valuable asset.

In July 2000, the city again erupted, this time in a smaller *incidente*, which seems to have been easily controlled and eventually resolved. This time, however, the Hong Kong press was totally silent about it, even though there were police in the streets fighting against demonstrators (*Ponto Final*, 11/07/00). There were strikes and manifestations against the importation of cheap labour from across the border at a time when unemployment in the city was relatively high. This *incidente* is significant for our argument, because it corroborates the opinions expressed earlier that the field of ethnic differentiation in Macao is changing and that the opposition between *boon dei yan* and Mainland Chinese is becoming increasingly consolidated in ethnic terms. In this sense, the Macanese no longer function as a third force, but seem to have become part of the *boon dei yan*.

CONCLUSION

Historically Macao has functioned as a sort of rearwindow to the Empire of the Centre. Although it is not unique in performing this function, it has done so longer and more continuously than any other place. Thus, in this book, we have looked at China from its margins.

As the Triad Wars *incidente* clearly demonstrates, the Chinese State, like any other system, does not constitute a coherent, self-sufficient, rectified entity. On the contrary, the system only finds its capacity for survival (its fertility, so to speak) in a relationship with its margins. This is a contradictory relationship of recurrent appropriation and suppression, which questions the system's own systematicity.

Elsewhere, I have argued that 'we must adopt a view of sociocultural life as a field of negotiation of meanings which is only partially structured by the greater legitimation of some agents and some cultural artefacts'. In line with this, then, marginality must be seen 'as the basic condition of social and cultural relations, whilst centrality is something constructed and delimited, constantly at risk of being dethroned' (1999b: 47).

Centrality – understood as the condition of hegemonic agents – is never absolute. All centres have other centres within them; and all centres are only partly and passingly so. Whilst permanently working at silencing the margins in order to strengthen their hegemonic condition, the agents of centrality are constantly having to engage the margins. Otherwise centrality would not manage to survive.

Modern social theory has inherited a view of sociocultural life that emphasizes structure, orderliness, coherence and definite meaning. This has proved to be a major hindrance to understanding. We have inherited a view of sociocultural relations that opposes marginality to centrality. This, however, seems incorrect in the light of the phenomena we have studied in this book. Rather, marginality must be seen as the basic condition of sociocultural life, whilst centrality is never completely achieved and is always temporary.

The logical contrary of centrality, thus, is not marginality but *anomie* – an equally unrealistic condition of normlessness, of absolute breakdown of standards and values. Now, it can be argued that humans are endowed with a disposition to believe that other humans make sense (a corollary of Donald Davidson's notion of 'interpretative charity' [1984: 197–8 and 2001: 211]). Thus, much as centrality is always an ideal and never an absolute condition, so is anomie always a phantasmagoria.

I believe that part of the reason why we find it so difficult to abandon a sociocentric view is that it is deeply implanted within the very analytical concepts we inherited from modern socio-scientific discourse. In this book, I have consciously explored a series of concepts – such as 'paradox', 'equivocal compatiblity', 'organized amnesia', 'identitary ambiguity', 'embarrassment of limits', 'self-betraying stratification', 'correlate asymmetry', 'habits of the heart' – which I consider useful both to describe the situations which we traditionally treat as 'marginal' and to help us see that 'marginality' is in fact the basic condition of all social existence.

Thus, from this perspective, Macao is not as exceptional as at first it might seem. Being in the margins of both China and Europe, Macao becomes an expeditious example for the study of a more general condition of all sociocultural life.

APPENDIX

GOVERNOR'S TELEGRAM CONCERNING STATUES
(Cf. Chapters 4 and 6)

Secret telegram from General José Manuel Nobre de Carvalho (Governor of Macau 1966–74) to Dr J. M. da Silva Cunha (Overseas Minister of Salazar 1965–73) sent and received on 15 March 1967, reference number 95 SEC, subject-matter heading 'Statue Coronel Mesquita'.[153] Author's translation:

> In reference to [telegram] 78 SEC, I inform Your Excellency that Macau has witnessed in the course of its history a repetition of events of a politico-social nature. Thus, it has also witnessed very special facts concerning statues, as was observed in [telegram] 36 SEC of 4 November 1955 and [telegram] 1 SEC of 12 January 1956, from this Government. The installation of the statue of *Cristo Rei* referred to in 1 SEC was not followed through and its pedestal was also destroyed. A few years ago, the figures of Chinese men thrown to the ground under the horse of the statue of Ferreira do Amaral were also removed. The statue of Coronel Mesquita, hero of [Fort] *Pantaleão* on Chinese territory, was also initially meant to be placed near the *Portas do Cerco*. Due to Chinese pressure the idea was abandoned and later it was placed near the Leal Senado where it stayed. I fully agree with the opinions expressed in Your Excellency's 78 SEC but the matter has to be very carefully considered and we have to wait, as Your Excellency says, for a more opportune moment. Right now, it is not easy to tell when this will be.

GLOSSARY OF CANTONESE WORDS

Cantonese terms have been transcribed using Sidney Lau's system of romanization (without indication of derived tones – cf. Lau 1977). Mandarin terms (*putonghua*, the official language of the People's Republic of China) have been written in the officially recognized *pinyin* system. The characters provided in this glossary are written in the non-simplified version of Chinese writing used in the Territory.

Cantonese is a tonal language that has six basic tones. In Sidney Lau's system these are indicated in the following way: 1 = high falling; 2 = middle rising; 3 = middle level; 4 = low falling; 5 = low rising; 6 = low level. Further complexities do exist (such as clipped tones and derived tones), but they have been simplified in this book as they do not affect the understanding of the word.

白鴿票	*baak6 gap3 piu3* (lit. white pigeon ticket) – a type of lottery
百家姓	*baak3 ga1 seng3* – the hundred most frequent Chinese surnames
本地人	*boon2 dei6 yan4* (Mand. *bendiren*) – local people
沉迷	*cham4 mai4* (lit. sink into obsession) – addiction
娶	*chui2* – to take a wife
大哥	*daai6 goh1* (lit. big brother) – elder brother, boss, leader
大細	*daai6 sai3* (lit. big small, Mand. *daxiao*) – game played with three dice
蛋家	*daan6 ga1* (Port. *Tancareiros*) – Tanka, fishing folk
賭	*do2* – to gamble
番攤	*faan1 taan1* – (Port./Eng. *fantan*) – a game played with buttons

GLOSSARY OF CANTONESE WORDS

快艇	*faai3 teng5* (Port. *faitiões*) – fast transport boats
風水	*fung1 sui2* (lit. wind and water) – geomancy
嫁	*ga3* – to get married (for a woman)
家長	*ga1 jeung2* – family seniors
嫁妝	*ga3 jong1* (lit. marriage property) – dowry
街坊會	*gaai1 fong1 wooi2* – neighbourhood associations
拐子佬	*gwaai2 ji2 lo2* (lit. child snatcher) – kidnappers of children
鬼	*gwai2* (Mand. *kuei*) – soul, ghost
鬼佬	*gwai2 lo2* (lit. ghost fellow) – European foreigners
字花	*ji6 fa1* (lit. character flower) – a type of lottery
佐堂	*joh2 tong4* (Port. *tso-tang,* Mand. *zhotang*) – assistant mandarin resident in Macao
爛賭鬼	*laan6 do2 gwai2* (lit. fellow rotten with *do2*) – compulsive gambler
禮金	*lai5 gam1* (lit. courtesy or ceremony gold) – bridewealth
利是	*lei6 si6* – red envelopes for money gifts
靈魂	*ling4* or *ling4 wan4* (Mand. *linghun*) – soul, spirit/power
奴婢	*lo4 pei5* – female slave
賣身契	*maai6 san1 kai3* (lit. sell body deed) – receipt for purchase of persons
民族	*man4 juk6* (Mand. *minzu*) – 'nationalities', officially recognized ethnic groups
妹仔	*mooi6 jai2* – a young girl who is purchased in order to work for her master or mistress and whose future husband must pay a brideprice to her master
南洋人	*Naam4 Yeung4 yan4* (lit. South Seas people) – Chinese migrants from Southeast Asia
澳門	*O3 Moon4* (lit. bay gate) – Macao
澳門街	*O3 Moon4 Gaai1* (lit. Macao road) – Macao's Chinese quarter, the old bazaar
澳門人	*O3 Moon4 yan4* – Macao resident
魄	*paak3* (Mand. *po*) – soul, 'the animal or inferior soul; the animal or sentient life which pertains to the body' (Lau 1997: 642)

GLOSSARY OF CANTONESE WORDS

琵琶仔	*pei4 pa4 jai2* – a young musician being initiated into prostitution
舖票	*po3 piu3* (lit. shop ticket) – a type of lottery
山票	*saan1 piu3* (lit. mountain ticket) – a type of lottery
神	*san4* (Mand. *shen*) – soul, spirit, deity, fairy, immortal
細佬	*sai3 lo2* (lit. small fellow) – younger brother, junior associate
私己	*si1 gei2* (lit. [for] private self) – property belonging personally to the bride
體己	*tai2 gei2* (lit. [for] own body) – property belonging personally to the bride
土生仔	*to2 saang1 jai2* (lit. land-born child) – Macanese, Macao's Eurasians
颱風	*toi3 fung1* – typhoon
銅馬像	*tung4 ma5 jeung6* (lit. bronze horse statue) – equestrian statue of Ferreira do Amaral
玩	*waan2* – to engage in 'healthy' recreational games in sociable contexts
闈姓	*wai4 seng3* (lit. examination compound and family name, Mand. *wei xing*) – a type of lottery, *vaeseng*
會	*wooi2* – gathering or association
黑社會	*hak1 se5 wooi2* (lit. black or dark social organization or gathering) – secret society
三合會	*saam1 hap9 wooi2* – triad
天地會	*Tin1 Dei6 Wooi2* – Heaven and Earth Society
陰	*yam1* – shadow, (yin) female, negative principle in nature
飲茶	*yam2 cha4* – drink tea, go to a *dim sum* restaurant
陽	*yeung4* – sun, (yang) male, positive principle in nature

NOTES

CHAPTER I. MACAO BAMBOO

1. The word is apposite – after all it was invented there, denouncing the Malay influence that characterized the *patuá*, the local Creole dialect: '**man.da.rin** n [Pg *mandarin*, fr. Malay *menteri*, fr. Skt *mantrin* counsellor, fr. *mantra* counsel – more at mantra] (1589) **1 a**: a public official in the Chinese Empire of any of nine superior grades **b** (1): a pedantic official (2): bureaucrat **c**: a person of position and influence often in intellectual or literary circles; esp: an elder and often traditionalist or reactionary member of such a circle **2** cap **a**: a form of spoken Chinese used by the court and the official classes of the Empire **b**: the group of closely related Chinese dialects that are spoken in about four-fifths of the country and have a standard variety centering about Beijing' (*Merriam-Webster's Collegiate Dictionary*).
2. The usual problem of transcription of Chinese words and names was solved in the following way: (a) for personal names, the most common public version was used (for example, Mao Tse-tung but Deng Xiaoping) – the common practice of transferring the names of Cantonese people into Mandarin was systematically avoided; (b) for place names that have become part of European languages, the English spelling was used (for example, Peking and Macao); (c) for place names in Guangdong Province, the Cantonese version most common in Macao was used; (d) for common terms in Cantonese, Sidney Lau's system of transcription (1977) was used – sometimes the numbering of the tones was left out or simplified – these words and the corresponding characters are found in the Glossary of Cantonese Words; (e) otherwise, for Mandarin words, *pinyin* was used.
3. It has been argued that, compared with other colonial regimes, the situation in Macao was not characteristic, as the Portuguese were never fully in power. Although this is certainly the case, I have nevertheless opted for classifying this period as 'colonial' for two reasons: (a) because the formal terms of government were phrased in typical colonial manner; (b) because ethnic relations in the city acquired a distinct 'colonial' tone, which they had not had before and would lose after 1967.
4. Pina-Cabral and Lourenço 1993b; Chinese edition, 1995; see also Pina-Cabral 2000a.

NOTES

5. In fact, he was merely elaborating on a long line of Portuguese commentators. This is a variant of the traditional Chinese proverb, for which the image of the grass is used, as it is thought that bamboo breaks too easily. In Portuguese eyes, however, the exotic bamboo describes Macao better than the vulgar grass. Teresa Sena called my attention to the fact that Silva Rego (1947: 107) had already used the image and that Graciete Batalha repeated it (1991: 59).
6. English translation based on Anne Cheng's French translation, cf. Confucius 1981: 99–100.
7. What Boaventura Sousa Santos has called 'a deficit in social citizenship' (Santos 1991: 142).
8. The *Tanka* (*Daan6 Ga1*, Port. *Tancar* – also known as 'boat people') are an ethnic sub-group of the broad Chinese universe – a maritime people of very low social prestige. In the past, they were sea-dwellers. They were forbidden access to the academic examinations that were necessary to enter into the Qing Imperial bureaucracy (cf. Peixoto 1988).
9. 'There is a tendency for the breach to widen and extend until it becomes co-extensive with some dominant cleavage in the widest set of relevant social relations to which the conflicting parties belong' (Turner 1957: 91).
10. Albert Yee has argued that the Chinese feel 'misruled' and thus are prone to looking for stepping-stones such as Macao and Hong Kong, cf. 1989.
11. His son and heir – Ho Haw-Wa – was appointed the first Chief Executive of the Special Administrative Region of Macao of the People's Republic of China.
12. Chinese Mainland commentators are also difficult to read as they are characteristically dependent on peculiarly rapid changes in official policy. For instance, in the early 1990s, the 'Portuguese-were-pirates' theory prevailed. But after the Hong Kong handover in 1997, the 'Macao-as-a-leased-land' theory, which was considered anathema up till then, became dominant overnight in the writings of Peking and Shanghai scholars.

CHAPTER 2. THE CITY'S PROFILE

13. Cf. some notes on the issue of the ethnographic present as applied to my research in Macao (Pina-Cabral 2000b).
14. I will not develop a discussion concerning the definition of ethnicity here, as the short theoretical statement included in Pina-Cabral and Lourenço (1993b: 41–51) still represents my present views. Bentley's definition of ethnicity may prove a useful guideline: 'ethnicity is, at base, a claim to common identity based on putative shared descent. Wherever we find an 'ethnic' category or group of people, we will also find a myth that they all originated in some primordial person, place or event. Membership in the category or group is validated by pointing to some set of shared attributes, usually overt culture traits, the members believe they share in common' (1991: 169). In this definition, I only take exception to the use of the word 'descent' which, to my mind, is better substituted by the word 'origin'.
15. Portuguese Ancient Regime legislation, in fact, contemplated this in an interesting way. In the *Ordenações Filipinas* (Vol. II, § LV), those who converted to Catholicism in the King's territories became naturalized (*naturaes do Reino*) in accordance with a combination of the legal principle of *jus soli* with the canonical principle of baptism as a 'second birth' – cf. Araújo 2000: 25.

16. This is in no way a denial that there were internal forms of 'self-destructive discrimination' once the person entered the community, cf. Chapter 8.
17. Lynn Pan's memories of the city are worth reading as they are very suggestive of the sort of experience of dislocation that was at stake (1992: 28–9).
18. Some estimates are considerably higher, cf. Teixeira 1986: 14.
19. Portaria n. 390, *Boletim Oficial de Macau* n. 26, 30/06/1934: 693.
20. These were carried out in Lisbon during the visits organized by the Missão de Macau in 1997–9.
21. These figures should be taken as merely indicative, as it is generally agreed that Macao's censuses are not particularly reliable.
22. The estimate of the number of Macanese persons living in the Territory is a matter of high political import. Prof. Jean Berlie, for example, states that I estimated the number as being 2000 (1999: 23) which is a most surprising reading of what I wrote (cf. Pina-Cabral and Lourenço 1993b: 20) and a figure at least three times smaller than any reasonable estimate.

CHAPTER 3. HOLLERING IN BRONZE: MEMORY AND CONFLICT

23. Ch'ien-shan, Tsin-san or, in *pinyin*, Qian Shan, a town upriver from Macao on the West River in front of Lappa Island, cf. Boxer 1965: 51. For a good map see Fay 1997 [1975].
24. The city had been conquered by Afonso de Albuquerque in 1511, at which time it had been a central and vital focus in the South Asian trade routes – both with Gujarat in India and with China (cf. Chaudhuri 1998, I: 175–6).
25. This was the term used for such customs officials by English merchants. Portuguese sources usually spell it *ho-pu*, cf. Conceição 1988: 48. The term is based on the word *haiguanbu* (Mand.), meaning Customs Services, and incorrectly applied to the men that staffed it.
26. The Chinese Rites Controversy concerned the debate as to whether the ceremonies honouring Confucius and the family ancestors were compatible with proper Christian practice. The Jesuits were in favour and the Dominicans led the opposition. The first ban by the Congregation for the Propagation of the Faith in Rome dates back to 1645 but was later lifted in 1656. Another ban was proclaimed by Clement XI in 1715 and confirmed by Benedict XIV in 1742. In 1939, the issue was again reconsidered and Chinese Catholics were allowed to practise the rites of ancestral reverence. This was finally confirmed during the II Vatican Council (1962–5).
27. Conceição's dates differ; instead I follow Gonçalves Pereira here (1995: 25).
28. For an even lengthier list, cf. Conceição 1988: 48–9. The same events are reported separately and in a yet more heated tone by Montalto de Jesus 1990 [1926]. See also Henrique Lisboa's chapter on Macao in *A China e os Chins* for a description of how the humiliation was felt still at the end of the nineteenth century, cf. 1888: 103ff. Goçalves Pereira's report is more recent and scholarly (1995: 17–27).
29. For the following summary of events, recourse was taken to Caldeira 1997 [1852/31], Montalto de Jesus 1990 [1926], Fay 1997 [1975], Conceição 1988 and, particularly, to Gonçalves Pereira 1995.
30. Legend has it that having had his arm torn off by a cannon ball, he yelled out: 'Forward, brave comrades! I still have one arm left!' cf. Montalto de Jesus

NOTES

1990 [1926]. By the 1920s, when Montalto de Jesus, a Macanese historian, enthused over this and other acts of rash bravery practised by Ferreira do Amaral, the latter had become a Macanese hero.

31. After the war, this man – a Timorese-Chinese Eurasian who assumed a central role during this terrible period as negotiator between the Administration and the Japanese – was to make a fabulous fortune in the gold trade. He would pass on the control of this profitable trade to Ho Yin and Y.C. Liang, the principal 'Red patriot capitalists' of Macao at the time of the Cultural Revolution. Ironically, according to a local historian, the British chief of the Chinese Customs, re-established in the city after the 1887 Treaty, handed over the control of the buildings to Pedro José Lobo during the war (Teixeira 1986: 20). Later on the site was used for the headquarters of Ho Yin. Today it is a guesthouse for official visitors from the Mainland.
32. For these dates I rely on Hsü (1990).
33. See the Governor's telegram to the Overseas Minister, Appendix I. I am grateful to Moisés Fernandes for his help in finding this and other central pieces of information for this chapter.
34. See Appendix I.
35. And, incidentally, next to the place where one of Sun Yat-Sen's residences in the city used to stand, over which the modern Post Office was built.
36. The officers who were in charge of the Indian possessions when they were invaded by Indian armies in 1961 had been most unfairly treated by Salazar. Many were court-martialled and demoted. They were used as scapegoats for a situation created by the dictatorship's own lack of foresight. This memory seems to have hung over the heads of many of the military men during the last decades of Portuguese colonialism. Governor Nobre de Carvalho, an army officer, found it more expeditious to suffer the humiliations to which he was subjected in Macao than to threaten to leave the city honourably. He knew that, if the Chinese agreed, he would be received dishonourably in Lisbon. Ironically, with hindsight, it could well be argued that had he been capable of making that threat the Chinese negotiators would have backed down.

CHAPTER 4. GAMBLING AND THE IMPERIAL CIVIL SERVICE EXAMINATION

37. I am grateful to Luís de Pina Cabral and Graça Fernando for their hospitality at the time we were carrying out this research. I would also like to thank the personnel of the Library of the Leal Senado, Mrs Julie Senna Fernandes, the Public Relations Officer of STDM, and Carla Araújo, then of the University of Macao, for their help and cooperation. This paper was first presented at the conference 'Macao in Historical Perspective' organized by the Portuguese Studies Program, University of California, Berkeley, in March 1996.
38. The English text reads: 'No one can win all the time. We advise you to play merely for pleasure and to risk only what you can spare. Management'.
39. Pronounced as 'dow' with a rising tone.
40. The names of the main Chinese games are written in the alphabetic form that is most common in Macao.

NOTES

41. Letter from Governor Roçadas to Deputy Marques Pereira, quoted in *A Verdade* 31/03/1910, p. 3.
42. There are some collections of materials, namely by Amaro (e.g. 1992) and the green book by the Inspecção dos Contratos de Jogos (1985), but there are practically no systematic analytic studies.
43. This applies equally to private contexts and to casinos, where different tables have different ranges of stakes – these being clearly indicated to the gambler.
44. Cantonese *daai6 sai3*, lit. large small (Mand. *daxiao*), a game played with three dice where the bettor has to chose between large and small numbers.
45. I have opted for citing names of famous historical figures in their most commonly encountered form in Macao and names of Chinese people whom I was acquainted with via Macao's nineteenth-century newspapers (and whose written Chinese names I often could not determine) in the most common way in which these newspapers referred to them. It is worth noting that these may well not be in Standard Cantonese.
46. In Cantonese *faan1 taan1* (Mand. *fantan*).
47. In 1890 this prohibition was still not in force, but by 1897 it was considered normal, *Echo Macaense*, 08/08/1897, n. 56, p. 56.
48. *O Independente*, 14/08/1888, n. 462, pp. 1–2. I rely here on information taken from the Portuguese-speaking newspapers of Macao and Hong Kong of the last three decades of the nineteenth century. Two newspapers in particular were systematically combed for information on gambling, *O Independente* and *O Macaense*. The latter was directly controlled by the Hos for most of this period, cf. *O Independente*, 29/08/1883, n. 204, pp. 1–2. The former had a more anti-gambling, Republican posture.
49. The word *piu3* means 'ticket'. Pacapiu: Cantonese *baak6 gap3 piu3*, lit. white pigeon ticket (Pinyin *bái ge piào*) was a lottery of eighty words that found its distant origin in pigeon racing (cf. Culin 1958 [1891], Lo 1978: 28). Sanpiu: Cantonese *saan1 piu3*, lit. mountain ticket (Pinyin *shan piào*) was a lottery based on the first 120 words of the classical *Primer of One Thousand Characters* (cf. Lou and Wang 1992: 65ff.). Poupiu: Cantonese *po3 piu3*, lit. shop ticket (Pinyin *pù piào*) was also a lottery of 120 words based on the names of the shops that subscribed to it (cf. Lou and Wang 1992: 66; *Va Kiu*, Macao, 14/03/1994). Of all of these only pacapiu continues to be practised in Macao today, albeit in a very different style. Jifá: Cantonese *ji6 fa1*, lit. character flower (Pinyin *zi hua*) was a lottery based on thirty-six numbers each associated with a person (all of them with particularly unfortunate life histories) as well as an animal (Lu 1978: 84).
50. For the sake of simplicity, we use the most common Portuguese transcription for the name in question at the time. Another Portuguese transcription encountered is *vaisém*, lit. in Portuguese 'goes without', although that was used by the newspapers with a depreciative intention. In Cantonese the term is *wai4 seng3* (Mand. *wei xing*), where the first word appropriately means 'examination compound' and the second 'family name'.
51. For the following description I was inspired by Miyazake (1982) as well as a series of very interesting articles which appeared in *Va Kiu* newspaper, Macao, between 13 January 1994 and 13 September 1994, signed by Lu Jin.
52. *Va Kiu*, Macao, 13/01/1994 to 13/09/1994.

NOTES

53. We are told it was 10 per cent, Lu Jin, *Va Kiu*, 01/08/1994.
54. E.g. *Echo Macaense*, 05/03/1899, p. 2; 12/03/1899, p. 3; 19/03/1899.
55. See the statue of him that was erected by 'his Chinese friends' and that is presently preserved in the grounds of the Casa Garden in Macao, the headquarters of the Orient Foundation.
56. That is, the sites of their households, as opposed to their *yin* homes – their family burial sites.
57. Cf. *O Independente*, 21/05/1885, p. 4; *O Macaense*, 24/08/1889, n. 5, p. 1.
58. We encounter considerable difficulty in interpreting the significance of these figures, as it is not stated precisely what value was being attributed to the *pataca*. We transcribe them here merely as an indication of the enormity of the difference between the Macao monopoly and the Canton monopoly.
59. Cf. *O Independente*, 03/09/1885, n. 309, p. 3; *O Independente*, 10/09/1885, n. 310, pp. 2–3.
60. Brother of the famous Pedro Nolasco da Silva, who was *Procurador dos Negócios Sínicos* for long periods and was later, together with Lou Lim-Ioc, one of the principal drafters of the Code of Law 'Rights and Duties of the Chins of Macao relative to their Ways and Customs', cf. Chapter 8.
61. In 1887, he actually handed over the official title to the monopoly to Senna Fernandes, *O Independente*, 16/04/1887, n. 393, p. 2.
62. Cf. *O Macaense*, 07/04/1892, n. 20, p. 1; 09/04/1892, p. 4; *O Independente*, 27/10/1894, n. 12, p. 4.
63. This time the amount agreed on was 5 320 000 *patacas*, *O Macaense*, 01/03/1890, n. 9, p. 4.
64. Cf. *O Independente*, 30/06/1892, p. 1; 23/06/1892, n. 3, p. 2; 06/08/1892, p. 2; 27/10/1894, n. 12, p. 4; and *Echo Macaense*, 09/04/1899, p. 2.
65. I acknowledge that the present discussion addresses gambling as practised by the general population, leaving aside the issue of serious gambling addicts.
66. See Kusyszyn's fortunate formulation of the similar notion that gamblers 'are playing *with* money rather than *for* money and [.. .] they are betting on the *possibility* rather than on the *probability* of winning' (1977: 23).
67. The point is made by Lorraine Datson in terms which are most relevant to the present analysis, when she claims that 'despite the ideology of the meritocracy that blossomed in the eighteenth century . . . the reality was quite different for the mass of the people. They were imprisoned within a static social and economic order that no amount of talent, resolution, patience, and audacity could unlock. . . . The only hope of moving up in the world was suddenly to acquire a vast sum of money, and practically the only hope of such a windfall in a non-meritocratic society was to buy a lottery ticket. Where industry and talent counted for little, buying a lottery ticket might have been the one escape from passivity' (quoted in Kavanagh 1993: 59–60).
68. I approach here Terradas' notion of 'antibiography': 'Antibiography reveals to us the silence, the emptiness, and the chaos that a civilization has projected on a person, making him or her conventionally insignificant. If we follow that route backwards, we suddenly realize how much that civilization had to do in order to achieve that reductibility in the life of that person' (1992: 13).

NOTES

CHAPTER 5. EQUIVOCAL COMPATIBILITIES: PERSON, CULTURE AND EMOTION

69. I am grateful to Mme Jeanne Féblot-Augustins for her suggestions while translating this chapter into French, some of which I have incorporated in the present version.
70. I am grateful to Carlos Alberto Afonso for having called my attention to this topic (cf. Afonso 1994).
71. The police documents call it 'a man's house' (*casa de homens*). I am not quite certain of the meaning of this term. Could it have been something akin to the bachelors' houses which Spencer and Barnett, for example, described in a village near Sekkei (1948: 463–78)?
72. *Boletim Oficial do Governo da Província de Macau*, vol. IX, no. 31, 31/07/1909. It was subsequently republished in Chinese and Portuguese versions in *Boletim Oficial*, n. 36, 04/09/1909, and in the *Anuário de Macau, 1927*, pp. 149–53 and remained valid until 1948.
73. The principal Macanese member of the committee that drafted this document was a man who occupied the post of *Procurador* for lengthy periods, Pedro Nolasco da Silva. The principal Chinese member was Lou Lim-Ioc, the son of Lou Can (who was the *vaeseng* boss, cf. Chapter 4 – see Araújo 2000: 146).
74. Newspaper article, *Vida Nova*, 17/04/1910, n. 68, quoted by Araújo 2000: 171–2.
75. This happened in 1894. After the implementation of the Chinese Courts in 1919 (*Tribunal Privativo dos Chinas de Macao, Decreto*, n. 3.637 of 29/11/1917, published *Boletim Oficial*, no. 14 of 06/04/1918, cf. Araújo 2000: 195), the *Procuratura* was closed down, but a *Departamento de Negócios Sínicos* continued to exist. The Chinese Courts operated until 1948, after which time the courts in Macao started using the codes of law of the Republic of China (Kuomintang) to judge all cases of Chinese residents who were Chinese nationals.
76. The extremely ambiguous role they played in the city can be assessed from the following news item taken from a local Portuguese newspaper (*O Macaense*, 18/01/1890, p. 2): 'The arrogance of these *loucanes* (agents) in their relations with the Chinese and the normal clients of brothels is not to be tolerated. We must get rid of this! We can have a notion of the importance of their position if we consider that any Chinese without means is bound to be taken away to prison for preventive custody. Whoever provokes their anger or refuses to tip them is immediately imprisoned and taken before the *Procurador* with the accusation of being a pirate. Then he is sent to prison whilst the inquiry takes place. It is common for people to stay there for months. These imprisonments are very often directly or indirectly carried out at the instance of agents of the Chinese government'.
77. It should be absolutely clear that none of the arguments developed here – nor any of Pessanha's arguments – should be taken as justifying (or worse even, condoning) the practices of kidnapping children for the purposes of adoption or prostitution, as still allegedly happens (cf. *Newsweek*, 07/09/1998, p. 31).
78. My translation, quoted in Veiga de Oliveira 1993: 388, n. 180.
79. The principal judge claims that, 'In China, the purchase and sale of children occurs with daily frequency. Even today, in the province of Kiang Si, there are open markets dealing with that trade: such is the horror of hunger that the parents sell their sons and daughters and even husbands sell their wives in

NOTES

order not to see them . . . die of hunger!' (quoted in Veiga de Oliveira 1993: 380).
80. *Lei6 si6*. The pronunciation of Chinese words given by these judges corresponds to the Sekkei (Mand. *shiqi*) dialect, cf. Woon 1987: 111.
81. *Gratificação*, alternatively to be translated as 'gratuity' or 'tip'.
82. One may presume this *nou pi* to be a dialectal version of the Standard Cantonese *lo4 pei5* – female slave. As to *kou kong*, doubt remains as to the precise meaning of this transcription. J. M. Potter, who studied a village of the Delta where the condition of slave was recognized right up to the Communist takeover, makes no reference to this term (Potter and Potter 1990: 56).
83. Incidentally, this was perhaps the argument which Pessanha considered most definite against the existence of slaves in China. He claimed that there could be no slaves, as labour was so cheap, that it would be more expensive to have to look after the labourer by means of a permanent relationship such as slavery (Veiga de Oliveira 1993: 340–1).
84. Pessanha again: 'prostitution in China is a vile profession but not an infamous one, from where women leave to be the companions and near equals of principal wives, in the wealthier families, where they become secondary wives' (Veiga de Oliveira 1993: 341).
85. He exemplifies this, arguing that it is particularly meaningless to call slavery to the 'boring negotiations, sometimes taking months or even years, by means of which, in some seedy and remote back alley of this city (. . .) an old witch transfers to another old witch her granddaughter, in return for a few *patacas* so that the assignee finds someone to succeed to her estate, so that the assigned receives protection during her youth, and so that the assignor may experience the voluptuous satisfaction of purchasing and possessing whilst she is alive, a worthy coffin where, once dead, she may honourably be buried' (Veiga de Oliveira 1983: 345).
86. Olga Lang quotes a Shanghai factory worker who told the researcher: 'We had no daughters, so we decided to buy a little girl in order to marry her later to our son. A little girl is cheaper than a grown-up one and we send her to work in the factory in the meantime' (1946: 127).
87. See also Rubie Watson: 'In Hong Kong's New Territories under the Ch'ing, male slaves (*hsi min*), whose status was inherited through the male line, were attached to many wealthy households. With their emancipation at the time of the Republican Revolution in 1911, however, male slavery ceased to exist as a viable institution in this area (. . .). Pawning and indenture, nevertheless, continued to be part of the labour scene until World War II, and women, it would appear, were well represented, perhaps over-represented, among Hong Kong's unfree population' (1991: 234).
88. Cf. Watson (1980a: 243): 'Until now I have deliberately avoided using the term "slave" in the context of female servitude because there was considerable variation in the relationship between "bought women" and their owners. The fact that they were bought and sold like chattels is not enough, in my view, to categorise these women as slaves (. . .).' My own argument is that, as a matter of fact, the notion that they were sold by the Chinese like chattels is one of the sources of these misunderstandings.
89. See Maria Jaschock (1988), Teixeira (1965) and Boxer (where he spells it *muitsai*, 1948, ch. 13). Venceslau de Morais, a friend of Pessanha, who became

NOTES

very famous for his prose writings on Japan, where he eventually died, lived in Macao for a while. During that time he purchased a *mooi1 jai2* with whom he had two sons whom he legitimated. These events have been studied by Danilo Barreiros 1990 [1955].

90. Cf. the letters of pirates to villagers demanding a ransom for stolen boys which Pessanha translated (or helped translate, Pires 1992: 177–9). Such piracy was very common in the waters of the Delta near the city, until World War II, cf. Lilius 1991 [1930]. In fact, in Macao today, there is a family of Macanese (Eurasians of Portuguese culture) who have descended from two boys who were raised as brothers because they were found by the police after a raid in a cave previously occupied by pirates in Coloane. In the 1950s, children in Macao were admonished by their mothers to be careful, in order to avoid *gwaai2 ji2 lo2* – lit. child snatchers. See the report concerning the military occupation of the Island of Coloane in 1910 and the fight against a group of kidnapper pirates (*Tribuna de Macao*, 24/06/93, p. 24, article by Leonel de Barros).

91. I am grateful to Susana Matos Viegas for discussions concerning the notions of personhood and self.

92. Let it be understood that I am not claiming that he would have *necessarily* done so. A number of idiosyncrasies and other contributing factors may have resulted in a different set of events. All I am claiming is that it is probable that he would do so and that all of the persons involved had good reasons to expect him to react in that way.

93. This is emphasized by Jesus himself, who casts into a secondary role his human bonds of filial piety in favour of his spiritual filiation. The following passage of the Gospel according to St Luke is exemplary of this: 'His mother and his brothers arrived but could not get to him for the crowd. He was told, "Your mother and brothers are standing outside, and they want to see you". He replied, "My mother and my brothers – they are those who hear the word of God and act upon it"' (Luke 8:19–21). Such a response would be deeply problematic for a Confucian mind.

94. Mayfair Yang gives perhaps the most comprehensive definition I have encountered of Chinese personhood: 'it appears that the Chinese subscribe to a relational construction of persons. That is to say, the autonomy and rights of persons and the sense of personal identity are based on differential moral and social statuses and the moral claims and judgements of others. Chinese personhood and personal identity are not given in the abstract as something intrinsic to and fixed in human nature, but are constantly being created, altered and dismantled in particular social relationships. Furthermore, the boundaries of personhood are permeable and can easily be enlarged to encompass a scope beyond that of the biological individual' (1989: 39).

95. We must, however, take into account de Bary's warning against 'dubious modern Western antitheses between the individual and the group, between rights and duties'. He calls our attention to the fact that Confucian ethics start from the notion of self-cultivation, not from any kind of group ethic. This points to the importance of emotion: 'Insofar as family relations have served as the paradigm for such a system and have been conceived primarily as affective, emotional ties rather than as legalistic and contractual ones, the language of rights or of legal entitlements does not fit the case well' (Bary 1996: 33).

NOTES

96. A word I borrow, perhaps abusively, from Meyer Fortes, e.g. 1983 [1959]: 33.
97. In his poems, he called her *Águia de Prata*, Silver Eagle.
98. His relations with his Eurasian son by her, however, were characterized by tension, distrust and incomprehension.
99. Like Venceslau de Morais' Chinese companion, who was originally purchased by him as a *mooi6 jai2* (cf. Barreiros 1990 [1955]).

CHAPTER 6. STONE SILENCE: ORGANIZED AMNESIA

100. This chapter was first presented as a paper at the Winter Term Seminar, Department of Anthropology, London School of Economics, February 2000. I am grateful to Charles Stafford and to Stephan Feuchtwang for their encouragement on this occasion. In writing it, I depended heavily on the generous collaboration of Moisés Fernandes, at the Institute of Social Sciences, University of Lisbon (cf. Fernandes 2000b).
101. For a detailing of the sources, see Fernandes 2000b: 59.
102. Cf. *Boletim Oficial de Macao*, no. 2, 08/01/55.
103. See the Governor's telegram to the Overseas Minister concerning statues of 15 March 1967, that is transcribed below (Appendix).

CHAPTER 7. NAMES: PERSONAL IDENTITY AND ETHNIC AMBIGUITY

104. This chapter was first delivered as a paper at the Graduate Seminar of the Department of Social Anthropology of the University of Oslo, Norway, March 1993. I am grateful to my colleagues in Oslo for the opportunity to discuss these issues with them.
105. Interestingly, judging by Francis Hsu's comments, Chinese racial prejudice is, in some sense, more akin to Portuguese prejudice than to that of other European colonialist nations: 'The Chinese had always regarded all non-Chinese as "barbarians". Yet this fact had not prevented intermarriage, residential mixing, social intercourse, and entry into officialdom by Muslims and members of other minorities' (1983: 993). See, however, Dikötter 1992.
106. In Goffman's terms, 'an individual who might have been received easily in ordinary social intercourse possesses a trait that can obtrude itself upon attention and turn those of us whom he meets away from him, breaking the claim that his other attributes have on us' (1963: 15).
107. 'Surnames are chosen from among those that belong to both parents or to one of the parents of the registered person or to the use of which they have a right; it being possible, in the case of there being no surnames, to choose one of the names by which the parents are known' (Vilhena de Carvalho 1989: 108, my own translation).
108. It is worth noting that the French system is far more constraining, markedly favouring the father's name. Although attitudes to this are changing in accordance with changes in gender roles and family practices, opinion polls indicate that there too the symbolic precedence of agnatic links has survived. However, there being less choice, the potential for contradiction between the ideal system and the actual naming practice is lesser than in Portugal. 'Le nom de l'homme conserve sa prépondérance parce que lui sont encore associées

des valeurs symboliques du passé, que de nouvelles vertus lui sont parfois attribuées et qu'enfin, pour apparaître comme nom de famille, le nom de la femme doit entrer en concurrence avec le nom de l'homme' (Valetas 1992: 29).
109. As seems to be the case in the United States, here too the naming of male children is more conservative and less varied than of female children, cf. Lieberson and Bell 1992: 519.
110. Thus, the mother's name is forgotten, particularly if she is Chinese. Concerning the 'amnesia' of Chinese names in Macanese genealogies, cf. Pina-Cabral and Lourenço 1992. See also R. Watson 1986.
111. Already in 1958, Graciete Batalha was quite clear about this, stressing also the importance of schooling: 'if a Chinese [chinês puro] is baptized, uses a Portuguese name, frequents our schools, assimilates our language and our culture, he passes automatically to be considered by the Macanese as one of them' (1974 [1958]: 9). Interestingly, she claims that, nevertheless, they will not be referred to as *filho da terra* (*to2 saang1 jai2*, lit. land-born child) by other Macanese. I myself have certified that now they are.
112. 'The legal status of a marriage did not determine the status of heirs, who could inherit at their father's will' (Ebrey 1991: 6).
113. A clear sign of this change is the election of a pro-democracy member for the Legislative Assembly in 1992, in spite of the strenuous efforts to prevent this undertaken by the conservative sectors of the Chinese community of the city (who are pro-PRC since 1966/7).

CHAPTER 8. CORRELATE ASYMMETRIES: GENDER, CLASS AND ETHNICITY

114. I opted for the use of the word 'matrimonial' as a way of avoiding the more specifically legal term 'marriage', so as to indicate that many relations that cannot be considered marriage in terms of the Portuguese legal system do have a founding function in terms of family life. Therefore, in this argument, matrimonial refers to the more general definition of marriage provided by the dictionary: 'the institution whereby men and women are joined in a special kind of social (. . .) dependence for the purpose of founding and maintaining a family' (*Merriam-Webster's Dictionary*).
115. For a development of the concept of *continued identities*, see Pina-Cabral 1997: 78.
116. The tight-collared, side-buttoned, slit-skirted dress that was characteristic of Chinese women during the first half of the twentieth century and that Deolinda da Conceição used as the name of her book and the symbol of the condition of the women she depicts.
117. In this case, diverging in religious belonging, in phenotypic appearance, in cultural values and even in political affiliation – as, even during the colonial period (1849–1967), the Chinese never fully claimed allegiance to the Portuguese State.
118. Cf. '*O refúgio da saudade*', Conceição 1987a: 107–22.
119. See the Bishop's declaration concerning these women, written in order to establish their right to Portuguese citizenship, cf. Pina-Cabral and Lourenço 1993a, Appendix I.

NOTES

120. These were the family histories of nine informants. Overall, I carried out twenty family histories.
121. I have left out people with a Portuguese name of whom I was told something like: 'he/she is Chinese, but it's as if he/she were a Portuguese'.
122. I am grateful to Marcelo Poon, at the time student of Law at the University of Macao, for his help in unearthing the legislation that made sense of these comments, which had taken me by surprise.
123. *Decreto-Lei* 31: 107 of 18/01/1941.
124. For a fuller explanation of the methodological procedures utilized and a more detailed analysis of the results, cf. Pina-Cabral and Lourenço 1993a: 119–57. For consultation of the database, cf. Pina-Cabral 1991b.
125. Macanese with Chinese or Portuguese with Chinese.
126. Macanese with Macanese or Portuguese with Macanese.
127. Between 1987 and 1990, the male spouse was Chinese in 46 per cent of the cases.
128. This is a non-standard form of written Chinese with adaptations that transcribe colloquial Cantonese.

CHAPTER 9. HABITS OF THE HEART: MODERN WOMEN AND FILIAL PIETY

129. I am grateful to Nuno Fernando Neves Pereira for the invaluable help he gave me in researching some issues discussed in this chapter.
130. One is reminded of Professor de Bary's comment that 'Much that was identified (sometimes mistakenly) with the Neo-Confucian family system was severely criticised in the liberal and liberation movements of the early twentieth century, and many old customs were abandoned. Notwithstanding this, the family system, or at least some vital core of it, has shown a surprising resilience to the rapid changes and pressures of modern life, as if it still could provide, in intensely demanding and trying times, a moral, emotional, and corporal support that nothing else has' (1988: 113).
131. Contrary to what one can find in the rural areas of the Pearl River Delta, where lineages as local interest groups and as cult units have survived the various revolutionary attempts to destroy them, cf. Göran Aijmer and Virgil K.Y. Ho (2000: 19–42).
132. Cf. *Boletim Oficial*, no. 31, IX, 31/07/1909, see note 72 above.
133. Again this is the old pronunciation. Today the pronunciation is *tai2 gei2*, as explained above.
134. This, rather than any intrinsic distaste for baby girls, would explain the prevalence of female infanticide that continues to be reported in rural areas. For example, *South China Morning Post*, 26/09/97, quoting a report by the World Health Organisation.
135. I am grateful to Mónica Chan for carrying out these, as well as many other interviews that my condition as male and as Portuguese would have completely invalidated.
136. I take recourse here to Carmelo Lisón-Tolosana's notion of 'generation', cf. 1988 [1966].

NOTES

137. A similar process has occurred at least once before. During the sericultural boom of the early twentieth century, according to Janice Stockard, 'The economic value of bridedaughters in sericultural areas led to longer periods of postmarital separation, as natal families and lineages sought to retain their married daughters for the valuable labour they performed. Even in the pre-mechanization era, bridedaughters must have enjoyed enhanced prestige within their natal homes as a result of their labour contributions' (1989: 167–8).
138. The questionnaire was conceived by a team led by António Hespanha at the Institute of Social Sciences of the University of Lisbon. I am grateful to him and to Carla Araújo for their generosity in granting me access to this material.
139. I am grateful to José Maria Moreira da Silva for allowing me to use his study of these cases.
140. Interestingly, this is the second term that the legislators of the *Usos e Costumes* did not feel they could translate into Portuguese. The term implies a corporateness of the family (presuming, of course, an exclusion of uterine relatives) that makes no sense in the Portuguese context.
141. Cf. David Ownby's discussion of the relevance of the concept for the general development of 'secret societies' in China: 'Of course, the idea of brotherhood can and frequently does suggest egalitarianism, which clearly clashes with the hierarchical orientation of Confucianism, but many examples of brotherhood contain their own hierarchies (including those within biological families). Even small brotherhoods in South China generally chose 'elder brothers' as well as 'second elder' and sometimes 'third elder' brothers, presumably to maintain discipline and facilitate common action, and the elaborate hierarchy within larger secret societies is well known. Indeed, anthropologist David Jordan notes that in modern Taiwan, brotherhoods are sometimes seen as superior to mere friendships in part because the built-in hierarchy of the brotherhood supposedly works to reduce conflict' (Ownby 1993: 16–17).
142. Mand. *Kuan Yin*, Avalokiteshvara's female representation.
143. The ambiguity of the story of the Kitchen God – one of China's most famous comments on the nature of conjugal relations – again points to this interpretation, cf. Pina-Cabral 1999b.

CHAPTER 10. TRIAD WARS AND THE END OF PORTUGUESE ADMINISTRATION

144. *Polícia Judiciária* – in the Portuguese system this is a body of detectives which investigates processes that are going to be presented to the courts.
145. In the midst of public outcry concerning these traditional disagreements, a joint task force was created that, as the handover approached, functioned increasingly in collaboration with 'liaison officers' and 'experts' from China's Ministry of Public Security.
146. 'Li Kuok-hoi has made an accusation against me, Cheong chi-fat, born in Pun-iü, saying that I owe him $20, which amounts to two months of his salary. Before these gods, I cut the head of the cock and I swear that the accusation is false. If, nevertheless, the debt does exist and I am trying to cover it up, may the gods make me, Cheong chi-fat, unhappy; may a thunderbolt fall on me;

NOTES

may the fire consume me; may my children and grandchildren die. If, however, the oath is true, then may Heaven make me happy. Let the Emperor of Heaven and the Empress of the Earth be observant of these words of mine' (*Boletim Oficial*, no. 31, 1909, p. 18).

147. In 1994, a floor room manager told me that the casino took roughly 2.5 per cent of all money played on baccarat tables and that junket chip dealers received a discount of 10 per cent per chip sold. In 1998 *Público* (30/05/98) claimed that the percentage was 22.5 per cent. I believe, however, that these quotas are prone to conjunctural variation.
148. In order to save the currency (RMB) from depreciation, the PRC tightened control of internal credit, which had an immediate impact in Macao.
149 Supposedly based on the ancient tradition of the Hung Moon society in the seventeenth century, 14K was founded in Canton by General Kot Siu Wong in the 1940s, so as to support the Nationalists in their fight against the Communists (Posner, 1990: 39). Today, it is said to have branches in Japan, Macao, Taiwan, Europe and Southeast Asia. It is one of the main sects of Hong Kong (cf. Chin 1992: 50) on a par with Sun Yee On (lit. 'new and correct security'), formed mostly by members from Chiwchow.
150. Her backers, however, eventually got into political trouble, the casino was closed by the police and she had to spend some time in prison (*Ponto Final*, 15/05/98).
151. Lit. Water Room, in Port. *Gazosa*.
152. One source claimed that Li Peng's son was one of his business partners (*Visão*, 28/05/98, p. 32).

APPENDIX

153. From the 'Archive Salazar' at the National Archives *Torre do Tombo*, Lisbon: AOS/CO/UOL – 85, Folio 535, Pt. 2, 7th Subdivision. I am grateful to Moisés Fernandes for having placed at my disposal this valuable document, which he unearthed during his extensive research in Salazar's personal archive.

BIBLIOGRAPHY

(All quotations in English of texts in other languages are translated by the author)

Afonso, Carlos Alberto, 1994. '*O poder do espaço: dominação simbólica, território e identidade nas Montanhas de Trás-os-Montes*', Ph.D. thesis, Faculty of Science and Technology, University of Coimbra.
Aijmer, Göran and Ho, Virgil K.Y., 2000. *Cantonese Society in a Time of Change*. Hong Kong: The Chinese University Press.
Alleton, Viviane, 1993. *Les Chinois et la passion des noms*. Paris: Aubier.
Amaro, Ana Maria, 1988. *Filhos da Terra*. Macao: Instituto Cultural de Macau.
Amaro, Ana Maria, 1992. *Jogos, Brinquedos e Outras Diversões Populares de Macau*. Macao: Imprensa Nacional.
Amaro, Ana Maria, 1992. 'Os Macaenses como grupo. Alguns dados antropobiológicos', *Revista de Cultura* **16**: 95–103.
Araújo, Maria Carla, 2000. 'Direito português e populações indígenas (Macau 1846–1927)', unpublished MA thesis, Institute of Social Sciences, University of Lisbon.
Ariès, Philippe, 1983. 'O casamento indissolúvel', in Philippe Ariès and André Béjin (eds), *Sexualidades Ocidentais*. Lisbon: Contexto Editora.
Ataíde, D. António de, 1957 [1608–12]. *Viagens da India para o Reino e do Reino para a India: Diários de Navegação coligidos por D. António de Ataíde no Século XVII*. Lisbon: Agência Geral do Ultramar.

Barreiros, Danilo, 1990 [1955]. *A Paixão Chinesa de Wenceslau de Morais*. Macao: Livros do Oriente.
Bary, Wm Theodore de, 1988. *East Asian Civilizations: A Dialogue in Five Stages*. Cambridge, MA: Harvard University Press.
Bary, Wm Theodore de, 1996. 'Confucian education in premodern East Asia', in Tu Wei-Ming (ed.), *Confucian Traditions in East-Asian Modernity*. Cambridge, MA: Harvard University Press.
Basto da Silva, Beatriz, 1986. *Elementos de História de Macau*, 2 vols. Macao: Dir. Serviços Educaçao.
Basto da Silva, Beatriz, 1988. 'Macau: o exército e a cultura', *Revista da Cultura* **5**: 87–94.
Basto da Silva, Beatriz, 1994. *Emigração de Cules: Dossier Macau 1851–1894*. Macao: Fundação Oriente.
Batalha, Graciete Nogueira, 1974 [1958]. *Língua de Macau – O que foi e o que é –*. Macao: Imprensa Nacional.

BIBLIOGRAPHY

Batalha, Graciete Nogueira, 1991. *'Bom Dia S'Tora!'*. Macao: Instituto Cultural de Macau.
Bentley, G. Carter, 1991. 'Response to Yelvington', *Comparative Studies in Society and History* **33**(1): 169–75.
Berlie, J.A., 1999. 'Society and economy', in J.A. Berlie (ed.), *Macao 2000*. Hong Kong: Oxford University Press.
Bettencourt, Francisco, 1998. 'Competição entre impérios europeus', in Francisco Bettencourt and Kirti Chaudhuri (eds), *História da Expansão Portuguesa* II. Lisbon: Círculo de Leitores.
Billeter, Jean François, 1977. 'Contribution à une sociologie historique du mandarinat', *Actes de la Recherche en Sciences Sociales* **15** (June): 3–30.
Boxer, C.R., 1948. *Fidalgos in the Far East, 1550–1770*. The Hague: Martinus Nijhoff.
Boxer, C.R., 1963. *Race Relations in the Portuguese Colonial Empire, 1415–1825*. Oxford: Clarendon Press.
Boxer, C.R., 1965. *Portuguese Society in the Tropics: The Municipal Councils of Goa, Macao, Bahia and Luanda, 1510–1800*. Madison: University of Wisconsin Press.
Braga, José Maria (Jack), 1952. 'A Projecção do Português no Extremo Oriente através de Macau', *Boletim da Sociedade de Geografia de Lisboa* **70**(4–6): 79–97.
Brito, Ana, 1994. 'Religion, politics and the construction of ethnic identity in Macao.' M.Phil. dissertation, Dept. of Anthropology, Chinese University of Hong Kong.

Caldeira, Carlos José, 1997 [1st edn 1852/3]. *Macau em 1850 – Crónica de Viagem*. Lisbon: Instituto de Ciências Sociais/Quetzal.
Cayolla, Lourenço, 1912. *Sciencia da colonização*. Lisbon: Tipografia da Cooperativa Militar.
Chan Shek-Kiu and Tan Weiguang, 1990. 'Urban development and pollution in Macau', in D.Y. Yuan, Wong Hon-Keong and Libânio Martins (eds), *Population and City Growth in Macau*. Macao: Centre of Macau Studies, University of East Asia.
Chaudhuri, Kirti, 1998. 'O estabelecimento no Oriente', in Francisco Bettencourt and Kirti Chaudhuri (eds), *História da Expansão Portuguesa* I. Lisbon: Círculo de Leitores.
Cheng M.B., Christina, 1999. 'A historical and cultural prelude', in J. Berlie (ed.), *Macao 2000*. Hong Kong: Oxford University Press.
Chin Ko-Lin, 1992. *Chinese Subculture and Criminality: Non-traditional Crime Groups in America*. Hong Kong: United Publishers (Chinese edition).
Chun, Allen, 1996. 'The Lineage-Village Complex in Southeastern China' and comments by John Clammer, Patricia Ebrey, David Faure, Stephan Feuchtwang, Ying-Kuei Huang, P. Steven Sangren and Mayfair Yang, *Current Anthropology* **37**(3): 429–50.
Clarence-Smith, Gervase, 1985. *O Terceiro Império Português (1825–1975)*. Lisbon: Teorema.
Clayton, Cathryn H., 1999. 'MACAU – Notes from the field: On belonging and the city', *Portuguese Studies Review* **7**(2): 93–111.
Coates, Austin, 1978. *A Macao Narrative*. Hong Kong: Oxford University Press.
Cohen, Abner, 1981. *The Politics of Culture: Explorations in the Dramaturgy of Power in a Modern African Society*. Berkeley: University of California Press.
Conceição, Deolinda da, 1987a [1956]. *Cheong-Sam (A Cabaia)*. Macao: Instituto Cultural de Macau.

BIBLIOGRAPHY

Conceição, Deolinda da, 1987b. *Fotobiografia de Deolinda Salvado da Conceição*, collected by António da Conceição Jr. Macao: Instituto Cultural de Macau.
Conceição, Lourenço Maria da, 1988. *Macau entre dois tratados com a China, 1862–1887*. Macao: Instituto Cultural de Macau.
Confucius, 1981. *Les Entretiens de Confucius*, trans. Anne Cheng. Paris: Editions Seuil.
Culin, Stewart, 1958 [1891]. *The Games of the Orient: Korea, China, Japan* (reprint). Rutland: Charles E. Tuttle.

Davidson, Donald, 1984. *Inquiries into Truth and Interpretation*. Oxford: Clarendon Press.
Davidson, Donald, 2001. *Subjective, Intersubjective, Objective*. Oxford: Clarendon Press.
Dikötter, Frank, 1992. *The Discourse of Race in Modern China*. Stanford, CA: Stanford University Press.
Douglas, Robert, 1894. *Society in China*. London: A.D. Innes & Co.

Ebrey, Patricia Buckley, 1991. 'Introduction', in Rubie S. Watson and Patricia Buckley Ebrey (eds), *Marriage and Inequality in Chinese Society*. Berkeley: University of California Press.
Elliot, Alan J.A., 1955. *Chinese Spirit–Medium Cults in Singapore*. London: Department of Anthropology, LSE (Reprint, Southern Materials Center, Inc., Taiwan).
Elman, Benjamin A., 1994. 'Changes in Confucian Civil Service Examinations from the Ming to the Ch'ing Dynasty', in Benjamin A. Elman and Alexander Woodside (eds), *Education and Society in Late Imperial China, 1600–1900*. San Francisco and London: University of California Press.
Endo, Shusako, 1988 [1976]. *Silence*. Harmondsworth: Penguin.

Fairbank, John King, 1989. *La Grande Revolution chinoise, 1800–1989*. Paris: Flammarion.
Fay, Peter Ward, 1997 [1975]. *The Opium War, 1840–1842*. Chapel Hill: University of North Carolina Press.
Fei Hsiao-Tung, 1953. *China's Gentry, Essays in Rural-Urban Relations* (M.P. Redfield, rev. edn). Chicago: University of Chicago Press.
Fernandes, Henrique de Senna, 1978. *NamVan: Contos de Macau*. Macao: Author's edition.
Fernandes, Henrique de Senna, 1996. *A tranca feiticeira*. Macao: Instituto Cultural de Macau.
Fernandes, Moisés, 2000a. 'Confluência de interesses. Portugal, Macau e a China', *História* **21**: 56–67.
Fernandes, Moisés, 2000b. *Sinopse de Macau nas Relações Luso-Chinesas*. Lisbon: Fundação Oriente.
Feuchtwang, Stephan, 1991. 'A Chinese religion exists', in H. Baker and S. Feuchtwang (eds), *An Old State in New Settings: Studies in the Social Anthropology of China in Memory of Maurice Freedman*. Oxford: JASO.
Feuchtwang, Stephan, 1992. *The Imperial Metaphor: Popular Religion in China*. London: Routledge.
Fok, K.C., 1991. 'The Ming debate on how to accommodate the Portuguese and the emergence of the Macau formula', *Revista Cultural* **13/14**: 328–44.

BIBLIOGRAPHY

Fortes, Meyer, 1983 (1959). *Oedipus and Job in West African Religion*, with an introduction by Robin Horton. Cambridge: Cambridge University Press.
Franke, Wolfgang, 1960. 'The reform and abolition of the traditional Chinese examination system', *Chinese Economic and Political Studies*. Harvard University: Centre for East Asian Studies.
Freedman, Maurice, 1979. *The Study of Chinese Society: Essays by Maurice Freedman*, edited by G. William Skinner, Stanford, CA: Stanford University Press.
Fry, Peter, 2000. 'Cultures of difference. The aftermath of Portuguese and British colonial policies in southern Africa', *Social Anthropology* **8**(2): 117–43

Gernet, Jacques, 1962. *Chine et Christianisme*. Paris: Gallimard.
Godlove Jr, Terry F., 1989. *Religion, Interpretation and Diversity of Belief: The Framework Model from Kant, to Durkheim, to Davidson*. Cambridge: Cambridge University Press.
Goffman, Erving, 1963. *Stigma: Notes on the Management of Spoiled Identity*. Harmondsworth: Penguin Books.
Gonçalves Pereira, Francisco, 1995. *Portugal, a China e a 'Questão de Macau'*. Macao: Instituto Português do Oriente.
Goody, Jack, 1990. *The Oriental, the Ancient and the Primitive: Systems of Marriage and the Family in the Pre-industrial Societies of Eurasia*. Cambridge: Cambridge University Press.
Grantham, Alexander, 1965. *Via Ports: From Hong Kong to Hong Kong*. Hong Kong: Hong Kong University Press.
Guedes, João, 1991. *As Seitas: Histórias do Crime e da Política em Macau*. Macao: Livros do Oriente.
Guimarães, Ângela, 1996. *Uma Relação Especial: Macau e as Relações Luso-Chinesas (1780–1844)*. Lisbon: Edição CIES.

Hall, Peter, 1992. *In the Web*. Wirral, England: Author's edition.
Herzfeld, Michael, 1982. 'When exceptions define the rules: Greek baptismal names and the negotiation of identity', *Journal of Anthropological Research* **38**(3): 288–302.
Honig, Emily, 1992. *Creating Chinese Ethnicity: Subei People in Shanghai, 1850–1980*. New Haven: Yale University Press.
Hook, Brian (ed.), 1991 (2nd edn). *The Cambridge Encyclopedia of China*. New York: Cambridge University Press.
Hou Ching-Lang, 1975. *Monnaies d'offrande et la notion de tresorerie dans la religion chinoise*. Paris: Institut des Hautes Etudes Chinoises, Collège de France.
Hsieh Yu-Wei, 1967. 'Filial piety and Chinese society', in Charles A. Moore (ed.), *The Chinese Mind: Essentials of Chinese Philosophy and Culture*. Honolulu: University of Hawaii Press.
Hsu, Francis L.K., 1981 [1st edn 1953]. *Americans and Chinese: Passage to Differences*. Honolulu: University Press of Hawaii.
Hsu, Francis L.K., 1983. Review article in *American Anthropologist* **85**: 993.
Hsü, Immanuel C.Y., 1990. *The Rise of Modern China*. Oxford: Oxford University Press.

BIBLIOGRAPHY

Jaschok, Maria, 1988. *Concubines and Bondservants: The Social History of a Chinese Custom.* London: Zed Press.

Jun Jing, 1996. *The Temple of Memories: History, Power and Morality in a Chinese Village.* Stanford, CA: Stanford University Press.

Kavanagh, Thomas M., 1993. *Enlightenment and the Shadows of Chance: The Novel and the Culture of Gambling in Eighteenth-Century France.* Baltimore: Johns Hopkins University Press.

King, Ambrose Y.C., 1996. 'The transformation of Confucianism in the Post-Confucian era: the emergence of rationalistic traditionalism in Hong Kong', in Tu Wei-Ming op. cit.

Kusyszyn, Igor, 1977. 'How gambling saved me from a misspent sabbatical', *Journal of Humanistic Psychology* **17**(3).

Lang, Graeme and Ragvald, Lars, 1993. *The Rise of a Refugee God.* Hong Kong and New York: Oxford University Press.

Lang, Olga, 1946. *Chinese Family and Society.* New Haven: Yale University Press.

Lau, Sidney, 1977. *A Practical Cantonese–English Dictionary*, Hong Kong: Government Printer.

Levenson, Joseph, 1965. *Confucian China and Its Modern Fate.* Berkeley: University of California Press.

Liang Peiyuan, 1996 [1968]. 'Poemas de Macau', *Revista de Cultura* **29**: 143–50.

Lieberson, Stanley and Bell, Eleanor O., 1992. 'Children's first names: An empirical study of social taste', *American Journal of Sociology* **98**(3): 511–54.

Lilius, Aleko E., 1991 [1930]. *I Sailed with Chinese Pirates.* Hong Kong: Oxford University Press.

Lisboa, Henrique, 1888. *A China e os Chins. Recordações de Viagem*. Montevideo: Tipografia a Vapor de A. Godel.

Lisón-Tolosana, Carmelo, 1988 [1966]. *Belmonte de los Caballeros*. Princeton, NJ: Princeton University Press.

Livingstone, David, 1982 [1857]. *Missionary Travels and Researches in South Africa* (Time-Life Books reprint). London: John Murray.

Lo Jung-Pang, 1978. *Kang Yu-Wei: A Biography and a Symposium.* Tucson: University of Arizona Press.

Lou Fu Qing and Wang Ming Kun, 1992. *Smoking, Gambling and Prostitution in Old Canton* (text in Chinese). Hong Kong: Chung Wa Publisher.

Lu Jin, 1994 (July). 'Once upon a time in Macau', daily column in *Va Kio Daily* (text in Chinese), Macao.

Lu Yan, 1978. *Dissection of the Hong Kong Society (3) – Gambling in Hong Kong* (text in Chinese). Hong Kong: Wide Angle Publisher.

Macau, Governo de, 1979–88. *Anuários Demográficos.* Macao: Serviços de Estatística e Censos de Macau.

Macau, Governo de, 1984. *Caracterização da Economia de Macau.* Macao: Gabinete de Comunicação Social.

Macau, Governo de, 1985a. *O Jogo em Macau.* Macao: Inspecção dos Contratos de Jogos.

BIBLIOGRAPHY

Macau, Governo de, 1985b. *A Educação em Macau*. Macao: Direcção dos Serviços de Educação e Cultura.
Macau, Governo de, 1993. *XIII Recenseamento da População/III Recenseamento da Habitação*. Macao: Serviços de Estatística e Censos.
Macau, Governo de, 1997a. *Intercensos 96. Resultados Globais*. Macao: Serviços de Estatística e Censos.
Macau, Governo de, 1997b. *Boletim Mensal de Estatística/Agosto 1997*. Macao: Serviços de Estatística e Censos.
Matos, Alice Delarue, 1989. 'Elementos para o estudo das características demográficas de Macau', *Administração* 5(3): 447–54.
Miyazaki, Ichisada, 1982 [1963]. *China's Examination Hell*, trans. Conrad Schirokauer. Yale: Yale University Press.
Montalto de Jesus, C.A., 1990 [1926]. *Macau Histórico*. Macao: Livros do Oriente.
Morbey, Jorge, 1990. *Macau 1999. O desafio da transição*. Macau: author's edition.
Morbey, Jorge, 1994. 'Alguns aspectos em torno da identidade étnica dos macaenses', *Revista de Cultura* 20: 199–210.
Moreira, Adriano, 1955. 'A conferência de Bandung e a missão de Portugal: Conferência realizada na Sociedade de Geografia', n.e., Luanda.
Moreira, Adriano, 1986. *De Bandung aos problemas Norte-Sul*. Lisbon: Instituto Democracia e Liberdade.
Murray, Dian H., 1987. *Pirates of the South China Coast. 1780–1810*. Stanford, CA: Stanford University Press.

Newman, Otto, 1972. *Gambling: Hazard and Reward*. London: Athlone Press.
Ng Chun-hung, 1989. 'Familial change and women's employment in Hong Kong', paper presented at the conference on 'Gender Studies in Chinese Society', Centre for Hong Kong Studies, The Chinese University of Hong Kong, November 1989, MS.
Nunes, Isabel, 1991. 'Bailarinas e Cantadeiras. Aspectos da prostituição em Macau', *Revista de Cultura* 15: 95–117, Port. edn.

Oliveira, Fernando Correia de, 1998. *500 Anos de Contactos Luso-Chineses*. Lisbon: Público/Fundação Oriente.
Olmstead, Charlotte, 1962. *Heads I Win, Tails You Lose*. New York: Macmillan and Co.
Ownby, David, 1993. 'Introduction: secret societies reconsidered', in David Ownby and Mary Somers Heidhues (eds), *'Secret Societies' Reconsidered: Perspectives on the Social History of Modern South China and Southeast Asia*. Armonk, New York: M.E. Sharpe.

Pan, Lynn, 1992. *Tracing It Home: Journeys Around a Chinese Family*. London: Secker & Warburg.
Peixoto, Rui Brito, 1988. 'Arte, lenda e ritual: elementos da identidade dos pescadores Chineses do sul da China', *Revista de Cultura* 5: 7–24.
Pereira, J.F. Marques, 1984 (1889). *TA-SSI-YANG-KUO*. Lisbon: Antiga Casa Bertrand e José Bastos [Facsimile edn, Macao, Arquivo Histórico de Macau].
Pina-Cabral, João de, 1986. *Sons of Adam, Daughters of Eve: The Peasant Worldview of the Alto Minho (NW Portugal)*. Oxford: Clarendon Press.

BIBLIOGRAPHY

Pina-Cabral, João de, 1990. 'A viagem: dentro e fora', in Ana Marchand, *Viagem do Reino para a India*. Lisbon: Fundação Calouste Gulbenkian/Centro de Arte Moderna.

Pina-Cabral, João de, 1991a. *Os contextos da antropologia*. Lisbon: Difel.

Pina-Cabral, João de, 1991b. *Relatório Descritivo sobre o Casamento Católico em Macau*. Macao: Instituto Cultural de Macau (limited photocopied edition available from the Institute).

Pina-Cabral, João de, 1992. 'The Gods of the Gentiles are demons', in Kirsten Hastrup (ed.), *Other Histories*. London: Routledge.

Pina-Cabral, João de, 1993. 'A lei e a paternidade: as leis da filiação portuguesas vistas à luz da antropologia social', *Análise Social*: 123–4.

Pina-Cabral, João de, 1994. 'Personal identity and ethnic ambiguity: naming practices among the Eurasians of Macao', *Social Anthropologist/Anthropologiste Social* 2(2): 115–32.

Pina-Cabral, João de, 1997. 'Houses and legends: family as community of practice in urban Portugal', in Marianne Gullestad and Martine Segalen (eds), *Family and Kinship in Europe*. London and Washington: Pinter.

Pina-Cabral, João de, 1998. 'Traffic humain à Macao', in *Ethnologie Française* (2), vol. XXIX, pp. 225–36.

Pina-Cabral, João de, 1999a. 'A composição social de Macau', in Francisco Bettencourt and K. Chaudhuri (eds), *História da Expansão Portuguesa*, vol. 5, pp. 235–301. Lisbon: Círculo de Leitores.

Pina-Cabral, João de, 1999b. 'The threshold diffused: margins, contradictions and hegemonies in contemporary anthropology', in Patrick MacAllister (ed.), *Essays in Honour of W. D. Hammond-Tooke*. Johannesburg: Witwatersrand University Press.

Pina-Cabral, João de, 2000a. 'How do the Macanese achieve collective action?', in João de Pina-Cabral and Antónia Pedroso de Lima (eds), *Elites: Choice, Leadership and Succession*. Oxford: Berg.

Pina-Cabral, João de, 2000b. 'The ethnographic present revisited', *Social Anthropologist* 8(3): 341–8.

Pina-Cabral, João de, n.d. 'Mater semper certa: the conditions for the access to paternity', paper delivered as Distinguished Lecturer of the Society for the Anthropology of Europe, American Anthropological Association meeting, San Francisco, November 1992.

Pina-Cabral, João de and Lourenço, Nelson, 1992. 'A questão das origens: família e etnicidade Macaenses', *Revista de Cultura* 16: 104–25.

Pina-Cabral, João de and Lourenço, Nelson, 1993a. 'Macau Bambu – um estudo sobre a identidade étnica macaense e a sucessão de gerações', *Administração* 21(3): 523–58 (Portuguese and Chinese versions).

Pina-Cabral, João de and Lourenço, Nelson, 1993b. *Em Terra de Tufões: Dinâmicas da Etnicidade Macaense*. Macao: Instituto Cultural de Macau. (Chinese edition, Macao: Instituto Cultural de Macau, 1995.)

Pires S.J., Father Benjamim Videira, 1994. 'Fonte do Nilau ou Poço da Avó (À busca da identidade de Macau)', *Revista de Cultura* 20: 5–10.

Pires, Daniel (ed.), 1992. *Camilo Pessanha: Prosador e Tradutor*, Macao: ICM/IPOR.

Posner, Gerald L., 1990. *Warlords of Crime. Chinese Secret Societies: The New Mafia*. Harmondsworth: Penguin Books.

BIBLIOGRAPHY

Potter, Sulamith H., 1990 [1986]. 'The cultural construction of emotion', in Sulamith H. Potter and Jack M. Potter, op. cit.
Potter, Sulamith H. and Potter, Jack, 1990. *China's Peasants: The Anthropology of a Revolution*. Cambridge: Cambridge University Press.
Price, John A., 1972. 'Gambling in traditional Asia', *Anthropologica* 14(2): 156–80.

Quine, W.V., 1966. *The Ways of Paradox and Other Essays*. New York: Random House.

Radcliffe-Brown, A.R., 1952. *Structure and Function in Primitive Society*. London: Cohen and West.
Rego, A. Silva, 1947. *A Presença Portuguesa em Macau*. Lisbon: Agência Geral das Colónias.
Rego, A. Silva, 1995. 'Relações directas entre Macau e o Brasil: um sonho irrealizável? (1717–1810)', *Revista de Cultura* 22: 7–30.
Report of the Advisory Committee on Gambling Policy. Hong Kong Government Press, June 1965.
Russell-Wood, A.J.R., 1998. 'Comunidades étnicas', in Francisco Bettencourt and Kirti Chadhuri (eds), *História da Expansão Portuguesa* II, pp. 151–68. Lisbon: Círculo de Leitores.

Sangren, P. Steven, 1987. *History and Magical Power in a Chinese Community*. Stanford, CA: Stanford University Press.
Sangren, P. Steven, 1991. 'Dialectics of alienation: individuals and collectivities in Chinese religion', *Man* n.s. 26: 67–89.
Santos, Boaventura Sousa, 1991. 'A justiça e a comunidade em Macao: problemas sociais, a administração pública e a organização comunitária no contexto de transição', *Administração* 13/14: 447–76.
Santos, Boaventura Sousa, 1998. *Macau. O pequeníssimo dragão*. Oporto: Afrontamento.
Scott, Ian, 1989. *Political Change and the Crisis of Legitimacy in Hong Kong*. Hong Kong: Oxford University Press.
Scheid, Frédéric, 1987. 'Mariages mixtes et ethnicité: le cas de Macao', *Cahiers d'Anthropologie et Biométrie Humaine (Paris)* V (3–4): 131–50.
Sider, Gerald and Smith, Gavin, 1997. 'Introduction', in Gerald Sider and Gavin Smith (eds), *Between History and Histories: The Making of Silences and Commemorations*. Toronto: University of Toronto Press
Silva, António de Andrade e, 1991. *Eu estive em Macau durante a Guerra*. Macao: Instituto Cultural de Macau.
Smith, James F. and Abt, Vicki, 1984. 'Gambling as play', *Annals of the American Academy of Political and Social Science*, pp. 122–32. Beverley Hills: Sage.
Smith, Robert J., 1996. 'The Japanese (Confucian) family: the tradition from the bottom up', in Tu Wei-Ming, op. cit.
Spence, Jonathan D., 1974. *Emperor of China: Self-Portrait of K'ang-hsi*. London: Pimlico.
Spencer, Robert F. and Barnett, S.A., 1948. 'Notes on a bachelor house in the South China area', *American Anthropologist* 50(3): 463–78.

Spitzer, Leo, 1989. *Lives in Between: Assimilation and Marginality in Austria, Brazil, West Africa, 1780–1945.* Cambridge: Cambridge University Press.

Stafford, Charles, 1995. *The Roads of Chinese Childhood: Learning and Identification in Angang.* Cambridge: Cambridge University Press.

Stafford, Charles, 2000. 'Chinese patrilineage and the cycles of *yang* and *laiwang*', in Janet Carsten (ed.), *Cultures of Relatedness: New Approaches to the Study of Kinship.* Cambridge: Cambridge University Press.

Stockard, Janice, 1989. *Daughters of the Delta: Marriage Patterns and Economic Strategies in South China, 1860–1930.* Stanford, CA: Stanford University Press.

Teixeira, Manuel, 1965. *Os Macaenses.* Macao: Imprensa Nacional.

Teixeira, Manuel, 1976. *O Comércio de Escravos em Macao/The So-Called Portuguese Slave Trade in Macao.* Macao: Imprensa Nacional.

Teixeira, Manuel, 1986. *Macau Durante a Guerra.* Macao: Imprensa Nacional.

Ter Haar, Barend J., 1993. 'Messianism and the Heaven and Earth Society: approaches to Heaven and Earth Society texts', in David Ownby (ed.), op. cit.

Terradas, Ignasi, 1992. *Eliza Kendal: Reflexiones sobre una antibiografía.* Bellaterra: Publicacions d'Antropologia Cultural, Universitat Autònoma de Barcelona.

Topley, Marjorie, 1970. 'Chinese traditional ideas and the treatment of disease: two examples from Hong Kong', *Man* n.s. **5**(3): 421–37.

Tse Hon-Kong, 1990. 'Population and economic development in Macau', in D.Y. Yuan, Wong Hon-Keong and Libânio Martins (eds), *Population and City Growth in Macau.* Macao: Centre of Macau Studies, University of East Asia.

Tu Wei-Ming (ed.), 1996. *Confucian Traditions in East Asian Modernity: Moral Education and Economic Culture in Japan and the Four Mini-Dragons.* Cambridge, MA: Harvard University Press.

Turner, Victor, 1957. *Schism and Continuity in an African Society.* Manchester: Manchester University Press.

Valetas, Marie-France, 1992. 'Le nom de famille ou l'éviction du nom de la femme. Analyse socio-démographique des représentations', in Ana Nunes de Almeida *et al.* (eds). *Familles et contextes cociaux.* Lisbon: CIES/ISCTE.

Veiga de Oliveira, Celina, 1993. *Camilo Pessanha: O Jurista e o Homem.* Macao: Instituto Cultural de Macau/IPOR.

Vilhena de Carvalho, Manuel, 1989. *O Nome das Pessoas e o Direito.* Coimbra: Almedina.

Wakeman Jr., Frederic, 1995. *Policing Shanghai 1927–1937.* Berkeley, CA: University of California Press.

Wang Chaoson, Deng Hanzeng and Huang Junxin, 1997. *Atlas de Macau/Macau Atlas.* Macao: Fundação Macau.

Wang Gungwu, 1991a. *The Chineseness of China: Selected Essays.* Hong Kong: Oxford University Press.

Wang Gungwu, 1991b. *China and the Chinese Overseas.* Singapore: Times Academic Press.

Ward, Barbara E., 1985. *Through Other Eyes: An Anthropologist's View of Hong Kong.* Hong Kong: The Chinese University Press.

BIBLIOGRAPHY

Watson, James L., 1980a. 'Transactions in people: the Chinese market in slaves, servants and heirs', in James L. Watson (ed.), *Asian and African Systems of Slavery.* Oxford: Blackwell.

Watson, James L., 1980b. 'Slavery as an institution', in James L. Watson (ed.), op. cit.

Watson, James L., 1993. 'Rites or beliefs? The construction of a unified culture in late imperial China', in L. Dittmer and S. Kim (eds), *China's Quest for National Identity.* Ithaca: Cornell University.

Watson, Rubie S., 1986. 'The named and the nameless: gender and person in Chinese society', *American Ethnologist* **13**(4): 619–31.

Watson, Rubie S., 1991. 'Wives, concubines, and maids: servitude and kinship in the Hong Kong region, 1900–1940', in Rubie S. Watson and Patricia Buckley Ebrey (eds), *Marriage and Inequality in Chinese Society.* Berkeley: University of California Press.

Weng Eang Cheong, 1997. *The Hong Merchants of Canton: Chinese Merchants in Sino-Western Trade.* Richmond, Surrey: Curzon.

Woon W.L., 1987. 'Chinese dialects in Macao', in R.D. Cremer (ed.), *Macao: City of Commerce and Culture*, pp. 110–13. Hong Kong: UEA Press.

Yang C.K., 1961. *Religion in Chinese Society.* Berkeley: University of California Press.

Yang, Mayfair Mei-hui, 1989. 'The gift economy and State power in China', *Comparative Studies in Society and History* **31**(1): 25–54.

Yee, Albert, 1989. *A People Misruled: Hong Kong and the Chinese Stepping Stone Syndrome.* Hong Kong: API Press/UEA.

Zhang Wenqin, 1996. 'Intercâmbio cultural sino-ocidental reflectido nas poesias das dinastias Ming e Qing sobre Macau', *Revista de Cultura* **29**: 55–62.

INDEX

adoption 108–9, 119, 166, 197
Ai-ling Chin 121
Álvares, Jorge 73
anomie 221
Anran Co. 214
'antinomies' (Quine) 102
Apolinário, Manuel António 215
Ariès, Philippe 185
Arriaga, Ouvidor 13–14
D'Assumpção, Carlos 6, 14
Australia 132

bambinos 166–7, 169
Bandung Conference (1956) 133
'Bang Nga' Koi 205–7, 213–19
Bank of China 70
de Bary, W. T. 121, 179
Basic Law of Macao 16, 76
Basto da Silva, Beatriz 12
Billeter, Jean François 100
blood oath 210
boat people (*tancares*) 2, 11, 43, 74, 89, 164
the Bogue 1, 56
Boxer Rebellion 14
Braga, Jack 130–1, 136
bribery 92
bridewealth payments 181–4
Britain and British influence 10–11, 14, 55, 59–62, 67, 107, 113–14
Brito, Ana 34
Buddhism 34–5, 45

Cai Yin Yuan 2
Caldeira, Carlos José 65
Calderon, Arturo Chiang 214

Cannossian Sisters 166–7
Canton 4, 69, 88–91, 97
Casa Branca 2, 22, 54, 58
Casino Lisboa 79, 85
Catholicism 22–3, 34–6, 115, 120, 137, 142, 152–3
Cayolla, Lourenço 112
centrality (of hegemonic agents) 220–1
Cha, Louis 201
Chan Lok 96–7
Chang Pao 14
Chinese community in Macao 42–7, 171
Chinese New Year 84–6, 88, 211
Chinese Rites Controversy 36, 56
Chiong-On society 96–8
Chow Tse-Tung 70–1
Christianity, conversion to 23, 152–3
citizenship rights 13, 156, 219
class differences 176
Clement XIV, Pope 56
Coates, Austin 14
colonialism 11, 66–71, 80, 130, 170, 173
Conceição, Deolinda da 160–3
Conceição, Lourenço da 57
Confucius and Confucianism 7, 23, 36, 117–20, 123–4, 152, 179, 193, 200–1
coolie trade 23–4, 80
corruption 92, 212–13
Costa, Almeida e 30, 41
Couto, Diogo de 114
Creole community and culture 22, 37, 66–7, 141
Cruz, Gaspar da 114

INDEX

Cuba 23–4
Cultural Institute of Macao 6, 17
Cultural Revolution 7–8, 14, 26, 73, 136

Davidson, Donald 221
death penalty 215
democratic deficit 16
Deng Xiaoping 26, 75, 87, 139, 172–3, 211
discrimination 146
divorce 186–7
Douglas, Robert 89
dowry 183–5, 197, 200

East India Company 4, 55, 57
economic activity in Macao 28–31
education 32–4, 75, 154, 191
elites 46–7
Elliot, Alan 123
emigration from Macao 23–4, 45
emotion, management of 121–5, 144
Endo, Shusako 107
English language 40–2
equivocal compatibility 105–8, 116, 126, 168
Esparteiro, Marques 132, 134, 138–9
ethnic composition of Macao 21–3, 36–48
ethnic identity 141–5, 152–7
ethnocentrism 148

familism 180
family size 191–2
fantan 88–9, 94–5, 98–9
Far Eastern Economic Review 208
Father of the Christians 115–16
Fay, Peter Ward 56
Ferreira do Amaral, João Maria 5, 51–3, 60–77 *passim*, 80, 94, 139
Feuchtwang, Stephan 84–5
Fok, Henry 30, 208
Fok, K. C. 9
Fong Heng-Seng 96
14K triad 213–16, 218
France 55
fraternal submission 200–1
free port status 61, 66
Freedman, Maurice 123–4
Freud, Sigmund 129
fright neurosis 124
Fry, Peter 17
Fu Tak-Iam 30, 86, 172

gambling 28–31, 79–82, 172–3, 205, 208–12
  alternative concepts of 83–7
  forms of 87–9
  history of syndicates 93–9
  paradoxes of 100–3
  see also vaereng lottery
Gernet, Jacques 86
globalization 177
Goa 4, 115, 133
Goffman, Erving 141–5, 153, 157, 166
gold, trade in 29, 73–5, 135–6
Grantham, Sir Alexander 132–4
Group of Four United 218–19

Haley, John 194
Han Chinese 42–3
Hideyoshi, Shogun 4, 107
Ho, Stanley 6, 30, 70, 75, 85, 95, 208, 214–15, 219
Ho Hau-Wah 48
Ho Lin-Vong 95
Ho Lok-Gwai 95
Ho Yin 14, 29, 46, 74–5, 136–7, 172, 176
Holy Infancy Asylum 166
Hong Kong 5, 9, 11, 16–17, 22, 30, 37, 59–60, 67, 80, 85, 88, 107, 131–2, 135–6, 171, 175–6
Hong Kong and Shanghai Banking Corporation 132
hoppo officials 55, 57, 62, 66
Hou Ching-Lang 124
Hsieh Yu-Wei 124
Hsu, Francis 121
Hsü, Immanuel 133, 136–7

identity building 128–9
illegitimate children 154, 156, 165, 189
immigration to Macao 27–8
Imperial Civil Service Examinations 79, 81 89–96, 99–102
incidente 123 73–4, 136, 172
incidentes 9, 11–14, 26, 41, 44, 61, 206, 218–20
inheritance patterns 195–200
intermarriage 22–3, 42, 120, 132, 145, 174
isolation of China 135
isomorphism in social reproduction 108–9

Japan 4, 69
Jesuits 36, 56, 115–16, 123

INDEX

Jiang Zemin 48
Joint Declaration, Luso-Chinese (1987) 5
Jun Jing 129

'Kai-si' Wai 213–16
Kang Yu-Wei 24
Kangxi Emperor 4, 54, 57
kidnapping 117, 119
Kou Ho-Neng 30, 46, 86, 172
Kou Kong class 118
Kowloon Village 88
Kui, Broken Tooth 47
Kuoc Ngan Ieng 125
Kuomintang, the 73–4
Kusyszyn, Igor 101

Lang, Graeme 86
language 32–3, 38–42, 46, 67, 142, 174–6
Leal Senado 8, 54–9, 62–4, 73, 107
legal system of Macao 110–14
Lei Gang-chun 94, 96
Levenson, Joseph 94
Li Hung-Chang 97, 99
Liang, Y. C. 29, 136
Liang Peiyuan 1
Lobo, Pedro José 14, 29, 68, 136, 166, 169, 172
Lou, Fu Qing 93
Lou Gao 92–8 *passim*
Lou Lim-Ioc 46, 92, 95–6, 100, 185
Lourenço, Nelson 6, 17
Lu Jin 90–2, 96
Lu Ping 76, 217

Macanese community 37–42, 66–8, 71–2, 75, 107, 129, 132, 141–6, 153, 156–7, 175–6
'Macao Formula' 9, 11
mahjong 83, 85–7
Malacca 4, 55
Mao Tsetung 136–8, 173
marginality of social existence 221
Marques, Jaime Silvério 30
marriage, age of 191
marriage patterns and practices 163, 172–3, 176, 181–2
master narratives 129, 132, 139
matrimonial context of production and reproduction 160–74
matrimonial insecurity 185–90
Melancia, Carlos 30

Mendes Pinto, Fernão 131
Mesquita, Vicente Nicolau de 63, 68–73 *passim*, 77
migration of population 15, 23–8, 47–8
Mo Peng Deng 214
modernization (of China) 71
monopolies, granting of 80–1, 95
Montalto de Jesus, C. A. 7
Moreira, Adriano 133
music 4

Nam Kwong 15–16, 74, 135
naming practices 141, 146–56
Nanking Treaty (1843) 60
nationalism 42, 71, 132, 137
Nativity metaphor 202
NATO 135
Nehru, Jawaharlal 133
New Century Hotel 216
New China News Agency (*Xinhua*) 16, 212
Newman, Otto 82, 101
Newsweek 216
Ng Chun-Hung 191

Olmstead, Charlotte 79, 101
opium trade 4, 28–9, 66, 81
Opium Wars 5, 59–60
optional inventories 199–200
Ownby, David 210

Pacific War 26, 68
  see also Second World War
passing 144, 151–6
Pereira, J. F. Marques 40–1
person, concepts of 120–5
Pessanha, Camilo 109–19 *passim*, 125
piracy 209
polygamy 183, 188
Pombal, Marquis of 56, 116
population of Macao 26–8, 37
Portas do Cerco 1, 14, 61, 63, 69–70, 72, 74, 173, 188
Portas do Entendimento 137–8
Portuguese community in Macao 36–7
Portuguese merchants 2, 4
Portuguese navigators 107
Portugueseness, capital of 67, 75, 132, 141, 145–6, 151, 156, 168, 176
Potter, Sulamith H. 121–2
Price, John 88, 101
Procuratura system 110–13

INDEX

prostitution 48, 119
public works 30

Qian Qichen 217
Qianlong Emperor 57
Queiroz, Eça de 24
Quine, W. V. 80, 102–3

racism 67, 169–70
Radcliffe-Brown, A. R. 117
Ragvald, Lars 86
Red Guards 73–4
Redinha, José 214
refugees 15, 26, 68
Rego, A. Silva 10, 59
religion 34–6, 39
Remédios, Maximiano António dos 98
Rua da Felicidade 14

Saint Lazarus parish 23, 35, 152–3
Salazar, Antonio de Oliveira 68, 130, 133–4, 170, 172
Sampaio, Jorge 48
Sangren, P. Steven 34, 124, 141
Santos, Boaventura Sousa 198
Second World War 69
 see also Pacific War
self, concept of 120–2
Senna Fernandes, Henrique de 44–5, 95, 98–9, 164
Si Tou Iok Lin 213–14, 216
Silva, Miguel Ayres da 98
Silva, Pedro Nolasco da 185
Silva Pedrosa Guimarães, da D. Alexandre 10
Singapore 123
slavery 113–19
social dramas 11–12, 16
social theory 221
Sociedade de Turismo e Diversões de Macao (STDM) 30, 208–13 *passim*, 218–19
sociocultural change 156
soul, the, concept of 123–5
sovereignty over Macao 8, 13, 16, 53, 59–60, 65–6, 129, 219
Spitzer, Leo 67
stabilitas tradition 185–6, 189
Stafford, Charles 193
stigma, concept of 143–5
Sui Fong triad 215–16

Sun Yat-Sen 14, 24–5, 71, 209
Superintendent of Maritime Customs 55

Taipa 69, 73
Taiwan 85, 124, 175
tancares, *see* boat people
Tanka community 43
Tao Siju 211
Taoism 34–5, 45
Texeira, Manuel 138–9
Tientsin Treaty (1858) 65–6
Time magazine 216
Topley, Marjorie 124
tourism 31
trade 9–10, 16, 106
 in persons 108–10, 115–20
traditional families 145–6
Trench, Sir David 16
Triad Wars 14, 31, 207, 218–20
triads 29, 47, 87, 209–16
Tu Wei-Ming 179
Turner, Victor 11–12

unemployment 31

vaeseng lottery 81, 89–102
Videira Pires, Benjamin 2
VIP rooms 212–14, 216
Vong da Conceição, Mariano 155

Wan Kuok-koi, *see* 'Bang Nga' Koi
Wang, Ming Kun 93
Wang Gungwu 71
Ward, Barbara 121, 123, 191–2, 195
Watson, James 116, 118–19
Watson, R. 168, 183–4
wedding practices 181–2
Weng Eang Cheong 54, 57, 106–7
women's employment 191–5
Wong Man-fong 211
Wong Tai Sin 86

Xinhua, *see* New China News Agency

Yang, Mayfair 123
yang cycle 193–4
Yee, Albert 2, 8

Zhou Enlai 133–7
Zhu Rongzi 218

LONDON SCHOOL OF ECONOMICS MONOGRAPHS ON SOCIAL ANTHROPOLOGY

1 & 2 The Work of the Gods in Tikopia
RAYMOND FIRTH
0 485 19501 1 (2nd edn in 1 vol) hb

14 Chinese Spirit-Medium Cults in Singapore (Second Edition)
ALAN J. A. ELLIOTT
With a new Preface by Sir Raymond Firth
0 485 19514 3 hb

17 Indigenous Political Systems of Western Malaya
J. M. GULLICK
0 485 19417 1 Rev edn hb

19 Political Leadership among Swat Pathans
FREDRIK BARTH
0 485 19619 0 pb

20 Social Status and Power in Java
L. H. PALMIER
0 485 19620 4 pb

22 Rethinking Anthropology
E. R. LEACH
0 485 19622 0 pb

24 Legal Institutions in Manchu China
A Sociological Analysis
SYBILLE VAN DER SPRENKEL
0 485 19624 7 Rev edn pb

28 Essays on Social Organization and Values
RAYMOND FIRTH
0 485 19628 X pb

33 Chinese Lineage and Society
Fukien and Kwantung
MAURICE FREEDMAN
0 485 19633 6 pb

37 Kinship and Marriage among the Anlo Ewe
G. K. NUKUNYA
0 485 19637 9 pb

38 Anthropology and Social Change
LUCY MAIR
0 485 19638 7 pb

39 Take Out Hunger
Two Case Studies of Rural Development in Basutoland
SANDRA WALLMAN
0 485 19539 9 hb

40 Time and Social Structure and Other Essays
MEYER FORTES
0 485 19540 2 hb

41 Report on the Iban
DEREK FREEMAN
0 485 19541 0 hb

42 The Political Structure of the Chinese Community in Cambodia
W. E. WILLMOTT
0 485 19542 9 hb

44 Political Systems of Highland Burma
A Study of Kachin Social Structure
E. R. LEACH
0 485 19644 1 pb

LSE MONOGRAPHS

45 Pioneers in the Tropics
The Political Organization of Japanese in an Immigrant Community in Brazil
PHILIP STANIFORD
0 485 19543 3 hb

47 West Indian Migration
The Montserrat Case
STUART B. PHILPOTT
0 485 19547 X hb

48 Land and Family in Pisticci
J. DAVIS
0 485 19548 8 hb

49 Beyond the Village
Local Politics in Madang, Papua New Guinea
LOUISE MORAUTA
0 485 19549 6 hb

51 Metamorphosis of the Cassowaries
Umeda Society, Language and Ritual
ALFRED GELL
0 485 19551 8 hb

52 Knowledge of Illness in a Sepik Society
A Study of the Gnau, New Guinea
GILBERT LEWIS
0 485 19552 6 hb

53 White Nile Arabs
Political Leadership and Economic Change
ABBAS AHMED MOHAMED
0 485 19553 4 hb

54 Ma'Betisék Concepts of Living Things
WAZIR-JAHAN KARIM
9 485 19554 2 hb

55 Forest Traders
A Socio-Economic Study of the Hill Pandaram
BRIAN MORRIS
0 485 19555 0 hb

56 Communications, Social Structure and Development in Rural Malaysia
A Study of Kampung Kuala Bera
WILLIAM D. WILDER
0 485 19556 9 hb

57 Sacrifice and Sharing in the Philippine Highlands
Religion and Society among the Buid of Mindoro
THOMAS P. GIBSON
0 485 19559 3 hb

58 Ritual, History and Power
Selected Papers in Anthropology
MAURICE BLOCH
0 485 19658 1 pb

59 Gods on Earth
The Management of Religious Experience and Identity in a North Indian Pilgrimage Centre
PETER VAN DER VEER
0 485 19510 0 hb

60 The Social Practice of Symbolization
An Anthropological Analysis
IVO STRECKER
0 485 19557 7 hb

61 Making Sense of Hierarchy
Cognition as Social Process in Fiji
CHRISTINA TOREN
Fijian hierarchy and its constitution in everyday ritual behaviour
0 485 19561 5 hb

62 The Power of Love
The Moral Use of Knowledge amongst the Amuesha of Central Peru
FERNANDO SANTOS-GRANERO
0 485 19562 3 hb

63 Society and Politics in India
Essays in a Comparative Perspective
ANDRE BETEILLE
0 485 19563 1 hb

LSE MONOGRAPHS

64 The Harambee Movement in Kenya
Self-Help, Development and Education among the Kamba of Kitui District
MARTIN J. D. HILL
0 485 19564 X   hb

65 Hierarchy and Egalitarianism
Caste, Class and Power in Sinhalese Peasant Society
TAMARA GUNASEKERA
0 485 19565 8   hb

66 Leadership and Change in the Western Pacific
Edited by RICHARD FEINBERG and KAREN ANN WATSON-GEGEO
0 485 19566 6 hb

67 The Art of Anthropology
Essays and Diagrams
ALFRED GELL
0 485 19567 4   hb
0 485 19660 3   pb

68 Conceiving Persons
Ethnographies of Procreation, Fertility and Growth
Edited by PETER LOIZOS and P. HEADY
0 485 19568 2   hb

69 Those Who Play with Fire
Gender, Fertility and Transformation in East and Southern Africa
Edited by HENRIETTA L. MOORE, TODD SANDERS and BWIRE KAARE
0 485 19569 0   hb

70 Arguments with Ethnography
Comparative Approaches to History, Politics and Religion
IOAN M. LEWIS
0 485 19570 4   hb

71 The Performance of Gender
An Anthropology of Everyday Life in a South Indian Fishing Village
CECILIA BUSBY
0 485 19571 2   hb
0 485 19671 9   pb

72 Chinese Sociologics
An Anthropological Account of the Role of Alienation in Social Reproduction
P. STEVEN SANGREN
0 485 19572 0   hb
0 485 19672 7   pb

73 The Earth Shakers of Madagascar
An Anthropological Study of Authority, Fertility and Creation
OLIVER WOOLLEY
0 8264 5750 9   hb

74 Between China and Europe
Person, Culture and Emotion in Macao
JOÃO DE PINA-CABRAL
0 8264 5748 7   hb
0 8264 5749 5   pb